RADICAL WRITING
CENTER PRAXIS

RADICAL WRITING CENTER PRAXIS

A Paradigm for Ethical Political Engagement

LAURA GREENFIELD

UTAH STATE UNIVERSITY PRESS
Logan

© 2019 by University Press of Colorado

Published by Utah State University Press
An imprint of University Press of Colorado
245 Century Circle, Suite 202
Louisville, Colorado 80027

 ASSOCIATION of UNIVERSITY PRESSES   The University Press of Colorado is a proud member of the Association of University Presses.

The University Press of Colorado is a cooperative publishing enterprise supported, in part, by Adams State University, Colorado State University, Fort Lewis College, Metropolitan State University of Denver, University of Colorado, University of Northern Colorado, Utah State University, and Western State Colorado University.

∞ This paper meets the requirements of the ANSI/NISO Z39.48–1992 (Permanence of Paper).

ISBN: 978-1-60732-843-8 (paperback)
ISBN: 978-1-60732-844-5 (ebook)
DOI: https://doi.org/10.7330/9781607328445

Library of Congress Cataloging-in-Publication Data

Names: Greenfield, Laura, author.
Title: Radical writing center praxis : a paradigm for ethical political engagement / by Laura Greenfield.
Description: Logan : Utah State University Press, [2019] | Includes bibliographical references and index.
Identifiers: LCCN 2018050269 | ISBN 9781607328438 (pbk.) | ISBN 9781607328445 (ebook)
Subjects: LCSH: Writing centers—Political aspects—United States. | Writing centers—Social aspects—United States. | English language—Rhetoric—Study and teaching (Higher)—Political aspects—United States. | English language—Rhetoric—Study and teaching (Higher)—Social aspects—United States. | Academic writing—Study and teaching (Higher)—Political aspects—United States. | Academic writing—Study and teaching (Higher)—Social aspects—United States. | Education—Political aspects—United States. | Social justice and education—United States.
Classification: LCC PE1405.U6 G735 2019 | DDC 808/.402071173—dc23
LC record available at https://lccn.loc.gov/2018050269

Cover illustration © Lay Some Eggs Pics / Shutterstock

For my grandpa Robert Greenfield

CONTENTS

ACKNOWLEDGMENTS

Thank you to Michael Spooner for believing in me and in this project. I am grateful for your willingness to support my desire to be bold and unapologetic in my message and for showing me where I needed my arguments to grow. Thank you to all the folks at Utah State University Press and University Press of Colorado for bringing this book to life, especially Rachael Levay, Kylie Haggen, and Laura Furney. Thank you also to Kami Day for the outstanding copyediting and Daniel Pratt for the great cover design.

Thank you to Megan Durling, my former student turned colleague, who challenged my thinking in vital ways many years ago and who has stuck with this project after all that time. It is a gift to have your writing included here.

Thank you to Karen Rowan, Kathy Shine Cain, and George Fourlas for your conversations about and feedback on drafts of this text. Your insights, questions, and suggestions have undoubtedly made it a stronger book. Thank you to the anonymous reviewers who helped me, among other things, to be more generous to my reader-colleagues.

Thank you especially to my many students in both my classrooms and in my writing and speaking centers. You are, in fact, my teachers. Years ago, my wonderful students at Mount Holyoke College in the Speaking, Arguing, and Writing Program explored many radical questions with me and helped create a community of practice infused with the values explored in this book. My amazing students at Hampshire College in the Transformative Speaking Program have grappled explicitly with designing an intentionally radical program and have challenged me to put my own beliefs into action, even when to do so has been politically risky. I am grateful especially to those who have also pushed back, challenging me to deepen my own thinking, clarify my ideas, and engage in greater nuance.

My colleagues and students at Women's Voices Worldwide, Inc. helped stretch my awareness of the implications of justice in the "real world" and have also reinforced my belief that the classroom is indeed the real world. Thanks especially to Maggie Baumer, who has been a vital colleague and reflection partner in that work.

Thank you to Lois Brown for always believing in me and to Bonnie Diamond for reminding me how much people matter. Thanks to my graduate-school buddies Soma Kedia and Tiffany Bailey, who played a foundational role in helping shape my early thinking.

Thank you to my colleagues with the Ethics and Common Good Project, especially Javiera Benavente and Teal Van Dyck, who have inspired a new lens into these questions and who have brought me deeper into my understanding of the radical notions of community, relationship, and embodiment. Thanks to Wilson Valentín for your mentorship and advocacy for my work.

Thank you to my many teachers, from kindergarten through graduate school, who have inspired me and played a role in instilling in me the courage to stand up for my beliefs: Mrs. Spangler, Mrs. Bell, Mrs. Ringler, Mrs. Livisay, Mr. Babcock, Mr. Bledoe, Mrs. Towers, Mr. Van Schoten, Mr. Millard, Mr. Roberts, Mr. Springer, Mr. Culbertson, Mrs. Rich, Ann Romines, Robert McRuer, Patty Chu, and Marshall Alcorn. And many others too numerous to name.

Of course, thank you to my wonderful family: Dad, who tells me to follow my dreams (and that people who say it cannot be done should not interrupt those who are doing it), and Mom, who always says if it were easy everyone would do it (and then never doubts I will). How fortunate I am to have the support of parents who believe I can achieve anything. Thank you to Hannah, Tine, Grandma, Grandpa, Rachid, Tarek, and all my relatives and friends who are my rock. I love you.

And finally, thank you to Doreen Salli, the director of the writing center at Washington University, where I got my first job as an undergraduate peer tutor two decades ago. You changed my life.

To live is to live a life politically, in relation to power, in relation to others, in the act of assuming responsibility for a collective future.

—Judith Butler

Introduction

JUSTICE AND PEACE ARE EVERYONE'S INTEREST
Or, the Case for a New Paradigm

During a recent school break, I found myself in a conversation with another mother at an indoor hotel swimming pool. Our young sons had befriended each other in the water and were entertaining themselves with a competition for the best jump into the deep end. Between judging the biggest splash or the wildest midair dance move, we discovered our different careers were leading us to grapple with strikingly similar questions about justice, writing, and free speech. This kindred spirit turned out to be Joy Peskin, the editorial director of Ferrar, Straus and Giroux for Young Readers, an imprint of Macmillan Children's Publishing Group. Joy published an essay in *Publishers Weekly* titled "Why the Milo Yiannopoulos Book Deal Tarnishes the Publishing Industry" (2017). Her essay offers a radical contemporary commentary on the politics of publishing and hate speech—a piece that gives voice to an important perspective shared by many in the publishing world. It also got her in hot water.

If you weren't otherwise familiar with Milo Yiannopoulos, consider yourself lucky. He is an editor at Breitbart who takes pleasure in being the "supervillain of the internet" in his explicit and outrageous promotion of racism, misogyny, and other forms of violence. His dangerous rhetoric has earned him a popular following primarily among disillusioned young white American men who are quick to scapegoat society's most vulnerable and marginalized as the reason for their own hardships. When Simon & Schuster offered him a deal to publish his book *Dangerous*, the publishing house found itself the center of significant controversy as people disgusted by his message came out to protest. At the same time, many liberals found themselves torn: should they protest the publishing of this book in rejection of its vile content, or should they support his right to free speech?

While many concluded that Yiannopoulis has a right to publish his views, no matter how unpopular, Peskin argues that "when a major publisher legitimizes old-fashioned hate and lies rebranded as alternative,

DOI: 10.7330/9781607328445.c000

our authors lose, our books lose, and our country loses" (2017). Indeed, as Joy and I discussed, everyone has a right to free speech, but not everyone has a right to a book contract. Publishers have not only a right but also an ethical obligation to determine which ideas to promote through publication and which to reject. Antifascists take this view a step further and argue that there should be no platform for hate, the ultimate ends of which are exclusion, violence, and genocide. No one should have the right to incite genocide. When one voice is calling for the death of the other, there is no common ground for democratic speech or debate (Bray 2017).

Scholar-activists Christopher M. Tinson and Javiera Benavente make an important case for the need to "distinguish between free speech claims that promote justice and those that protect the right to any kind of speech at all, especially speech of the willfully uninformed or intentionally harmful variety" (2017). Citing a willingness to engage, a commitment to getting and staying informed, a commitment to developing a shared understanding of shared history, and a commitment to "collective courage"—which requires listening as much as it does speaking—as characteristics of democratic speech, Tinson and Benevente make it is easy to see that Yiannopoulis' speech does not fit the bill. Hate speech by definition is antithetical to democratic speech. Indeed, Peskin argues convincingly that Yiannopoulis is "more than a provocateur. He is a terrorist, shouting 'fire' in a crowded theater. The fire is otherness—that which is not white, Christian, and male; the crowded theater is America" (2017).

If being tasked with editing a book for publication that contains hate speech, Joy and I discussed, an editor would face an ethical dilemma: if their job is to make the text better, wouldn't it be unethical to help an author be more effective in communicating their racism or misogyny, for example? You can see how our conversation quickly turned to writing centers. This dilemma is precisely at the center of many debates among writing center tutors: how should they respond when a student writer is working on a text containing violent views? Just as the publishing industry does not have a universal standard in response to such a question (thankfully, public pressure compelled Simon & Schuster eventually to withdraw the book deal from Yiannopoulis, although a copy of the manuscript with the editor's notes has been leaked), the writing center field does not have a universal answer to this question either. Indeed, just as Peskin experienced significant pushback from others in her field for advocating against the publishing of Yiannopoulis's book, folks who argue on behalf of a values-based, rather than a writer-based, approach to writing centers are not universally well received either.

The current paradigm of writing centers, I argue, leaves us in a bind. Our privileging of writers over righteousness risks in both small and large ways our field's complicity in enabling or even promoting systems of injustice many of us personally reject. In her critical history of writing centers, "'Our Little Secret': A History of Writing Centers, Pre- to Post-Open Admissions," Elizabeth H. Boquet juxtaposes the ways many writing center people "find it difficult to believe that the writing center may be a site of regulation rather than liberation, though it is often that" yet at the same time fail to "envision it as a source of radical or liberatory pedagogy, though it is often that" (1999, 479). Reading Kenneth Bruffee's foundational work as "foreshadowing the radical thrust of later writing center theorists" (475), she equates the unanticipated oppressive or liberatory outcomes of everyday writing center work with Foucauldian accidents and asks what we are failing to envision for writing centers. A reading of history since Boquet's penning of "Our Little Secret" reveals that this unwitting ambivalence has continued. And although our radical thrust also continues, I argue, to build momentum, it remains, to draw on the language offered by Jackie Grutsch McKinney (2013), "peripheral" to the stories that dominate the field about what writing center work is, or better yet, what it *could* be.

We do have radical stories to tell. Nancy Maloney Grimm (1999) has offered us a powerful postmodern critique of the cultures of individualism that shape our institutions and our writing centers—a critique that continues to inspire many in our field. Anis Bawarshi and Stephanie Pelkowski (1999) have cautioned us against the colonialist assumptions underlying Stephen North's (1984) prevailing idea of a writing center and many of our individual centers' stated missions. Anne DiPardo (1992) has shared stories that compel us to recognize the importance of conscious engagement across racial differences in writing sessions. Harry Denny (2010) has provided a broad examination of identity politics, including race and ethnicity, class, sex and gender, and nationality as it relates to one-to-one mentoring. Jay Sloan and Andrew Rihn (2013) have called on us to critically examine heteronormativity and homophobia in writing center work. Neil Simpkins has extended this work to focus our attention in particular on the needs of trans students in the writing center (blog post to *Another Word: From the Writing Center at the University of Wisconsin–Madison*, November 18, 2013). Rebecca Day Babcock (2015) has provided a comprehensive analysis of the field's scholarship on disabilities in the writing center, identifying the need for more significant empirical studies, particularly about tutors and directors with disabilities. Frankie Condon (2007) has given us the imperative to question white privilege and to see antiracism work in all its forms as central to writing centers. Karen Rowan and I, along with contributors to our edited collection, have called on the field to examine and sustain dialogues about institutionalized racism in writing centers (Greenfield and Rowan 2011b). Vershawn Ashanti Young (2011), specifically, has compelled us to resist dominant racist assumptions about language practices and to explore code meshing as a just alternative. Beth Godbee and Moira Ozias (2011) have offered frameworks for engaging in writing center activism. Boquet (2014) has challenged the writing center community to see our work as a potential intervention against deadly violence, while Rasha Diab (2008) has invited us to be proactive in creating conditions for peace. Indeed, when we flip through the pages of our journals and conference programs, we can see with excitement an increasing number of scholars and practitioners engaging questions of difference, oppression, and justice.

Implicit in this body of scholarship, be it through the lens of racism, sexism, homophobia, or other forms of violence, is an increasing recognition that the work of writing centers is implicated in these various systems of oppression and that we have an ethical responsibility to intervene purposefully. And yet, despite the growing number of these revolutionary arguments—arguments that call on us to be critically conscious of our identities, to examine unjust systems, and to seek opportunities for transformative action—the dominant discourse and practices of the field remain largely unchanged. Indeed, despite assertions by scholars such as Frankie Condon, for example, that we must consider antiracism work not to be "strange and tangential" but rather "central and pressing" (2007, 19) in writing centers, the work of antiracism and anti-oppression broadly remains, for the most part, in the margins as many struggle with how to put these ideas into practice. Though more prevalent and visible than even a decade ago, scholarship related to resisting oppression or building towards justice and peace in and through writing centers has not fundamentally unsettled the dominant stories of practice in the field.

We can see this tension between justice work and the field's status quo when the arguments made by people who direct what Denny has referred to broadly as "critical/activist" writing centers (2005, 40) about their values and visions are juxtaposed with the commonplace beliefs that circulate unquestioned in our everyday discourses. For example, despite Brian Fallon's (2011) powerful and well-received consideration of the fundamental value of tutor empathy and Grimm's (1999; 2011) enduring arguments about the need for the field to take collective responsibility for changing unjust institutions rather than merely acculturating individual students, respected scholars such as Les Perlman can still count on being able to make, without any controversy, comments like the one he made in a 2016 interview posted on the *WLN: Journal of Writing Center Scholarship* blog:

> *What students need* is to internalize the hidden conversations that are always present in any piece of writing. Writing tutors, by asking questions, making objections, requesting clarification—that is, being a reader that is present—help student[s] define and then internalize the reader who is almost always absent. *That is the writing tutor's most important and extremely vital role.* (emphasis added)

Indeed, it is safe to assume that many if not most writing center folks agree with this characterization. It conforms to what Grutsch McKinney, borrowing from Jean-Francois Lyotard, calls a "grand narrative" of writing center work (2013, 11). We recognize its familiar allusions to Kenneth Bruffee's (1984) celebrated theories of conversation, its implicit privileging of the experience of the reader, and its focus on the writing processes of individual students, and we are quick to agree with its praise for the valuable work of tutors. But critical/activist scholars have been asking us to do the radical work of questioning what we assume students most need, challenging implicit biases of readers, rethinking our beliefs about the work tutors do in relationship to the writer, and indeed imagining more ambitious possibilities—such as resisting injustice or promoting peace—for what a writing center as a community of people can achieve.

So how is it that our radical stories and our foundational assumptions remain in tension? Why are the critical/activist arguments embraced as important topics of interest without fundamentally disrupting business as usual? I argue that while the growing body of anti-oppression scholarship suggests a positive and hopeful direction for writing centers, such work does not merely represent an activist adaptation of existing writing center theories and pedagogies but rather emerges out of a *fundamentally different paradigm*, one predicated on a radical reading of the world. While the work of critical/activist scholars is implicitly rooted in this new paradigm, we have not yet explicitly named it and its influence on our vision. Instead, critical/activist scholars continue to assert new ideas and methodologies without accounting comprehensively for the change in world-view upon which such assertions depend. And would-be supporters across the field fail to fully hear these critical arguments because they are understandably interpreting them through their own different world-views. We are trying to fit a square peg into a round hole, as it were.

We can see this substantial internal miscommunication play out in the field in any number of ways. For example, we see two paradigms clash when student presenters at a recent Northeast Writing Centers Association conference attempt earnestly to draw on the radical possibilities in the work of Grutsch McKinney (2013) to describe a "peripheral" story of their work with ESL writers yet end up articulating a list of familiar assumptions and practices about their sessions that reinforce a grand narrative about such writers as inherently Other. Without access to a different paradigm, it is hard to tell a different story. We see two paradigms clash when writing center directors, working hard to invite their new tutors to engage critically with writing center scholarship on social justice and develop their own philosophies and pedagogies, are frustrated when at the end of the term tutors have by and large consumed common writing center practices, such as playing the devil's advocate, as the only means of engaging with ideological conflict in sessions rather than reinventing these practices. Without knowledge of a different paradigm, it is hard to imagine different practices. We see two paradigms clash when writing center scholars express genuine disgust at racism or homophobia but continue unintentionally to engage in and even celebrate practices that critical/activist scholars have explicitly denounced as perpetuating violence, such as privileging commonplace interpretations of code switching. Without the possibilities of a new paradigm, it is hard to imagine possibilities for sustainable change in action. We see two paradigms clash when anti-oppression efforts are relegated to "special-interest" groups rather than engaged throughout the field. Without a new paradigm, I argue, it is impossible for the field to take hold of transformative justice work.

For radical theories and methodologies to effectively take hold in writing centers, our task requires nothing less than to initiate an entire deconstruction and reinvention of the field. To do so is certainly a difficult task because the complete overhaul of a discipline is a massive and controversial undertaking to say the least but also because we lack the language necessary to describe this process. We need explicit language to comprehensively describe the political assumptions that dominate our field, assumptions that, despite our intentions to the contrary, provide a logic that leads us to continue business as usual. And we need explicit language to comprehensively describe the political assumptions that underlay the arguments by critical/activist writing center people who are deeply troubled by business as usual. Without a common language to fully articulate both our diversity of perspectives and our shared vision of change, we will never bridge the gap. We will continue to tell contradictory stories about writing centers. And we will never, collectively, make good on the radical promise of writing centers. That promise, I argue, is our ethical imperative.

Unapologetically ambitious in scope, *Radical Writing Center Praxis* is an argument for and an explication of a new paradigm for the writing center field. Critical of the ways the field has failed to recognize consciously and name explicitly the necessarily political underpinnings of its theories and practices, I challenge both the conservative values that have rendered writing centers complicit actors in numerous systems of oppression but also the failure of dominant liberal writing center practices to engage in transformative change making. Indeed, I argue that when relativism and neutrality are held up as virtues, the liberal practices that emerge serve to facilitate the very injustices many writing center people in theory despise. Accordingly, despite our many successes, the collective influence writing centers are having on the world is simultaneously violent. None of us, certainly, wants to facilitate violence. The question is, How do we come to recognize when we are facilitating violence, and how do we stop? How do we confidently create peace instead?

This book provides a comprehensive vocabulary for describing the contemporary state of the field in political terms and builds an argument using that vocabulary for what I present as a radical alternative for what our field can become. I use the term *politics* not to refer to specific social issues or contemporary elections but rather ideologies and practices rooted in beliefs about the nature and value of *power*. Drawing on the work of radical theorists and educators including Judith Butler, Henry Giroux, Paulo Freire, Ira Shor, Donaldo Macedo, Patricia Bizzell, bell hooks, Lucien Demaris, Cedar Landsman, and others, the theory of radicalism I put forth is rooted in ecological, humanizing, and liberatory values. Arguing that all "truths" are human constructions (all things consist in ideology), that power and authority are neither inherently good or bad (but rather terrains of struggle and potentialities to be exercised), and that ethical engagement transpires through human agency and reflective action, I propose love, justice, peace, compassion, community, and other similar values as an ethics to be engaged explicitly and actively. In doing so, I build a case for radical praxis compelling writing center folks—directors, scholars, tutors, students, and others—to recognize our daily activities as directly tied up in the stakes of ensuring the future of life on the planet. Necessarily, I examine the ways our beliefs and practices fail to align and propose ways to close that gap.

A radical praxis itself to be sure, this book encompasses the theoretical and the practical, a rigorous analysis of the larger ethical questions and an accessible offering of tangible everyday applications. Emphatic about the ethical imperative for a radical paradigm, this book is not prescriptive in its final answers about what a radical writing center field must look like or in its arguments about how individual centers, directors, and tutors might interpret its meanings. Indeed, there is no one-size-fits-all approach. Our experiences and strategies are necessarily and substantially contextual; the particularities of our navigations and negotiations will be different. Rather, the version of radicalism I propose requires a conscious, collective, ongoing, participatory dialogue within and beyond the field, the outcomes of which I cannot surely predict. Instead, I offer a common language for such dialogue, build a case for this radical engagement, and suggest possibilities for practices meant to inspire and spark the imagination of the field's scholars and practitioners.

Necessarily, what I envision is a long and perhaps never-ending process—one full of struggle, reflection, experimentation, messiness, and joy. This process entails looking back at our history—our scholarship, our practices, and our politics—in order to come to terms with our complicated origins and to more fully understand our present. This process requires that we look beyond our field to grapple with the important work and questions created by those engaged in various social movements, transformative projects, and varied disciplinary research that can provide new insights into our own experiences and inspire new possibilities for developing our work in writing centers. This process also requires that we take a courageous look inward—at the state of the field's scholarship and practices and at our own individual assumptions and behaviors—in order to gather a full and true picture of the strengths we must hone and the failings we must remedy. Finally, this process entails setting a new agenda—individually and collectively—a common language and vision for the field with countless local translations given our varied and diverse institutional contexts.

Our various institutional contexts are significant and will inform how each of us comes to engage with and enact radical praxes. During the two decades I have been involved in writing centers, I have been a tutor, teacher, consultant, or writing and speaking center director in small, medium, and large colleges and universities; in liberal arts and vocational schools; in urban and rural settings; in deeply conservative-leaning and liberal-leaning schools and schools with explicitly radical ambitions; in community-based nonprofit centers, struggling public high schools, and wealthy private international boarding schools; in coed and single-sex (women's) institutions; in secular and religious schools; in primarily white institutions and institutions serving primarily students of color; and in centers in four states and nearly a dozen countries spanning four continents.

In these varied contexts, I have experienced everything from curiosity and enthusiastic support for my radical politics and ambitions to resistance and downright abusive and illegal retaliation. Accordingly, I have learned many lessons along the way about the nature of political struggle, the complexity of negotiation, and the inequities of risk involved and have come to define radicalism in increasingly more nuanced terms. The challenges I have experienced have not weakened my fidelity to radicalism but have rather strengthened my resolve and affirmed my convictions as to the righteousness of such work. I have also learned that radicalism looks very different for different people in different times and places. For those with exceptional privilege, radicalism is often visible and bold and direct. For those targeted by the violence of the oppressive systems radicalism aims to destroy, survival and self-love are themselves radical acts. I emphasize this point to invite all readers to recognize their own radical potential and to assure you radicalism does not depend on finding yourself in the "right" context but rather offers a way to understand and negotiate, on your own terms, whatever context you may be in.

Given the chapter themes, the organization of the book might seem at a glance to move broadly from theoretical to increasingly more pragmatic questions. Seeking to model a radical praxis in the presentation of the text itself, however, the book in fact holds theory and practice in a purposeful tension throughout. The theoretical arguments motivating the earlier chapters are derived from specific, concrete observations about writing center practice; the explorations of pedagogy in the later chapters necessarily prompt new theoretical questions. Indeed, the structure of the book could best be understood as an iterative process bringing the reader closer and closer to the heart of radical praxis. The logic behind the organization itself is a progression of guiding the reader through an examination and dismantling of the dominant paradigm and the rebuilding of a new one.

To those ends, the first chapter, "The Politics of Contemporary Writing Centers," defines and offers politics as a framework through which to understand the history and status of the field, critiquing both the conservative and liberal values and practices that dominate it. Ultimately, this chapter makes a case for dismantling the old paradigm. The second chapter, "A Radical Politics for Writing Centers," offers a new paradigm in its place. I define and build an argument in favor of a radical politics and in so doing call on the field to boldly engage questions of ethics in its theories and practices. The remaining chapters walk the reader through a process of rebuilding the field from this new radical paradigm, exploring in turn the questions of *why*, *what*, and *how*? The third chapter, "Making a Better World," asks *why* we should do writing center work and offers, through an examination of theory and practice, a process of creating a radical vision and mission for writing centers. The fourth chapter, "Love-Inspired Praxis," asks *what* a radical writing center is. By considering a range of common disciplinary frameworks for locating meaning and practice, I offer a process of defining writing center work anew while simultaneously problematizing the activity of definition itself through a radical lens. Finally, the fifth chapter, "Radical Writing Center Practices," asks *how* we do radical writing center work. By examining radical principles and stories of practice, this chapter offers a starting point for the field in engaging new language and conceptions of writing center pedagogy.

Given the book's movement from past to present to future in deconstructing and rebuilding the field, the primary intended audience for this book is curious yet seasoned scholars, researchers, directors, teachers, and tutors currently engaged in writing studies broadly or writing center work specifically, as well as folks who collaborate regularly with writing centers or who do similar work in related programs including speaking centers, reading centers, multimedia centers, teaching and learning centers, English language resource centers, and other tutoring spaces. These seasoned readers will find challenging arguments to unsettle assumptions we often take for granted and new opportunities to imagine the potential of our work. Many in this audience are our leaders who play a substantial role in guiding the direction of the discipline—from regional to international representatives in our professional organizations, to hosts of our conferences, to journal editors and manuscript referees, to other people who control the agenda, the priorities, the discourse, and the grand narratives of the field. Many in this audience are also the field's everyday practitioners, people coordinating centers and programs or offering professional- or peer-tutoring resources at their institutions.

The values many in the writing center field hold dear, such as love, peace, and empathy, align with the same values at the foundation of radicalism. Often a primary obstacle keeping us from making the leap into radicalism is a desire for greater resources, support, and ideas for how to turn our values into tangible action. If compassionate scholars can have access to information about the ways systems of oppression are deeply embedded structures that shape our everyday lives, and tools for how to resist and recreate the world in practice, our potential for positive intervention will increase exponentially. The writing center field, because of its size and will, I argue, holds mighty potential to change the world.

Most of us committed to personal growth generally and justice work specifically recognize the rich learning potential that comes from embracing the discomfort we might feel when having our assumptions or behaviors called into question. Anne Ellen Geller, Frankie Condon, and Meg Carroll (2011) draw on Roland Barthes's notion of the *punctum*—a prick of shame—that "breaks through our notion of the normal and the civil" (Geller et al 2011, 108) to explore a painful but necessary experience for engaging in justice work (they write about antiracism specifically). Significantly, they note that the "stories we learn the most from are the stories most difficult to narrate, precisely because they exceed the bounds of civility, of polite interest, because they prick both conscience and consciousness, because they make visible that which has been hidden from us or that which we have attempted to hide from ourselves and others" (107). Their description resonates with my own experience as a learner. I know I am risking further vulnerability by putting my thoughts onto paper, and I know my readers are also taking a similar risk by engaging and reflecting. So if you feel a prick, seize the moment for what it promises: the opportunity to "name, interrogate, and intervene" (108) in the injustice otherwise at work. This is hard but necessary labor, and it is my intention therefore that the criticisms and challenges I offer throughout be received not as antagonistic but as committed and hopeful invitations. This book is meant to be both clarifying and inspirational, a model to encourage people to take risks to examine what is in their hearts and to take the leap together into radical praxis.

In addition to the courage it takes to look inward and grapple with opportunities to change our own thinking and behaviors, radicalism on the whole takes courage because by definition it speaks truth to power and will always be met with resistance. It is easy to internalize that resistance and to question whether we are doing the right thing or whether our vision of change is possible. For readers inclined towards this work but fearful of stepping into it wholeheartedly, this book is meant to provide enthusiastic support for you to unapologetically engage the ethics of writing center work and to take steps to build the better world you envision. If it is permission to be bold you are looking for, you'll find it here!

For readers who already have a background in social justice work, peace building, or other radical frameworks, be you new or seasoned directors, scholars, researchers, teachers, tutors, or collaborators, this book provides us with a language for extending the conversation beyond the closed spaces of our special-interest groups and out into the field for more meaningful dialogue with people across our political differences to increase our opportunities for real, transformative engagement. It can be tempting, particularly in the hostile contemporary climate of partisan politics in the United States, to dismiss those who disagree with us or whose practices seem ignorant or hopeless. Certainly, some may treat us this way. More often, however, we all have more complicated stories under the surface. Many folks are yearning for something different but are stuck. This book offers a new framework for engaging our colleagues rather than feeling isolated, ineffective, or even at odds. Together, with this language, we can better translate theory into practice as a larger community.

Included in this language is a conceptual framework for bridging the gaps between and among the various oppression-related "topics" (racism, sexism, classism, homophobia, language prejudice, etc.) around which our current scholarship tends to be structured. In addition to enabling our work to be intersectional, this paradigm will allow relationships among like-minded scholars and practitioners to form more readily and for conversations across the field to be more productive. This book offers a language from which we can connect our work and speak with a collective voice in the field. For radical newcomers, the book describes commitments and desires already swirling in your hearts, enabling you to move forward with your work in writing centers with greater reassurance, confidence, and ambition. And for seasoned readers, this book provides new ways of engaging our critical questions with greater nuance and bold ideas for pushing the boundaries of our work in practice. Ultimately, this book is a call to action to bring our work together so we can take it all further.

While some readers will likely disagree with the very premise of the book, that is okay. I do not imagine I will unsettle anyone's deeply held beliefs or convert every reader to radicalism (however much I might wish to!), but I do intend for this book to provide an articulation of why certain pedagogies often clash and a vocabulary for engaging in meaningful dialogue or discussion across our differences. When we have a shared language to more clearly identify those differences rather than speak across one another (and, as is often the case, dehumanize one another), the possibility for stronger communication, meaningful shared learning, and even points of agreement and positive change can more readily emerge.

Directors and other folks of any political persuasion who teach tutor-education courses or lead new-tutor orientations of various kinds may choose to use this text to initiate newcomers to the field. Although many sections of the book speak implicitly in purposeful ways to first-time tutors, if presented only as theory without a desire to experiment with its practical implications, the grand narratives this book critiques will likely prevail. In other words, my arguments are meant to be taken holistically. This book would best be used for tutor education in contexts in which the leadership is committed to radical praxis.

OPPRESSION 101

The purpose of the book, as explained above, is to walk the reader through a process of reinventing the writing center field in radical terms. Radicalism, as future chapters explore in detail, is rooted in hopeful action in resistance to systems of oppression and in service of creating a just and peaceful world. While resistance and radical hope are invoked frequently throughout the book, such invocations rely on a certain degree of familiarity with concepts related to oppression that I take for granted readers will understand. In other words, while the text only occasionally makes explicit reference to terms like *prejudice, discrimination,* or *institutionalized oppression,* a critical understanding of these concepts is an implicit and necessary premise underlying the claims I make. Accordingly, readers who are less familiar with these concepts, or who are working with disparate definitions than those I take for granted, may easily find themselves lost or misread my arguments.

I am using this introduction, therefore, not only to explain the larger aims of the book but in fact to articulate the unspoken readings of injustice upon which much of it rests. What follows here, therefore, is a cursory explanation of foundational concepts related to oppression, illustrated by manifestations in academic or local writing center contexts. The vocabulary offered below is not the explicit language of the book. Indeed, the shared vocabulary I promise is presented in subsequent chapters, not here. Instead, I offer here the conceptual knowledge one needs in order to move forward with the arguments I make. In describing these concepts, I implicitly defend the book's premise that creating a just and peaceful world is not a "special interest" limited to only a few of us but rather an ethical necessity for us all.

Prejudice and Discrimination

To understand the nature of oppression is to understand the differences between individual people's beliefs and behaviors and systems of power. Many readers will be familiar with the concept of *prejudice,* or a preconceived opinion about a person stemming from biases or prevalent stereotypes (generalizations) about the groups to which that person is perceived to belong. For example, a white monolingual English-speaking teacher, Professor Johnson, assumes on the first day of class that his student Emi will not be a very good writer based on her name, what she looks like, and his perception that most international students at his university struggle with English. Professor Johnson, however, has never met Emi, does not in fact know whether she is an international student, does not know what languages she speaks and writes or how well, and has not seen her work. This professor is exhibiting prejudice.

Important to our understanding of prejudice is that it is experienced at the level of the individual. *Anyone* can exhibit prejudice. Just as Professor Johnson makes assumptions about Emi, so too can Emi make assumptions about her professor. Based on her biases about white men, perhaps stemming from poor experiences with past teachers or pervasive beliefs in her peer group, she might assume on the first day of class that this particular teacher will be arrogant or perhaps scatterbrained. Without yet meeting Professor Johnson and experiencing his teaching, her assumptions are also prejudiced.

Also important to our understanding of prejudice is that these personal biases can be both conscious and unconscious. In other words, we might be very aware that we hold certain prejudicial views and are able to communicate them overtly (e.g., "You must be an idiot because all Republicans are idiots!" or "By talking to me you must be hitting on me because gay people want to turn everyone gay!"). With this awareness we may feel guilty and wish to abandon our beliefs yet find it difficult to do so (e.g., "I know not every single Republican could possibly be an idiot, but they just make me so mad . . . I can't imagine how a smart person could argue those positions!"). Or, with this awareness we may feel quite confident in our prejudicial beliefs and desire to cling to them tightly (e.g., "I am against the gay agenda and have no interest in getting to know a gay person!").

The above examples demonstrate individuals' awarenesses of their prejudices. Many of our biases, however, are in fact unconscious. For example, we might sincerely believe all people are equal and think overt expression of racial prejudice is terrible or even a thing of the past. At the same time, because we are bombarded with both subtle and direct messages throughout our lives (on the television, in our social circles, in school, in books, and so on) about who people are and who matters most, we cannot help but take in some of this messaging and incorporate it unwittingly into our beliefs. It is hard for many people to come to grips with the fact that *everyone* holds unconscious biases, even the most kind-hearted and well-intentioned people, because we are all conditioned to some degree by our environments. A Black writing tutor, Alia, might consciously believe Mexican students are no different from anyone else but still harbor unchecked negative assumptions based on stereotypes about Mexicans' cultural values towards education, leading Alia to believe her student Sara's challenge with her history paper has more to do with Sara's effort than the poorly crafted assignment sheet. A phenomenon known as *confirmation bias* leads people in fact to search for and interpret information that confirms their preconceived ideas while disproportionately ignoring information that might contradict it. Alia may not realize her unconscious racial prejudice is the reason she is jumping to conclusions about Sara and may instead believe she is approaching Sara with an open mind.

This unconscious prejudice, just like conscious prejudice, cuts in all directions. Sara in the example above might just as easily feel doubtful about Alia's ability to help her with her writing because Alia is Black. She might consciously think anti-Black racism is wrong. She might even be an outspoken activist against it but nevertheless feel a twinge of discomfort when she is assigned to meet with Alia when a group of white male tutors, who fit the stereotypical image in her mind of academic high achievers, are sitting nearby in the writing center waiting for their students to arrive. She might not realize her own racial prejudice is at play in her desire to meet with one of them instead.

Because our choices in behavior are necessarily motivated by our conscious and unconscious beliefs, *discrimination* refers to the tangible types of treatment we exhibit towards another person based on our prejudice. If Professor Johnson in the first example gives Emi a low grade on her writing based on his prejudicial assumptions about her abilities rather than fairly assessing the quality of her work in its own right, his actions are discriminatory. If Sara, in the other example, asks to cancel her appointment with Alia and meet instead with a white tutor, her actions are discriminatory. Again, because we are talking about individual beliefs and behaviors, anyone can discriminate, and anyone can be discriminated against.

Oppression

Although the above discussion reveals any person—no matter their gender, race, class, age, religion, nationality, sexuality, ability, education, or any other social identity marker—can hold prejudicial views and can choose harmful behavior against another motivated by those views, the *impact* of those views and behaviors is decidedly *not* the same for everyone. When we move from a discussion of prejudice and discrimination to a discussion of *oppression*, we introduce the function of structural *power*. Power, in this case, refers to the ability (often due to financial resources, institutional authority, physical might, or networks of supporters, for example) of one's prejudice and discrimination against another to have a substantial material effect on a person's life.

In the earlier example of Emi and her teacher, given the context of the classroom, Professor Johnson has greater power than Emi because he has the authority to create the assignments, facilitate the class meetings, assess students' writing, and assign grades. By holding the power to assign grades, he implicitly also has the power to influence Emi's other needs outside class, such as maintaining a certain GPA in order to retain her financial-aid package, be eligible to apply for a TA position, or be competitive for graduate school. When the teacher discriminates against Emi by lowering her grade based on his false assumptions about her Japanese American identity, he negatively affects her life in substantial, material ways. Now, Emi might still hold prejudicial views about her teacher. She might even decide to act upon those views, speaking rudely to him or purposefully disengaging from class discussion, but because of her relative lack of power in that space, her choices will not harm him nearly to the same degree. Professor Johnson can oppress Emi whereas Emi can only inconvenience him, if that.

The function of structural power is critical. It is the failure to make this distinction that leads many people to refer inaccurately to prejudice, discrimination, and oppression synonymously. When we fail to consider how discrimination in the absence of power and discrimination in the presence of power are materially different in consequence, we end up talking across one another without resolution. This failed distinction is what leads some people to cry reverse racism or to advocate for men's-rights organizations. It is certainly true that people of color can harbor racial *prejudice* towards white people just as white people can harbor racial *prejudice* towards people of color. It is also true that women can hate men just as men can be misogynists. It is not true, however, that people of color can *oppress* white people, as white people collectively maintain greater structural power (access to financial resources, control of institutions, larger networks of people in some areas, and so on) than people of color. Likewise, women cannot *oppress* men, as men collectively maintain greater structural power. Individual people of color can hurt individual white people's feelings. Individual women can hurt individual men's feelings. Indeed, individual women of color can inflict certain kinds of serious interpersonal harm. But white men can, as a collective, by virtue of their positioning, destroy entire communities/populations.

Institutionalized Oppression

To make the above assertion relies on an understanding, you recall, that oppression is not about individual biases and behaviors but rather systems. In that way, oppression cannot be understood out of context or discerned with absolute certainty when considering any one-on-one interaction in a vacuum. Indeed, it is the context in space and time that creates the conditions of asymmetrical power. It is the context that gives the experience meaning. If oppression were understood as simply individual, isolated expressions of bigotry, we could look at all discrimination in a vacuum and conclude it is really no big deal. The person targeted could simply brush themselves off, leave the space, and go about their life. Indeed, it is this lack of attention to context that allows some people to be dismissive of people's experiences of *microaggressions*—pervasive insults and dismissals. A single insult tossed about on an otherwise equal playing field might be something to ignore, to shrug off. That same insult leveled against someone with less power, someone who has been the target of that same insult again and again and again, becomes a more painful, even traumatic, verbal assault.

Lest we be inclined to think overcoming oppression is simply a matter of growing a thick skin, we must understand oppression is not simply about hurt feelings. It is about material consequences, from lack of access to necessary resources (education, housing, food) to psychological trauma. It is about lacking freedom from intimidation and physical violence. It is about people's lack of ability to live life itself. As Ta-Nehisi Coates reminds us, in reference to racism, oppression is a visceral experience: it "dislodges brains, blocks airways, rips muscles, extracts organs, cracks bones, breaks teeth" (2015, 10). We must always remember, he goes on to stress, "that the sociology, the history, the economics, the graphs, the charts, the regressions all land, with great violence, upon the body" (10). When we look at oppression we must look at the context making the outcomes of the powerful expression of prejudice so devastatingly violent against people's bodies.

One such context is the *institution*. Institutions are organizations, establishments, or societies of people who have come together with a common purpose. They are also laws, practices, customs, structures, or mechanisms of order. Institutions include individual programs or spaces, such as a writing center, a school's biology department, or a university itself. Institutions also include hospitals, schools, television stations, police stations, churches, grocery stores, or banks. From the local to global, we can also understand institutions in their collective forms, such as the US system of higher education, the media, the healthcare system, the job market, the criminal-justice system, the government, Wall Street, and so on.

Institutional oppression, therefore, refers to the discrimination perpetuated by those who hold power within an institution and in fact by all people who participate in the institution's activities. This power is enforced through laws, rules, protocols, practices, and social norms that serve to maintain the existing order. Academic institutions, for example, are structured around certain practices for hiring, compensating, reviewing, promoting, dismissing, or providing resources for faculty and staff. They are structured around practices for admitting, funding, advising, supporting, teaching, retaining, expelling, assessing, and graduating students. They are structured around rules for teaching, conducting research, engaging with the community, and participating in service. They are also structured around cultural practices, extracurricular and social activities, residential life, commuting practices, food service, buildings and grounds maintenance, and rituals and traditions that shape the climate of the institution. All these practices are rooted in specific beliefs about who is valuable and who isn't, what kinds of activities are acceptable and what aren't, what ideas are welcome and what aren't, and how different people should therefore be treated. Sometimes these beliefs are explicitly written and followed as established rules, and sometimes these beliefs are unspoken but nevertheless communicated through cultural norms.

Institutional oppression comes into play when discrimination is inscribed into the very rules and norms of the institution itself. Such oppression might come in the form of sexist hiring practices, racist grading practices, or transphobic bathroom-use policies. It might come in the form of inaccessible buildings, inequitably distributed financial-aid packages, or the use of racist course evaluations by students in considering faculty promotion. Oppression can be perpetrated through the dominant language and discourse practices of the institution sympathetic to rape culture or unsympathetic to mental-health needs. It can also be found in the relative silence of the institution in responding to concerns about sexual assault or racist policing. Oppression can be inherent in the very construction of the institution on land stolen from the indigenous people who once inhabited it and in its continuation of colonizing practices that perpetrate violence against indigenous people who work or study in the institution, as well as against those who cannot or do not enter it. Independent of the personal feelings or values of individual people, the discrepancies in power among different populations are maintained through everyone's participation in the normalized activities of the institution.

For example, the chair of the physics department might himself be a very kind person but nevertheless contribute to oppression by teaching the same introductory course syllabus the department has taught for ages, which only features writings by white men; by unknowingly creating an exclusive climate in his classes by only calling on the people who raise their hands first, even though research shows women are less likely to do so despite having ideas of equal value to contribute; by holding his class in a beautiful but inaccessible old classroom in the library because past (nondisabled) students have enjoyed the charm of the space; by including policies on his syllabus that forbid eating in class, using a laptop, or wearing headphones even though such activities are vital to the health and learning needs of some disabled students; by voting against tenure for the one Latinx woman in the department because he is persuaded by his white male peers that her research on women of color in STEM is too subjective and not a sufficiently rigorous topic for the "hard sciences"; and through his failure to intervene when a group of physics students flyer the campus to advertise an upcoming student event with a poster featuring a homophobic joke—he doesn't want to discourage committed students from majoring in physics, an already small department, and then risk losing funding or faculty lines. This lack of action in response to hate is exactly the kind of institutionalized cultural value that cultivates the hostile conditions that lead bullies to target people like Tyler Clementi, a gay student at Rutgers University, to the point of suicide; or to brutally murder people like Matthew Shepard, a gay student at the University of Wyoming; or to massacre forty-nine young people at a gay nightclub in Orlando on Latinx Night. Oppression rips muscles, remember, and cracks bones.

If we consider the case of Emi and Professor Johnson in a vacuum, we might be tempted to argue that the low grade isn't really a big deal and that Emi actually has more power than I first attributed to her. Maybe she could confront her teacher and ask for a better grade. Or maybe she could rally her classmates to collectively put pressure on the teacher to change his views. Or maybe she could file a complaint against her teacher with the department head. Surely, she could work hard in her other classes and trust that her good grades across the

semester would outweigh the one low grade. Or perhaps in her application to graduate school she could simply explain why that one grade was
so low and trust that the strengths of her portfolio would shine. Indeed,
she could choose to do any of these things. And maybe one or even several of them would work. But more often than not, when considered in
a larger context of the power of the institution, to escape the effects of
oppression is impossible.

Emi's professor's prejudice is not an anomaly. Rather, because she
belongs to a targeted population—Japanese Americans—she is likely
to encounter professors in many of her classes who perceive her just as
unfairly. Japanese Americans historically have endured brutal injustices.
Most notoriously, during World War II, more than one hundred thousand Americans of Japanese ancestry were forced into concentration
camps when the United States government, utterly convinced by its
own xenophobia, justified stripping its own citizens of their freedom to
protect the state. Even before WWII, anti-Japanese sentiments led to the
creation of laws that prohibited Japanese people from becoming citizens, owning land, attending schools with whites, or enjoying civil rights.
In more recent history, the animosity towards Japanese Americans, often
fueled during periods of contentious US foreign relations with Japan
(and China), has continued in the form of physical violence, stereotypes
in popular culture, and the myth of the model minority (a rhetorical
move whereby Asian Americans are strategically pitted against other
racial groups even though they are all harmed by white supremacy). In
the education system, teachers who reject overt discrimination against
Japanese Americans might still harbor unconscious biases. They might
hold unfair expectations about the assumed innate intelligence of their
Japanese American students and fail to provide supports to students
who are genuinely struggling; simultaneously, teachers may nevertheless imagine such students as inherently foreign, their English-language
abilities therefore somehow unnatural, and fail to recognize their actual
achievements and help develop their strengths.

Professor Johnson's own prejudices towards Emi may very well be
shaped unconsciously by this climate. Emi's grades in other courses
might suffer for the same reason. She is likely to be a racial minority
in most of her classes, and in an institution whose curriculum does not
comprehensively integrate examinations of history, racism, and language diversity for all its students (like most predominantly white institutions), she is likely to find herself among students who harbor similar
biases, who lack empathy, or who simply lack the interest or will to
support her in resisting the injustice she experiences. The department

chair, who may have even hired her teacher and is presumably respon-sible for overseeing the curriculum and ensuring the quality of teaching, is unlikely to be her champion in a department dominated by white fac-ulty and largely ignorant of the experiences of students of color. Indeed, when an entire institution is structured around white supremacy, she is unlikely to find access to the supports she needs, except from a minority of sympathetic white teachers or teachers of color who, by serving with-out additional compensation as de facto advisors for many such students of color, are themselves exploited and oppressed by this same system. Perhaps she will find refuge in a multicultural center or a Japanese American student group on campus. But she is likely to find such pro-grams poorly resourced and to suffer the additional abuse of ignorant white students who call *her* racist in her attempt to find support through such affinity groups. In other words, because of the unequal power dynamics, Emi does not have the luxury of leaving this particular class and having the discrimination she experiences disappear. Rather, it has the potential to appear at every turn. It is that collective power of many people positioned to act upon their biases that creates institutionalized oppression. It is that pervasiveness, that insidiousness, that inescapabil-ity, that makes it so devastating.

Because institutionalized oppression depends upon networks of people and norms of behavior, not individual attitudes, even people targeted by the institution's oppression can participate in oppressive activities. Sometimes this participation is conscious and strategic, such as faculty choosing certain research agendas or students adopting par-ticular language practices to get the funding or grade that depends on those agendas or practices. Sometimes this participation is unconscious or uncritical, such as people subjected to oppressive norms believing the messages they receive about their own or their group's inferiority and idolizing the people in power. This phenomenon is known as *internalized oppression*. Indeed, sometimes people oppressed by an institution can be among its most outspoken supporters and the most vitriolic critics of their own community (hooks 2003). This self-hatred and lack of critical consciousness is a significant contributing factor to allowing institution-alized oppression to thrive.

Another way institutionalized oppression thrives, of particular sig-nificance to the audience of this book, is through our rhetoric. Indeed, institutionalized oppression works very hard to fly under the radar, to present itself as normal, natural, unremarkable ways of life. Institutions use language, therefore, that works to ignore, minimize, or obscure recognition of its unjust practices. Often leveled at women, rhetorical practices such as gaslighting, a form of mental abuse in which information is twisted around to take the blame off the abuser and make the victim question her own culpability or even sanity, is one such example of oppressive rhetoric. "Colorblind racism" and the "new racism," described by Eduardo Bonilla-Silva (2014), are other examples, strategies in which a person pretends they don't personally see race in order to avoid engaging with substantive issues around racial inequities and convince the listener racism no longer exists. Dog-whistle politics, similarly, is a way of employing coded messaging that appears abstract and benign but in fact signals a strong, often racist, message to a target group. More recently, terms such as *mansplaining* or *whitesplaining* or *whitemansplaining* have emerged to describe the patterned ways men speak, without regard to their own incomplete understanding, condescendingly towards women; or the ways white people speak, without regard to their own incomplete understanding, condescendingly towards people of color; or how white men speak towards women of color, often about matters of gender and race. In these ways, Emi's teacher might argue that he doesn't see color and that instead Emi's expression of concern about her treatment or grade is just Emi being paranoid, overly sensitive, or entitled. As a result, talking about oppression can be very, very difficult, not only because people in power have a lot to lose by acknowledging it but also because our discourses are rigged by the same oppressive values.

Systemic Oppression

If we continue our examination of the contexts that make the manifestations of discrimination so oppressive, we are compelled to look beyond local institutions or institutions writ large to consider the external environments that in fact shape the institutions themselves. Indeed, our communities, our nations, our global networks are structured by the purposeful interplay of many institutions, none of which could stand alone without the support of and for each other. When one institution is able to operate unjustly, it is because it has the support of many other institutions that allow it to operate unchecked. More often, institutions in fact encourage each other's oppressive practices because to do so is in the interests of those who control the entire network itself. Put differently, the practices of one institution necessarily influence the practices of other institutions. People's experiences of oppression or privilege in one institution necessarily influence their experiences of oppression or privilege in another. It is this interconnectedness, this massive web of institutions, that renders oppression *systemic.*

Consider, for example, the school-to-prison pipeline in which children of color are disproportionately suspended and expelled from school and arrested at significantly higher rates for infractions identical to those committed by their white counterparts, who receive much less severe punishments, if any. This early and disproportionate introduction into the juvenile justice system (whether directly via arrest by an in-school officer or indirectly as a result of criminal activity born of hopelessness after an expulsion) serves to make the reentrance into school difficult (as the student has fallen behind) and the likelihood of finding stable employment with a livable wage (as the student lacks a diploma and now has a criminal record) even more so. A self-perpetuating system, the lack of employment and resources can increase the chances of engaging in illegal activities, which increases the chances of reentrance into the criminal-justice system. This says nothing of the disproportionate policing and sentencing of people of color outside schools. Indeed, 68 percent of all men in state and federal prisons do not have a high-school diploma (Amurao 2016), and nearly that same percentage are people of color (NAACP 2016). Rather than facing each institution (the school system, the criminal-justice system, and the workforce) separately and on equal footing with their peers, children of color are subjected to systemic oppression when the injustices of one institution feed strategically into the injustices of the next. Attorney and civil-rights activist Michelle Alexander has written persuasively about the ways the contemporary criminal-justice system is strategically organized to determine a racial caste system in the United States, no less effective than slavery or Jim Crow at maintaining a legal basis for racial discrimination.

> Today it is perfectly legal to discriminate against criminals in nearly all the ways that it was once legal to discriminate against African Americans. Once you're labeled a felon, the old forms of discrimination—employment discrimination, housing discrimination, denial of the right to vote, denial of educational opportunity, denial of food stamps and other public benefits, and exclusion from jury service—are suddenly legal. (2012, 2)

Identifying mass incarceration as the definitive civil-rights crisis of our time (indeed, the United States has the highest rate of incarceration in the world, has the highest rate of incarcerating its racial or ethnic minorities, and currently imprisons more Black people than did South Africa during the height of apartheid [6]), Alexander exposes the systemic nature of contemporary race-based oppression.

Writer and activist Kevin Powell also paints a picture of how white supremacy and anti-Black racism is a devastating and totalizing system, helping us understand racism as inextricably bound with inequities in power, sustained across multiple institutions.

> Black folks do not control nor own the majority of politics and the government, education, the mass media culture, social media and technology, Hollywood, corporate America, sports teams, music and other entertainment, the arts, the book industry, police departments, anything that shapes the thinking of every single American citizen and resident during our waking hours. Not even close. We do not set the standards for what is considered beautiful or attractive, what is considered courageous or intelligent, nor do we dictate what becomes popular, visible, viable. And we certainly do not say what matters in history, what does not, what stories should be told, and which ones are irrelevant, not for the multitudes—not even close. Our stories, our versions of America, of our history, are marginalized, put to the side, specialized, ghettoized. (2016)

Although Powell is writing explicitly here about racism, our world is structured around many other systems of oppression, each of them intersecting with each other in significant and consequential ways. Powell and others have convincingly demonstrated the mutually constituted functions of imperialism, genocide, chattel slavery, racism, and economic exploitation. We could continue this list to include sexism, homophobia, transphobia, ableism, and many others.

For these reasons, when we return to a consideration of experience at the individual level, we see that real people embody many identities and therefore experience the connectedness of different systems in different ways. A wealthy white able-bodied transwoman, for example, experiences the world differently than a poor disabled transman of color, even though their shared trans identity creates a certain kind of affinity. There is no entirely universal experience, though some experiences are more salient to folks than others. Known as *intersectionality*, a term made famous by scholar Kimberlé Crenshaw (1991), the study of interconnected systems of oppression requires us to recognize, for example, that people do not exist as embodiments of singular identities (such as gender) but rather that our various identities intersect in dynamic ways that render our experience of any one identity (such as gender) different from someone else who might share that same identity. Put simply, as radical activist Alicia Garza has explained, intersectionality is a fancy word "just to say 'three-dimensional people'" (Hammond, *Windy City Times*, May 4, 2016).

Beyond simply a theory of difference, however, Crenshaw reminds us, intersectionality is a theory of oppression that compels us to "account for multiple grounds of identity when considering how the social world is constructed" (1991, 1245). For example, when feminist or antiracist practices "expound identity as woman or person of color as an either/ or proposition, they relegate the identity of woman of color to a location that resists telling" (1242). Failing to tell that location creates further marginalization. It is this observation that leads radical activists, for example, to reject feminist movements that implicitly privilege the experiences of heterosexual cisgender white women and that fail to account for the unique needs of queer women of color (see, for example, McKenzie 2014). Through a different lens, it is this same observation that leads radical activists to reject racial-justice movements that are not explicitly attentive to gender, sexuality, ability, and other forms of diversity (see, for example, Garza 2014) rather than explicitly centered on those most otherwise marginalized, such as disabled trans women. To interpret oppression through an intersectional framework is not to ignore or minimize the ways systems of oppression structure our world in powerful and dehumanizing ways but rather to examine those systems with a sensitivity to the complexity of human experience and, in fact, to build coalitions to resist oppression.

Finally, in coming to understand what systemic oppression is, we must necessarily circle back to the beginning where we first examined individual prejudice. Where does our prejudice come from? Surely, it is the context of systemic oppression, the unavoidable images, messages, practices, and experiences we encounter at every turn in our lives, that teaches us to dehumanize others and indeed to become disconnected from our own humanity, from the earth itself. When the very air we breathe is clouded by oppression, to engage in anti-oppression work is not merely a special interest but rather a vital interest of us all.

Building on this introductory set of concepts, I invite all readers—seasoned social justice scholars, curious beginners, and skeptics—to encounter the chapters that follow with the intention of examining the various ways not only our social identities but also our world-views lead us to interpret oppression differently and to choose different courses of action in response to what we understand, especially as it relates to our work with writing centers. Lest we get overwhelmed and feel defeated by the outline of concepts I've just presented, the vision offered by this book is one that assumes that because systems of oppression are created by people, people also have the capacity to dismantle these systems and build something better in their place. I offer tools to put hope into practice.

The current paradigm of writing centers, however, as the first chapter argues, is at best ambivalent and at worst indifferent to systems of oppression, relying on the premise that the work of writing centers is separate

1

THE POLITICS OF CONTEMPORARY WRITING CENTERS

A Critique of Conservative and Liberal Ideologies and Practices

*We must always take sides. Neutrality helps the oppressor, never the
victim. Silence encourages the tormentor, never the tormented.*
—Elie Wiesel

*If you are neutral in situations of injustice, you have chosen the side of
the oppressor. If an elephant has its foot on the tail of a mouse and you
say that you are neutral, the mouse will not appreciate your neutrality.*
—Archbishop Desmond Tutu

Many writing center directors are familiar with the ways our work over
the past century has been marked by significant shifts in how educators view the text and the production of texts, how we understand the
origins and processes of knowledge creation, and how we therefore
approach educational practices as they relate to the teaching of writing. The stories that tend to circulate in our field about our work are
primarily told through one of two instructive lenses: (1) the *histories*
of educational spaces—that is, the evolution of writing labs across the
twentieth and twenty-first centuries (e.g., Lerner 2009) and the student-
centered and "diversity"-driven practices compelled by the civil-rights
movement and open-admissions era of the 1960s and 1970s and beyond
(e.g., Carino 1996); or (2) the *composition praxis* that has been shaped
by those histories—that is, the evolution of writing pedagogy from
current-traditional rhetoric to expressivism to social constructionism
to postmodernism and so forth and the attending iterations of collaborative learning practices or metaphors inspired by these theories (e.g.,
Gillespie and Lerner 2008).

Building upon these important lenses, in this book I center an
explicit consideration of another prevailing influence I argue is critical
for the field to name: *politics*. To be sure, Jane Nelson and Kathy Evertz

DOI: 10.7330/9781607328445.c001

(2001) offered a valuable edited collection addressing the *Politics of Writing Centers* some time ago, but whereas the politics explored by the pieces in that collection fell under a range of definitions organized topically (from the negotiation of conflict generally to the preservation of writing centers in various institutional contexts specifically) and offered a range of conclusions and proposals in response, this book seeks to achieve something quite different. Specifically, this book engages with a very particular definition of politics and builds an argument in favor of a uniquely radical vision for writing centers.

So what do I mean by politics? I am not referring to national partisan politics (e.g., presidential elections or Republicans and Democrats) or classical political philosophy (e.g., the musings of Plato or Aristotle). Instead, I use the term *politics* to refer to the different ways people interpret, exercise, and value *power*. In other words, politics encompasses both ideologies and the practices that emerge from and reconstitute those ideologies. Similar to George Lakoff's interpretation of a political model characterized by a "cluster of . . . assumptions" (2002, 21), my use of the term *politics* in this book refers to *thinking* and *behavior* as opposed to individual *people* or political *parties*.

As I argue in this book, writing center work has up until now emerged out of politics I describe as conservative and liberal. Strongly critiquing those political frameworks, this book builds an emphatic case for reinvention within a radical political framework. It may be helpful, though, to consider my definition of politics—using Sharon Crowley and Debra Hawhee's terminology—as "commonplace"; my conclusions "may not apply at all times and in all places to people who identify themselves as liberals or conservatives" (2004, 115) or radicals.

This distinction is important because the political frameworks I discuss are merely idealistic—they seldom manifest consistently or "purely" in any real individual. As humans, we are complex and even contradictory beings who defy narrow categorization. While we may resonate strongly with the ideals of a certain framework, our values, beliefs, and behaviors often span many ways of being and doing. We move in dynamic ways across space and time. The particular political frameworks I offer here, despite my critiques of their various shortcomings and opportunities, are not meant to indict any one individual. Certainly, not all self-identified conservatives are authoritarian foundationalists (even though I build a case against conservativism itself for containing within it the blueprint for this possibility), and not all self-identified liberals are pluralists to a fault (even though I build a case against liberalism itself for the failures inherent in that quality). Rather, these political frameworks provide a set of lenses for understanding forces that shape people's thinking and explanations for certain behaviors.

To those ends, important in this definition of politics is the notion that our politics are not necessarily *conscious*. As human beings full of flaws, contradictions, and good intentions, we are each a work in progress. We differ in the extent to which we are aware of our own feelings, perceptions, fears, and desires. We do hold many explicit—or conscious—beliefs and values (e.g., "I believe I should love my neighbor"), but we also possess implicit—or unconscious—biases resulting from our socialization (e.g., "I am fearful of those people"). Our behaviors are an extension of these internal beliefs, both explicitly derived (e.g., "Because I believe I should love my neighbor, I volunteer at the local food bank") and implicitly motivated (e.g., "Because I am fearful of those people, my heart will pound involuntarily when they pass me on the street"). Often, our explicit values contradict the behaviors motivated by our implicit biases, as the example above reveals. As a result, we might profess a particular politics but in practice enact something different. Most of us who desire self-awareness and integrity seek to bring our values and practices into greater alignment, and this text offers tools for doing so.

In the context of this book, *politics* therefore refers to the collection of our views and practices—conscious and unconscious, intentional and unintentional, consistent and contradictory. We cannot escape our politics because all of us have perceptions and practices that stand in some kind of relationship to power, whether we realize it or not, care about it or not, or like it or not. We might, therefore, come to understand our politics as our complicated relationships to power: as negotiated potentialities. This book, however, is not simply about our individual politics. It is about our collective politics—the politics of the writing center field, our educational institutions, our communities, and ultimately the world.

Why examine the politics of writing centers? Doing so enables us to understand the ideologies that have informed the evolution of our theories and practices, and it is therefore a vital factor, as I will argue, in helping us set out a purposeful, effective, and—most important—ethical path for our future. This book is a call for the field to reexamine, redefine, and commit anew to writing center work through an explicitly political lens. Most important, this book puts forth an unapologetic case for privileging a radical politics of writing centers. But to get to that point, we must first examine where we have come from and where we are now.

The political frameworks I am using emerge out of debates that have persisted in the field of education across at least the past century, both in the United States and globally, among teachers and scholars who have found these frames useful in articulating educational philosophies, devising purposeful practices, and locating the reason for dissonant views. Notably, these frameworks have helped educators define and defend their views on the world, the function of education, and the ideal relationship among the student, the teacher, and society. Educators have found strength in the clear statement of virtues, knowledge, behaviors, and skills in service of a greater good that conservativism aims to offer through its fidelity to righteous truths, as well as in the opportunities for engagement with different views, enhanced critical thinking, and global citizenship liberalism aims to offer through its pluralistic reading of the world. When read purely in black-and-white terms, however, either of these frameworks is vulnerable to critique.

For those reasons, to complicate matters further, I also invoke the language of ethics throughout this text, which we might understand as the various means by which people come to make judgments about what is right and wrong. In the field of applied ethics, which examines ways in which people can create an equal and just society, philosophers observe that most people are not clear about the reasons for their own beliefs and indeed that our beliefs can overlap and diverge depending on context. This field of philosophy implicitly makes clear the sticking point of engaging conservativism and liberalism in binary terms: subscribing purely to relativism (a key tenet of liberalism), in which claims of right or wrong are prohibited given its valuing of diverse perspectives, can result in defeatism in the face of real-life problems; subscribing purely to universal truths (a key tenet of conservativism), in which our view of what is right renders other people stupid and wrong, can lead to domination via violence. Are we thus limited to only these two options?

How do we construct an ethics outside this binary? Some philosophers argue for alternative models—a third way (which becomes a binary itself). Others suggest that their models in fact resolve the binary. Materialism, for example, draws on the best of both political frameworks by suggesting humans do in fact have common needs even across cultures (such as love, food, shelter) that should be met while still valuing the diversity of views, contexts, and practices that shape our lives. The educators who have inspired me similarly offer an alternative politics—radicalism—which I simultaneously advocate as superior given my personal beliefs about right and wrong (recognizing, of course, that doing so makes me vulnerable to the same criticism leveled against conservativism) but which I propose for the whole writing center community because more than simply a third way, radicalism offers, I believe, a continuum of possibilities drawing on the best of both other frames (a confident assertion of values and an openness to difference and the unknown). What is important therefore is not the theory for its own sake but what the theory opens up for us. The following discussion explores the ways our prevailing politics have shut down opportunity for creating a just society.

AN EXPLICATION AND CRITIQUE OF CONSERVATIVISM IN WRITING CENTERS: OR, WRITING CENTERS ARE RIGHT AND GOOD (EXCEPT WHEN THEY'RE NOT)

Drawing on definitions found in both education and philosophy, *conservativism* in this book is defined as follows: a politics that (1) interprets power as a commodity or *possession* that enables access to an ultimate *truth*, (2) acquires power through absolute submission to *authority*, and (3) values power as something intrinsically *positive*. If we take each of the above components in turn, we can gain a fuller picture of conservative politics and understand how writing center work emerged from and continues to be influenced by this ideology.

The Commodification of Truth

The first component above maintains that conservativism interprets power as a commodity. In other words, power is understood as a *thing* one can acquire, seize, or hold. The function of power, in this model, is recognized as the means to identifying and actualizing the truth. Power is the authority to define, a window to view, a ticket to gain entrance to, or a weapon to defend that truth.

By this definition, then, conservatism relies on a *foundationalist* world-view—a belief in the existence of absolute, transcendent truths. Truth is immutable and intrinsically right and good. Depending on the particular community or historical moment, those named truths vary. In the United States, conservative politics has manifested in very specific historically and culturally situated ways. Truths have ranged from the devotion to a single omnipotent God, the reverence for a very particular family or social or economic structure, or the righteous fidelity to a virtue such as freedom or self-reliance. Critics of contemporary iterations of conservativism in the United States also interpret conservatism to mean that the more explicitly sinister idolization of systems such as white supremacy or patriarchy can be read as conservative understandings of truth.

Conservative politics can be read throughout the histories of the US political landscape. Relevant to our work in writing centers, we can trace that influence through the evolution of our school systems, and language instruction more specifically. Beliefs about the intrinsic rightness and goodness of Christianity, European supremacy, manifest destiny, and capitalism guided the colonization of the Americas and the systematic rape and genocide and enslavement of indigenous populations, Africans, and poor Europeans. Those same values reemerged through a rhetoric of white-supremacist beliefs in the truth of a singular American identity, religion, culture, language, and phenotype in order to justify the rightness and goodness of the postcolonial state (Horner and Trimbur 2002; Lu 2004; Yamamoto 1999). The founding of US schools and the literacy practices that have dominated those schools, for example, can be read through a conservative belief in singular truths. For example, the descendants of Puritan colonists were responsible for establishing many schools and colleges across the upper northern midland areas of the United States in order to advocate literacy as a means to reading the Bible (in English) and ultimately to salvation: that population's version of truth (Frazer 2006). At the same time, views about the righteousness of the new nation and white supremacy also motivated such atrocities as the US government's strategic policy promoting the removal of Native American children from their homes and its systematic, sometimes-deadly abuse and forced assimilation in hundreds of notorious boarding schools designed to strip those children of their culture (Amnesty 2007).

In this historical context, literacy has always been constructed as white property (Prendergast 2003) and used strategically as a tool to oppress populations who stand to threaten the idealized social order. Think, for example, of the ways African slaves were forbidden to learn to read and write; the ways English-only ideologies and legislation have spread like wildfire across state governments to the exclusion of the language practices of populations of color perpetually characterized as "foreign" (Horner and Trimbur 2002); and the ways the privileging of an imaginary standardized English in schools has been used to deny access to students of color who continue to use their various languages to wield their own power in the face of oppression (Greenfield 2011).

In writing centers, we can see how dominant composition theories at the turn of the twentieth century, and indeed in present times, have been influenced by a conservative belief in absolute truths. Current-traditional rhetoric, a theory of writing distinguished by its exaltation of the text, emerged out of a specific conservative interpretation of idealized form and mechanics. Fidelity not simply to the text writ large but to a specific kind of text—one that emulates the language practices, discourse patterns, and value systems of those who are in possession of power (i.e., white, standardized-English-speaking, Christian, heterosexual, able-bodied men)—is prized by a conservative ideology as ultimately right and good. While many compositionists and writing center practitioners today reject the explicit aims of current-traditional rhetoric, the conservative ideologies that once motivated this pedagogy can still be found flourishing in our everyday practices. Our subscriptions to the necessity of particular "academic" genres of writing (and our rigid interpretations of what those are), our privileging of standardized English, our use of standardized rubrics, our values about what makes for persuasive evidence, our plagiarism policies, our preference for certain linear organization structures or thesis statements or topic sentences, and so on, all rely on a culturally determined and idealized version of what counts as a right and good text—a decidedly conservative practice.

Submission to Authority

The second component of conservativism identified above is the belief that power is acquired through absolute submission to authority. Certain people, prophets, or texts are deemed the bearers of truth, and thus deferring to and emulating that authority is believed to be right and good as well as the path to righteousness itself. Lakoff interprets this ideation of conservativism as the "Strict Father" model in which children must obey their parents (the authorities) and build character through self-reliance and self-discipline (the true and righteous path) (2002). Other analogies might be used well in its stead, including the idolization of Jesus Christ (the authority) and the following of his teachings (the way, the truth, and the life); the idolization of patriarchy (the authority) and the following of its teachings (the adoption of sexist gender roles, policies, and cultural norms); or—with respect to literacy practices—the idolization of the white, heterosexual male teacher (the authority) and the following of his teachings (literacy practices and texts constructed in his own image such as the bildungsroman, the comedy, or the explicitly asserted thesis-driven argument).

Conservativism, therefore, is a closed system. In a self-fulfilling sense, it bestows power and authority upon those who uphold its principles. Because truth is defined as absolute, conservativism therefore structures a perception of the world by how well individuals, institutions, or societies uphold and perpetuate that truth. As a result, conservativism evaluates the world in concrete, binary terms: *right* and *wrong, good* and *evil, white* and *black.* When the authority of right and good people and institutions is threatened, conservativism becomes highly concerned with returning power to those it believes will reinstate the "natural" order. When power resides in the hands of right and true authorities, conservativism becomes exclusively concerned with maintaining the status quo; hence, the derivation of its name from *to conserve.*

In the context of US schooling, conservativism either rejects the authority of teachers and institutions it perceives as promoting values at odds with its interpretations of truth or submits to the authority of teachers and institutions who embody it. In these right and good institutions, where teachers are vested with the authority to define truth, students who struggle or fail to succeed are believed to do so as a result of their own inferior mental capacity, their substandard moral upbringing, or their lack of self-discipline. The trouble is always with the insubordinate or inadequate individual, never with the system.

In practice, conservative education is largely *positivistic,* viewing knowledge as empirical, scientific, objective, politically neutral, and accessible to all—which, its critics say, leaves no room for subjectivity, diversity in values or ethics, contextual qualifications, or self-criticism; and *technocratic,* identifying the acquisition of technical skills, or the kind of thinking that supports the legitimacy and value of those technical skills, as the primary purpose of schooling. In these classrooms the teacher, as bearer of truth, is meant to hold the ultimate authority as both expert and disciplinarian, and students are discouraged from asking questions that challenge either the authority of the teacher or the material presented, lest that material contradict conservative truths. Questions are encouraged only in the service of helping students better understand or learn to arrive at truth. The "banking" model of education, as critiqued by the radical Brazilian educator Paulo Freire (1970), in which teachers seek to deposit knowledge into the presumably empty minds of the students, is derived from conservative politics.

Radical theorist Henry Giroux critiques this positivistic mode of education, arguing that it

> operates so as to undermine the value of history and the importance of historical consciousness in other significant ways: First, it fosters an undialectical and one-dimensional view of the world; second, it denies the world of politics and lacks a vision of the future; third, it denies the possibility that human beings can constitute their own reality and alter and change that reality in the face of domination. (1997, 13)

The unqualified absolutism about how the world should be or, in Judith Butler's words, "who counts as human" (2004, 17) in a conservative model, as radical critics argue (and I agree with them), serves to reify both students and subject matter in a way that divests students of civic agency. Although a popular iteration of conservativism in the contemporary United States promotes an image of the nation as just and democratic, liberal and radical critics see those qualities as merely aspirational and instead characterize the present state quite differently. Radical theorist bell hooks has described US society as an "imperialist white-supremacist capitalist patriarchy" (2003, 11); other contemporary radicals frequently invoke this description, with some variation, including the addition of *militaristic, cis hetero,* and *settler colonial.*

Radical critics Peter McLaren and Ramin Farahmandpur argue more specifically that "all forms of social oppression under capitalism are mutually interconnected" and that "all of these forms of oppression [racism, sexism, classism] are linked to private ownership of the means of production and the extraction of surplus labor" (2005, 23). Agreeing with this characterization, most critics identify the curriculum imposed by conservative educators as serving to enforce a racist, sexist, and classist (and in other ways exclusionary) world-view in the service of capitalism. Accordingly, these systems of oppression are institutionalized in academia. Cary Nelson and Stephen Watt (1999), for example, observe the conservative trend of corporatizing the university as a site of technical production in service of the marketplace. Jonathan Neale summarizes this perspective succinctly:

> Universities do three central jobs in a capitalist system. First, universities and schools justify the division of labour in the whole society . . . The second job universities do is to interpret the world and train new professionals in ways that will be useful to business and governments. The third job is to confuse people about reality in order to keep the capitalist system going. (2015)

While many conservatives are critical of what they interpret to be the liberal views espoused in progressive classrooms across the nation, liberals and radicals are critical of the conservative ideologies they believe are maintained in practice. Rather than teaching to produce better democratic social activists—citizens working to make "the lives of others bearable" (Butler 2004, 17)—universities in practice, liberals argue, are conservative apparatuses interested in preparing subjects to function best within existing social and economic systems.

When we look at the history of writing center theory and practice, we can see the conservative ways the authority of the text, the teacher, and the institution has been and continues to be upheld, even when we struggle to create something different. Our writing centers are often situated within institutions that are themselves structured by policies and practices that limit our own authority. Consider the prevalence of the tenure system for scholars and educators who work in traditionally recognized disciplines and spaces, juxtaposed with the often contingent nature of writing center professionals (for further discussion, see Dawn Fels, Clint Gardner, Lila Naydan, and Maggie Herb's February 1, 2016, post on the *Writing Center Journal* blog). Students who visit the writing center are often coming from classrooms likewise influenced by conservativism, either because of a conservative professor or because of the limits faced by an otherwise liberally minded professor who must carefully negotiate their own stakes when it comes to employment, review, and promotion. Consider the ways institutions position teachers—even those of us who would like to reject this model—to maintain authority over students by creating the assignments, leading lectures or discussions, setting deadlines and rubrics, and evaluating and grading students. We can also see the conservative influences on writing centers that employ the notorious fix-it-shop model, which is a derivation of fidelity to the absolute authority of the institution, the teacher, and the text—whether for pedagogical reasons or to maintain their funding under pressure from the institution. Remedial, text-focused, skills-based instruction preserves the dominant power structure through its methods and goals.

While many contemporary writing center directors and tutors reject this antiquated model and desire to foster more progressive spaces, in practice we often nevertheless unwittingly still defer to conservative thinking that upholds the authority of the institution and the teacher. Stephen North, arguably the most influential voice shaping contemporary writing center discourse and practice, wrote in his pivotal text defining the discipline that tutors should never, out of professional courtesy, question the professor: "Hence we never play student-advocates in teacher-student relationships. The guidelines are very clear. In all instances the student must understand that we support the teacher's position completely . . . In practice, this rule means that we never evaluate or second-guess any teacher's syllabus, assignments, comments, or grades" (1984, 441). Although a decade later he questioned his earlier stance (1994, 13), the influence of that stance on the field could not be undone. Leigh Ryan and Lisa Zimmerelli, authors of one of the most widely used tutoring guides, similarly warn, "Be careful . . . never to comment negatively to students about a teacher's methods, assignments, personality, or grading policies. Recognize that you cannot know everything that transpires in a classroom" (2015, 3). Previous editions of the text asserted the value more overtly: "Even if you think you do [know what transpires in the classroom], it is unprofessional to pass judgment" (2010, 3).

This deference to the teacher's authority as a matter of professionalism (and, implicitly, also the authority of the writing center director who defines professionalism and enforces that interpretation), can be seen in similarly accepted truisms when the tutor is described as a middle person between the teacher and student helping translate the teacher's ideas and assignments into terms the student can understand (Harris 1995) and, implicitly, consume. Such descriptions covertly reassert the authority of the teacher, as the tutor's job is rarely described in terms of helping the teacher learn to better craft their assignment sheets or read the students' writing differently. Without this critical component, the tutor is not, in fact, a middle person but rather a tacit advocate for the teacher. In similar ways, the deference to the institution's authority can also be seen when the tutor is described as a cultural informant, helping the student/outsider learn to understand and adopt the accepted practices and discourses of the university, or a cultural collaborator, engaging across individual differences within the "contact zone" of the writing center (Severino 2005) but not helping the institution change to better meet the needs of marginalized students.

Many directors and tutors feel strongly about creating change and advocating for students but feel helpless in the face of the broader power of the institution. For some tutors, the writing center itself is another institution whose authority proves inhibiting to tutor agency. In particular, the student-centered focus advocated by many centers leaves some tutors in a bind when they feel simultaneously compelled to question institutional authority yet pressured to defer to the agenda of a student who expresses an urgent need to acquiesce to that authority. Writing about such a bind when mentoring multilingual writers, Bobbi Olson has argued persuasively about the need to consider such work through an ethical lens. Wanting to devise practices that change institutional conditions, she critiques the ways writing studies by and large focuses "too much on the needs of the institution at the expense of the needs of multilingual writers" (2013, 2). Nancy Barron (Barron and Grimm 2002) complicates this same question as she reflects upon her work with a fellow writing tutor of color navigating a double bind, one in which teachers expect active engagement and original writing but (sometimes implicitly, sometimes explicitly) punish students of color for writing critical analyses of race.

Because the reasoning for our beliefs is often unconscious, our practices at times may be guided by our implicit biases rather than our explicitly held values. In this way, even within its own systems of logic, the expressed aims of individual conservatives can break down when their explicit values contradict the absolutism of conservativism's tenets. When whiteness or patriarchy or capitalism is the unconscious motivation for a belief, for example, conservativism rejects practices that destabilize the power of those systems, even if individual people who identify as conservative sincerely feel compassion for people who suffer under those systems.

In the context of the writing center, for example, we can see how a conservative deference to authority can maintain contemporary systems of oppression despite our individually held beliefs about the importance of equality or compassion. The privileging of English only—and specifically "Standard English"/standardized English—is held fiercely by many directors and tutors, even when the psychological and social traumas perpetrated on students of color as a result are known. This is the case either because directors and tutors are convinced of standardized English's superiority or, more often, reject its superiority but are stuck about how to imagine and put into practice an alternative. Instead, deference to the authority of teachers (who demand standardized English in their classrooms or who tutors incorrectly imagine will demand standardized English in their classrooms) dominates the practices of many writing center tutors. This particular phenomenon has a substantial history in US education.

Despite often positing literacy as a path to truth (or salvation), US conservativism has historically rejected the very methods that in practice have demonstrated *greater* success for language acquisition for students of color. These methods are rejected, I argue, because to give power to people of color would contradict the authority—the righteousness—of a nation founded on white supremacy. For example, conservativism regularly rejects using students' home languages as a starting point from which to develop standardized English-language skills. John and Russell Rickford document the rejection of the significantly successful Bridge readers in 1977—reading materials meant to teach "students to read first in their native dialect, and then [switch] . . . to the standard language" (2000, 178)—due to the public's "hostile, uniformed reactions to the recognition of the [Black] vernacular in the classroom" (179). This action denied Black students access to the very textbooks that helped them develop standardized English-language skills at a significantly higher rate than did their counterparts learning by strict immersion. This same conservative ideology was evident in the public's outcry against the Oakland California School Board's 1996 decision to allow Ebonics to be used as a language of instruction in classrooms with predominantly Black students—not as course material but as a medium through which to teach standardized English (Smitherman 2001).

As these examples show, even though numerous scholars have argued that students learn a second language best when their home language is recognized and respected (Gilyard 1996; Jordan 1997; Smitherman 2001), many conservative educators vehemently resist this in practice. In his book *Literacies of Power*, radical educator Donaldo Macedo exposes the way such conservatives fulfill their desire to maintain the status quo by requiring the consumption of standardized English yet denying the pedagogical practices most needed to do so successfully.

> Education conducted in "English only" is alienating to linguistic-minority students, since it denies them the fundamental tools for reflection, critical thinking, and social interaction. Without the cultivation of their native language, and robbed of the opportunity for reflection and critical thinking, linguistic-minority students find themselves unable to re-create their culture and history. Without the reappropriation of their culture, the valorization of their lived experiences, the vacuous promise made to students by "English only" supporters that the English language will guarantee them "full participation first in their school and later in American society" can hardly be a reality. (1994, 135)

A conservative politics is at play in writing classes and centers where discussion is expected to be conducted in English only and standardized English specifically, where written work is required to be drafted, revised, and submitted in standardized English, and where students are given no opportunity to challenge these expectations or engage in conversation about the politics of language use. When such questioning is only welcomed at the service of encouraging students to see how the acquisition of standardized English is crucial to their success (e.g., Shafer 2001), a conservative politics is at play. We also see the influence of conservativism in centers where tutors are all or primarily monolingual standardized-English speakers and in centers where multilingual tutors are not allowed or not encouraged to speak in languages other than English when conducting sessions with students, including students who share a language in common with the tutor.

Grutsch McKinney reminds us that the stories we tell about our work are not necessarily reflective of what we actually do—that there are gains and losses associated with our decisions to censor our stories, resulting in "cognitive dissonance" (2013, 4). In this way, despite a dominant narrative initiated by North and perpetuated by many that "we are not here to serve, supplement, back up, complement, reinforce, or otherwise be defined by any external curriculum" (1984, 440), many commonplace writing center practices indeed do exactly that. Practices such as hosting sessions with uninterested students whose professors require them to visit the center, sending written reports back to professors who require their students to meet with a tutor, or focusing all the center's services on one-to-one instruction with students without also working with faculty on their pedagogy all uphold the absolutism of teacher and curricular authority. Such centers are engaged in conservative politics. When writing center tutors are not empowered to work with students to question the institution, question the teacher, question the assignment, or have agency over their own educational progress, such centers are engaged in conservative politics. When writing center directors and tutors see their work as stewards of, separate from, or on the margins of the institution rather than as a catalyst for or facilitator of change within and beyond the institution, such centers are engaged in conservative politics.

Certainly, our engagement may be against our will—the power of the institution has material influence on our opportunities and decision making and can limit the practical potential of our desires to create something different. Those desires are an important starting point, however, and radicalism, I argue, provides new ways to think about how to negotiate and realize them.

Power as Positive

The final component of conservativism identified above is its value of power as something positive. Because it is possessed by right and good authorities, and because it provides access to the truth, power is itself believed to be inherently right and good. As such, conservativism seeks to create, maintain, and expand power when it is in the hands of its established authorities. When it is held by those who express a different ideology, the bearers of that difference—not the power itself—are rejected and feared. Power does not become evil in its own right; rather power (this precious commodity to be protected) has fallen into the hands of evil people and must be wrestled back into the hands of the righteous. Such fear of power falling into the "wrong" hands explains the (unfounded) conservative fear by nineteenth-century slave holders that all emancipated enslaved people would seek vengeance and slaughter their former captors. A desire to limit the power of the government (which does not represent a right and good authority) but support the power of other institutions (such as the church) that uphold a specific version of truth also reveals a conservative perception of power as positive. In contemporary times, some critics argue that conservatives reject the authority of the government when liberally oriented politicians propose legislation conservatives see as encroaching upon their freedoms (e.g., gun reform) but are quick to invoke the authority of the government to endorse legislation that encroaches upon people's freedoms but does so in service of their own dearly held beliefs (e.g., women's reproductive rights). This goes to the point that people rarely fit squarely into a box, and the reasons for our beliefs are often unconscious and contradictory.

In our academic institutions, this aspect of conservativism is most apparent in the views expressed by people resistant to efforts to bring about structural or systemic changes to institutional norms or practices. Viewing the school or the faculty writ large as inherently authoritative bodies worthy of respect, conservatives see the maintenance of these bodies as a positive, constructive, and often moral endeavor. Less likely to question the institution as a structure itself, conservatives more often voice their dissent if an unworthy candidate assumes a position of power (such as a new president with liberal views) or proffers beliefs that threaten the absolute authority of the institution (such as faculty who support student protests or teach courses with social justice agendas).

In the writing center, this aspect of conservativism is revealed, as one example, in centers that employ graduate-student tutors, alumnae, professional tutors, or faculty to work with students and are resistant to undergraduate peer tutors (or even non-English majors or multilingual students) performing the work. Centers that do hire undergraduate peer tutors but who rely exclusively or primarily on hiring criteria sanctioned by the institution (such as a minimum GPA or a faculty recommendation) also fall into this category. In these ways, the authority of a writing tutor is recognized as positive, but certain people (those endorsed by the institution's standards) are deemed more worthy of serving in such a role. For example, at the 2003 IWCA/NCPTW conference, I attended a presentation by a writing center director who explained his impossibly rigid set of criteria for hiring undergraduate tutors in his center, making no effort to hide his distaste for and distrust of the majority of his students. His criteria had led to the hiring of one lone undergraduate peer tutor who he deemed came closer than any others to "analyzing writing" with the "same skill as faculty" and who was alone charged with the daunting task of providing peer-tutoring services to the entire student body. While many writing centers avoid peer tutoring due to the same skepticism this particular director embodies to the extreme, many other directors who do value peer tutoring are not empowered to make such decisions about their staffing. A common and insidious challenge directors face is the pressure to demonstrate their tutors' legitimacy to those who control the funding and to those faculty who remain skeptical of students' ability to help other students. In short, conservativism values the power that comes with authority and is thus very careful to guard it, the consequences be what they may.

Over the past century, as the next section shows, we can trace a significant movement from conservativism to liberalism as the dominant politics informing the theories and practices of the writing center field. Nevertheless, as the illustrative examples above have shown, our work in many ways still carries with it conservative practices informed by conservative ideologies.

AN EXPLICATION AND CRITIQUE OF LIBERALISM IN WRITING CENTERS: OR, IF YOU DON'T STAND FOR SOMETHING, YOU'LL FALL FOR ANYTHING

Though often revered by progressive writing center enthusiasts as the morally superior alternative to conservative ideologies, a liberal politics, which favors relativism, emerged as a dominant politics in the field out of practical necessity to protect those enthusiasts against marginalization or even eradication in higher education. Other scholars have readily noted this "pedagogy of self-defense" (Clark and Healy 1996), frequently interpreted as a strategy for alleviating institutional fears of plagiarism by seeking to minimize the tutor's role in relationship to the writer's ideas and the writing. This strategy of self-defense, however, does not account comprehensively for the ways the field's scholarship and lore rarely if ever make explicit mention of its liberal underpinnings. Not inconsequential, I argue, is the field's failure to explicitly name and grapple with its own politics, which has contributed to our often precarious positioning in the academy and has made us unintentionally passive facilitators of a host of unethical practices.

This de facto liberal politics came about, I argue, in response to our own fear. In many ways, as Harvey Kail (2009) has noted, the writing center field contributes to its own marginalization by perpetuating a particular narrative about itself devoid of a courageous vision statement—a statement that would necessarily clearly and firmly identify our significance. It takes courage to name our politics because doing so then requires accountability for enacting practices that align with the values we espouse. It makes sense that we would be fearful of stepping out of the margins. To step out of the margins would require the field to uncover its implicit biases and to change the ways we both conceive of and enact writing center work. Ironically, our reverence for the grand narrative about writing center work and our fear of challenging the authority of the field's traditions and discourses are themselves functions of a conservative politics.

Even though we rarely name our specific politics, writing centers are always engaged in power negotiations across our institutions. Our work often takes on both conservative and liberal (and radical) practices in an attempt to be welcomed within institutions that are themselves often champions of liberal ideology (e.g., "academic freedom" or "critical thinking") but immersed in conservative practices (e.g., "corporatizing" the university or rigid ranking, reporting, or funding structures). As such, we engage in practices and employ rhetoric that attempts to appease conservative and liberal stakeholders alike. As rhetoricians, we are in fact quite good at this! As a survival tactic, writing centers have sought to distance themselves in seemingly benign ways from the beliefs and values associated with contemporary conservativism but have been cautious about adopting counterhegemonic rhetoric too readily in public lest we become further vulnerable. Problematically (aside from the obvious participation in unjust practices we in theory despise), in doing so, many writing centers have come to define themselves not in terms of what we are or what we want to be but in terms of what we do *not* want to be.

Stephen North's (1984) exposition almost single-handedly provided an archetype for a global network of writing centers who, to this day, often articulate their missions not in clear support of liberal or radical principles but rather in rejection of conservative principles. The following kinds of statements, which employ language that rejects the authority of the teacher and tutor and rejects absolute truth (the rightness and goodness of an idealized text), are ubiquitous in writing centers, as a simple perusal of everyday writing center websites or conversations with folks at writing center conferences across the United States make clear:

> *The writing center does not support the curriculum.*
> *The writing center is not a fix-it shop.*
> *The writing center does not edit or proofread papers.*
> *The writing center does not correct grammar.*
> *The writing center does not do the work for students.*
> *The writing center does not grade papers.*
> *Peer tutors are not "experts."*

It's important to note these declarations are not minor footnotes to otherwise robust and visionary statements of purpose but rather frequently comprise the majority, if not the entirety, of a center's public description of its mission. It is no wonder our work continues to be misunderstood! When we do not explicitly name our politics, we are understood as merely the resulting tension among our vague articulations, our actual practices, and others' assumptions. A failure to recognize or name our politics does not somehow render us devoid of them.

Liberalism, I argue, despite our awkward dancing, dominates the contemporary field in practice. And while it represents, in my view, a positive alternative to conservativism, it too is insufficient. *Liberalism* in this book is defined as a politics that (1) rejects absolute truth, (2) is suspicious of authority (which it equates with power), and (3) views power as negative.

Relative Truths

Whereas conservativism values absolutism, liberalism values relativism. Liberalism departs dramatically from conservativism by refusing to privilege a singular conception of truth. With no fidelity to a universal rightness or goodness, liberalism avoids the promotion of a particular model of the ideal person, family, institution, society, religion, culture, nation, or virtue. It finds value in differences and is comfortable with competing interpretations and conclusions. Rather than reading the world in binary terms, liberalism is accepting of spectrums and hybrids and gray areas. It is responsive to context, history, and varied lenses. Accordingly, liberalism rejects the inherent righteousness of a single entity or system and seeks to interpret the successes, challenges, or failures of individuals as informed not only by their personal attributes and efforts but also by their relationships to broader social, cultural, and systemic influences.

In the US context, liberalism has translated into the denouncement of systems such as white supremacy, capitalism, and patriarchy, condemning them as fundamentally inequitable and unjust. This critical frame has been a driving force behind various social movements and policy changes such as affirmative action, voting rights, marriage equality, and others—movements in which protection of personal rights and opportunities has been sought within systems otherwise designed to advantage some and disadvantage others. Within the education system, liberalism has supported the creation of ethnic studies, gender studies, and other programs that provide a critical lens into history and society otherwise traditionally dominated by a single conservative narrative of experience and truth. Voicing a liberal politics, critic Donald Lazere argues, "College English courses have a responsibility to expose students to socialist viewpoints because those views are virtually excluded from all other realms of the American cognitive, rhetorical, semantic, and literary universe of discourses" (1992, 195).

Liberalism also provides alternative interpretations of a host of master narratives, including conservative accounts of the gross disparity in achievement between students of color and their white counterparts in US schools. Whereas conservatism identifies fault within the individual through theories such as biological essentialism (e.g., Black people are genetically inferior) or cultural racism (e.g., Latinx people don't value education), liberalism is willing to question the absolutism of the system and examine the ways white supremacy manifests in schools and their intersecting systems.

The composition theories informing dominant writing center pedagogies are likewise derived from a distinctly liberal relativism. Expressivism, for example, is a rejection of absolutism predicated on the assumption that each individual is in possession of their own unique internal truth. Social constructionism, likewise, rejects the existence of a primordial truth and instead sees knowledge as both situational and, as its name suggests, constructed through communal discourse. Significantly, one of the field's most privileged tenets—the ever-cited focus on the process, not the product or the writer, not the writing—is a rejection of an idealized text in favor of personal experience and growth.

Critical scholars such as Grimm (2011), Bawarshi and Pelkowski (1999), and Irene L. Clark and Dave Healy (1996) have called into question the ways the field's commitment to North's "better writers," however, raises concerning questions about the ends to which these changed writers are being produced. When a liberal politics prohibits the naming of a specific ethical imperative, believing instead that everything has value, the processes employed in writing centers become open to any and all significations. Put differently, without an articulation of what it *means* to be a better writer, for better or worse, writing centers simply facilitate the strengthening of whatever ideological agendas come through their doors.

To clarify, writers could in theory become better writers when they can independently produce texts that effectively inspire readers to be kinder and more compassionate, to think critically about social injustices, or to take meaningful action for positive change. Just as easily, writers could become better writers when they can write hateful arguments even more persuasively, inciting fear and violence. Better writers can become students who use homophobic language more eloquently in ways that contribute to an exclusionary and dangerous campus climate. As they leave our institutions, better writers can become even savvier at authoring textbooks that woefully misrepresent history and that miseducate a citizenry socialized into dangerous ignorance. Better writers can become journalists who can more effectively stoke the flames of Islamophobia across an entire country. Better writers can become politicians who can better pass legislation that tramples on people's civil rights. Better writers can become more articulate community leaders who mobilize mobs to commit hate crimes. Better writers can become presidents who more easily mislead their countries into war. Without a doubt, the most violent and oppressive dictators and genocidal maniacs across history have shared a very powerful tool of persuasion—indeed, they too could be understood as better writers (and speakers). Beyond the expressed commitments of select individuals courageously speaking out against the norm, a liberal politics prevents the field as a whole from articulating any kind of foundational language that rejects in no uncertain terms those kinds of ends.

Implicit in this liberal value of multiple relative truths is an assumption that neutrality is not only possible but is indeed desirable. In the writing center, the desire for neutrality becomes troubling when tutors rub up against matters of injustice. Indeed, an ongoing subject of concern among tutors in the field involves how to manage ideological conflict in their sessions (Durling, Wiessbuch, and Frank 2009). When taught to believe all ideas are valuable, tutors are often pressured to respect their students' rights to believe what they want to, to defer to the students to control the direction of the sessions, and to focus on the form rather than the content of the texts, even if the students' arguments are offensive or violent.

Liberalism, by its very nature, does not allow tutors to assume any sort of moral authority in challenging the ideas or goals of the writer. In rejecting a single truth, liberalism runs a bit too hastily to the opposite extreme by accepting everything as truth. Catherine McKinnon, a world-renowned lawyer and scholar (responsible for winning the first international recognition of rape as an act of genocide when Bosnian women survivors of Serbian genocidal sexual atrocities were awarded damages of $745 million), has offered a clarifying critique of liberal relativism. During a panel presentation on women's leadership and social justice, she challenged the liberal fear of denouncing traditional misogynist practices in different countries due to the belief that all cultures are equally valid by proposing that in fact all cultures are equally *in*valid and therefore should not be immune to criticism (2010). Nigerian author Chimamanda Ngozi Adichie makes a similar point: "Culture does not make people. People make culture. So if it is in fact true that the full humanity of women is not our culture, then we must make it our culture" (2013). When instead everything is perceived as right and good, tutors become uncritical in discerning between empirical evidence and opinion and unable to assert any kind of ethical position in response to the ideas and practices they encounter.

In some centers, if the students' arguments are particularly troubling, tutors may be invited to play the devil's advocate, adopting a practice that engages minimally with injustice at the level of depersonalized theory, something to be addressed indirectly and tentatively. This strategy is at best disingenuous, as the tutor's goal is usually to lead the writer to see the error in their logic and ultimately come to agree with the tutor's thinking. At worst, this strategy is dangerous if it serves to strengthen the writer's ability to argue on behalf of a violent view they will carry out into the world. Jay Sloan has written tellingly about his own experience feeling "personally and professionally defeated" (2003, 68) as a tutor conducting a failed session with a homophobic student who brought into the session "his steadfast conviction in the same ideology that had kept [Sloan] personally defeated, closeted, and culturally invisible for many years" (65). Expressing frustration in the "game-like stratagems" he was "forced to use" (68) by the dominant writing center paradigm, Sloan ultimately argues such strategies are a barrier to genuine collaboration.

In a liberal model, there is no clear theory by which tutors can show up in all their humanity, dialogue about or argue for what they believe is ethical, and try to effect substantive systemic change. In a liberal model, there are no clear practices for others on staff to intervene if the original tutor is disinterested, incapable, or in danger in the face of an ideologically troubling session. In a liberal model, there is no clear support for a tutor who refuses to engage with a student who is unwilling to have their violent rhetoric challenged to still be seen as a professional doing their job. Likewise, a liberal model offers no clear theory by which directors or tutor educators can argue for what they believe is ethical and necessary when building their programs or hiring, mentoring, or supervising tutors.

Instead, the liberal writing center is producing educators who say things like this graduate-student writing tutor at the 2012 Northeast Writing Centers Association conference: "I don't care if my students' writing is racist—it's not my job to make students better people." While the connotations of making "better people" can surely be interrogated critically, this tutor's indifference to promoting racism should be frightening to everyone. Such a sentiment sounds eerily like the words of people in violent mobs who commit brutal atrocities and then later hide behind the words "I was just doing my job" or "I was just following orders." We might personally object to this kind of sentiment, but it is a sentiment produced by the dominant writing center paradigm: liberalism finds virtue in neutrality, implicitly seeking refuge in the assumption that claiming neutrality excuses us from culpability for others' or even our own wrongdoings. For people who believe so sincerely that writing, tutoring, and learning directly influence people's real lives—as most writing center enthusiasts do—assuming a position of neutrality or indifference is an ironic and troubling stance indeed.

Suspicion of Authority

In contrast to the "Strict Father" model he attributes to conservativism, Lakoff describes the liberal world-view as deriving from the "Nurturant Parent" model. In this model children are allowed to question their parents and explore the world's diversity. They are encouraged to love, respect, and care for others. Liberals tend, in the classical sense, to believe "individuals are, or should be, free, autonomous rational actors, each pursuing their own self-interest" (2002, 19) rather than acquiescing to the will of a single person, institution, or deity. As such, liberalism views authority as something negative and therefore is critical of ways conservative educational practices, holding up the professor as sole expert, focus too much on technocratic training and not enough on democratizing.

In order to maintain "empathy for others" and "to explore the range of ideas and options that the world offers" (Lakoff 2002), liberalism seeks to allow the expression of different viewpoints and to celebrate the rights of all people to their diverse experiences, lives, and perspectives. This politics rejects the imposition of ideas—including the ideas of individual liberals—on others. Lazere, for instance, represents a liberal ideology in his resistance to "imposing" particular political values on his students:

> I am firmly opposed, however, to instructors imposing socialist (or feminist, or Third-World, or gay) ideology on students as the one truth faith—just as much as I am opposed to the present, generally unquestioned (and even unconscious) imposition, of capitalist, white-male, heterosexual ideology that pervades American education and every other aspect of our culture. (1992, 195)

Failing to critically distinguish between imposition and engagement, and fearful of being labeled as hypocrites by conservatives for advocating for the moral superiority of a position, liberal educators often retreat into practices of indifference. Indeed, some liberals fear any association with conservativism so severely they equate it with pure domination and therefore interpret the assertion of their own values as oppression. This fear doesn't come out of nowhere: some privileged conservatives claim to be oppressed when people different from them demand equal rights. Certainly, this is not what oppression means.

In writing classrooms, liberalism often translates into discussion-based, collaborative education models in which the intent of the teacher is that all students have the opportunity to speak and in which the teacher is a co-learner rather than a dictator of truth. Such teachers often seek to create democratic spaces within the classroom where students share a voice in the work of the class and sometimes are invited to vote on different materials or approaches to learning that will be used. The liberal influence on contemporary writing center work in this regard is abundantly clear. The field's rejection of the teacher and the class-room as the ultimate authority in favor of a student-centered model facilitated by peer tutors in individual conferencing is a distinctly liberal move in resistance to a traditional hierarchical model. The dominant practice of writing centers—what the field amorously terms *nondirective tutoring*—emerges from this liberal ideology, as tutors resist imposing their beliefs on students, ask leading questions to draw out writers' ideas, and allow writers to control the direction of the sessions.

Writing center practitioners, ironically, have been woefully unreflective when it comes to examining our own assumptions and practices, taking for granted, in a conservative way, the rightness and goodness of this liberal model. But if we turn a critical eye on the assumptions and effects of those liberal practices, we can see that a liberal writing center model is at best flawed and ineffective and at worst complicit in the oppressive systems it seeks to reject. How is this so? By refusing to privilege any kind of authority, liberal writing center directors and tutors are so fearful of imposing their beliefs on their students that they refuse to lead their students too directly into any kind of serious investigation, analysis, or practice that might be truly transformative in positive ways. Rejecting a conservative belief in absolutism, liberals' valuing of relativism is upheld so vehemently it often comes at the cost of positive social change. Despite good intentions, what comes out in practice is a fatalistic response to social inequality. As Giroux (1988) aptly observes, liberal scholarship commonly critiques schools as sites of domination and reproduction but ultimately maintains a sense of despair by failing to explore emancipatory possibilities.

By seeing oppressive social structures as problematic but nevertheless fundamentally unchangeable, liberalism compels teachers and tutors to try to create democratic "safe" spaces within the classroom or the writing center but focus their lessons and tutorials—just like conservatives—on helping students develop skills to navigate and survive within existing systems. Seeing it as futile to try to change their environments, many liberals work from a defeatist perspective in a way that serves to perpetuate the disparities in power they would otherwise critique. Influential compositionist Peter Elbow, for example, has argued that despite the injustice of language prejudice against students of color, the short-range goal of English teachers must be to help students "meet the demands of most teachers and employers" because, he insists, "we can't wait for a new culture of literacy" (2002, 129). This kind of logic rests on decidedly liberal assumptions. Freire, like most radicals, sees this as "an ideology that humiliates and denies our humanity" (1998, 27).

Given its largely antifoundationalist position, liberalism finds itself in a bind when it is unable to articulate a definitive political and pedagogical agenda. In the words of radical compositionist Patricia Bizzell,

> The anti-foundationalist critics [liberals] do point out the effect of historical circumstances on notions of the true and good which their opponents claim are outside time. In other words, the critics show that these notions consist in ideologies. But once the ideological interest has been pointed out, the anti-foundationalists throw up their hands. And because they have no positive program, the anti-foundationalist critics may end up tacitly supporting the political and cultural status quo. (1990, 265)

This insufficiently theorized political perspective, Bizzell goes on to observe, results in little improvement from the conservative classroom:

> We [liberal teachers] tell the students we are only teaching them about difference. Yet in order to do that, we must deconstruct ideologies the students hold as foundational, a very painful process that students often oppose no matter how egalitarian and nonauthoritarian the teacher tries to be . . . [Many] of us who try to make a pluralistic study of difference into a curriculum, are calling students to the service of some higher good which we do not have the courage to name. We exercise authority over them in asking them to give up their foundational beliefs, but we give them nothing to put in the place of these foundational beliefs because we deny the validity of all authority, including, presumably, our own. (269)

In the liberal classroom or writing center, practice risks devolving into an anything-goes, laissez-faire free-for-all where little critical work actually takes place. This phenomenon revealed itself in a writing center I directed where for several years the liberally oriented peer tutors' number one expressed concern was a fear that they were being too "directive," whereas the number one complaint found in student feedback reports was a frustration that tutors were in fact too passive in their sessions, withholding knowledge that would have been necessary and useful to their learning.

In that regard, a significant way liberalism fails students in our writing centers is in pedagogies about language learning. The oft-cited Students' Right to Their Own Language resolution by the Conference on College Composition and Communication in 1974 was a promising theoretical start but, in contrast to the radical vision of social change that prompted it and the radical scholars who have proposed creative and challenging practices and pedagogies (such as translingual writing [Canagarajah 2013] or code meshing [Young el al. 2013]) in response to it, liberal educators frequently invoke this same resolution to justify their existing practices that in effect ultimately privilege the consumption of standardized English. In other words, these educators cite the resolution to pay lip service to valuing difference without drawing a tangible road map for change. The liberal code-switching pedagogies developed in the wake of the resolution often maintain the status quo. Though willing to recognize the legitimacy of multiple languages and even to admit those languages (in moderation) into the classroom or the writing center, liberal educators nevertheless still resort to teaching standardized English; the acquisition of this language is configured as an inevitable need, often even by teachers who themselves are skeptical of such a conclusion but are uncertain about a practical alternative.

Put differently, liberal educators are willing to engage in some classroom and tutoring practices their conservative counterparts are not, but they are either unwilling or unsure how to put forth a vision for the future that contradicts the conservative model of truth. Liberal educators may seek to reject the authority vested in standardized English by conservative ideology by saying the standard derives its value not from its position as an intrinsically superior language but rather due to its function as a tool for linguistic-minority students to survive within an unjust system; this is an argument I have adamantly critiqued elsewhere (Greenfield 2011) because of its lack of grounding in linguistic evidence and failure to theorize systemic oppression effectively. Despite sounding more palatable, the ends of these code-switching pedagogies are the same as those put forth by conservatives who believe standardized English to be superior. In the liberal writing center, tutors may be taught, for example, that Black Englishes are legitimate and valuable and may even be encouraged to use translation as a tool in their sessions with speakers of these varieties, but ultimately they are expected to help multilingual students acquire the standard. As Christopher Schroeder, Helen Fox, and Patricia Bizzell rightly observe, "'The Students' Right to their Own Language,' whatever revolutionary sentiments may have animated its framers, turned out to espouse methods to make *assimilation to the dominant culture* easier, at least in theory, for students from politically marginalized social groups" (2002, vii; my emphasis). To be clear, I am not arguing that the resolution is inherently assimilationist but that it is vulnerable to such when taken through a liberal framework. Radical educators have derived different meaning from it and used it to different (better) ends.

In short, liberal education has yet to resolve the disparity between its ethical view and its practical pessimism. As a result, liberal writing centers are failing many of their students because they cannot commit in practice to what they claim to value in theory.

Power as Negative

Because liberal politics is suspicious of authority, and authority is equated with power, liberalism also tends to view power itself as something inherently negative. Like conservatives, liberals view power as a commodity and are fearful of what could happen when power falls into the wrong hands. But unlike conservatives, they experience profound guilt when confronted with their own power. Certainly, as our professed values and actual practices are rarely in perfect alignment, people professing liberal values are just as vulnerable to self-interested inconsistencies as are their conservative counterparts. In practice, then, many liberals profess a desire to share the wealth, so to speak, by supporting a range of social-welfare programs for people experiencing poverty or homelessness or hunger, for example, but are fearful of relinquishing their own power and thus resistant to engaging in practices that would fundamentally transform existing social systems. In this way, radical critics of liberalism applaud liberal educators' respect for difference but criticize their failure to theorize power effectively, to come to terms with their own relationships to power, and to develop transformative pedagogical methods.

In the contemporary US context, we can see the ways liberals' discomfort with their own power is detrimental, for example, to queer and racial justice efforts. Rejecting the abstract concepts of homophobia and white supremacy (imagined exclusively as white-robed clansmen burning crosses), many white liberals believe on a conscious level that racism and discrimination based on gender or sexuality are wrong and that all people should have equal opportunity. Unable to come to terms with their own positions of power within these asymmetrical systems, nevertheless, able-bodied middle-class white cis gay men often dominate the discourse about the diverse needs of LGBTQ people (such as centering marriage equality in national debates) while failing to advocate for the needs of "homeless queer youth or struggling elders" or resisting, the "invisibilization and erasure of queer and trans people of color" (McKenzie 2014). Further, such privileged white liberals often employ coded logic and language to absolve themselves of the need to explicitly grapple with the multiple institutional and state-sponsored practices that contribute to gender and race-based violence. By relying on rhetorics such as colorblind racism, liberals can appear reasonable and moral while simultaneously resisting almost all practical approaches to deal with de facto racial or other inequalities. For example, as Eduardo Bonilla-Silva explicates, the rhetoric of what he terms "abstract liberalism" enables people who consider themselves nonracist to invoke liberal principles of "equal opportunity" to reject affirmative action by arguing that people of color should not be provided with "unique opportunities" (2014, 79).

In the classroom or writing center, this liberal discomfort with power can lead privileged teachers and tutors to try to offer their students a voice while lacking a commitment to uncovering and working through the complexities of power dynamics in a way that would fundamentally change the system at large or threaten their own privilege with any tangible consequence. In other words, while privileged liberal teachers and writing center directors and tutors may desire in theory to have a more democratic society (and, certainly, liberally identified people have been responsible for significant social work throughout US history), they are resistant nevertheless to relinquishing their own power in the process.

In classroom practice, this conflict of interests often manifests in liberal teachers making helpful accommodations to students' differences without calling into question the unjust human activities that have rendered such needs as "different" in the first place. Radical scholars Donaldo Macedo and Lilia Bartolomé criticize these liberal practices of accommodation that demonstrate a fundamental misunderstanding about how asymmetrical power relations are reinforced: "By not understanding the critical role of cultural resistance as a learning tool and as an expression of voice, those well-intentioned liberal educators will, at best, embrace a form of charitable paternalism and, at worse, reproduce the very dominant ideological elements they purport to eradicate through the teaching of tolerance" (2001, 119). In other words, teachers cannot work successfully across differences if they themselves do not understand the "asymmetrical power relations that relegate certain cultural groups to a subordinate status" and instead view education as a purely technical issue (126) in which students are simply given the tools they supposedly need to succeed. As a consequence, Macedo writes elsewhere with Ana Maria Araújo Freire,

> by refusing to deal with the issue of class privilege, the pseudocritical [liberal] educator dogmatically pronounces the need to empower students, to give them voices. These educators are even betrayed by their own language. Instead of creating pedagogical structures that would enable oppressed students to empower themselves, they paternalistically proclaim, "We need to empower students." . . . While proclaiming the need to empower students, they are in fact strengthening their own privileged position. (Freire and Macedo 1998, 11)

Likewise, in a conversation with Paulo Freire, Macedo critiques liberal thought most explicitly.

> While we can conceive of diversity that never threatens our [white liberal teachers'] privilege in that we are always in a position to manage diversity (the case of white professors claiming to love diversity of students in their classes) we are still unable to imagine ourselves being managed by diversity. In other words, diversity is good so long it remains charitable and never threatens the privileged positions of white men and women. (Macedo and Bartolomé 2001, 82)

Indeed, Grimm (1999) is frequently quoted for making this very critique of writing centers. While Macedo here references white teachers specifically, liberal teachers of color are not immune to similar behaviors—whether derived from their own internalized oppression that resists the expression of agency of students of color or from a philosophy—which scholar Charles Mills attributes to Black liberalism—that assumes the "categories, crucial assumptions, and descriptive and normative frameworks of liberalism can be adopted with little change to the task of getting rid of [racism]" (blog post on *Pea Soup*, February 23, 2015). Giroux implicitly explains why this sort of paternalism or futility happens when he argues that liberals see their *consciousness* of problems in schools as a *resolution in and of itself;* while working to balance inequalities based on race or gender in the classroom, for example, liberals fail to ask how and why these imbalances are being reproduced as a result of social realities and how and why capitalism creates these inequalities of power (2001, 51). Bartolomé similarly observes that

> by not being willing to deconstruct the very ideology and by promoting a pedagogy of caring only, they [liberals] end up basically arguing for a comfort zone restricted to the classroom only. This position constitutes what Paulo Freire calls an entrapment pedagogy. It is also a process through which middle-class teachers deal with their own class guilt under

the guise of caring for these students either by promoting a false notion of social promotion that deskills students . . . [or] by indulging them in an overcelebrating of self that could lead to a level of narcissism. (Macedo and Bartolomé 2001, 103)

In the writing center, this paternalistic "entrapment pedagogy" is apparent in the way the field celebrates its separateness from the classroom and other institutional spaces, lauding itself as a "safe space" where hierarchies are turned on their heads, where students are centered and differences are celebrated, where the voices of the marginalized are included, and where unlikely relationships can be developed, while at the same time continuing to be run by a disproportionate number of white directors, staffed (at PWIs) primarily by white domestic monolingual English-speaking student tutors (and our professional organizations and published scholarship are dominated by the same), and functioning in ways marginalized tutors and students still identify as reproducing the same conditions and dynamics they experience elsewhere. The writing center, implicitly invested in its own marginalization as an insular program separate from and even antithetical to the problematic practices of the institution, uses this distinction in order to convince itself it is distanced from any kind of negative power. It is an attempt to absolve itself of its responsibility to name its own power, to come to terms with its space or program as an institution in and of itself, to name its relationship to the broader institution as something other than its hapless victim, and, most important, to confront the ways asymmetries in power operate by and through it. Liberals' fear of confronting the power they inevitably wield prevents them from exercising that power purposefully and ethically.

CONCLUSION

The writing center field's unwillingness or inability to name its liberal politics, to critically examine those politics, and to articulate an ethical point of view means that in practice our work is serving to perpetuate systems of injustice most of us in theory would reject. By implicitly though falsely claiming neutrality in relation to power and valuing process as though it is a virtue unto itself rather than a vehicle for any number of both liberatory and oppressive ideologies and practices, writing centers become complicit actors in the more conservative agendas of our institutions. Consequently, I argue that the dominant paradigm of writing centers is fundamentally unethical and must be changed. The following chapter is a call for a fundamental paradigm change in writing centers: an explicit commitment to radical politics.

2
A RADICAL POLITICS FOR WRITING CENTERS
Towards a New Paradigm

Is it possible to teach English so that people stop killing each other?
—Ihab Hassan

As an alternative to conservativism and liberalism in writing centers, this book argues a different politics—a radical politics—should be instituted in its stead. Important to emphasize, this radical politics requires that we not simply tinker with our existing pedagogies but rather that we completely transform the field. As Grutsch McKinney rightly observes, "Many involved in writing center work have internalized what I have called the writing center grand narrative and when confronted by new ideas, our instinct is to see how the new idea fits into our existing internalized, collective narrative. Failing this, we might reject ideas that we cannot place within our existing story of our work" (2013, 16). Indeed, in creating a new radical paradigm, we will necessarily need to commit to new values, articulate a new reason for being, define our work differently, and reinvent our everyday practices, ultimately writing new narratives for writing centers. I invite readers, therefore, to find meaning in the discomfort they may feel as I go off the old script, so to speak, to put forward a new vision, and to consider this vision on its own terms.

Conservative and liberal skeptics may be fearful of what they might interpret as my call for them to "be political." The previous chapter demonstrates that political neutrality is, in fact, an impossibility; power is always negotiated across all human activity. As Bobbi Olson puts it, "As language teachers, the politics of our work has always been present; we just haven't always acknowledged this fact" (2013, 4). What I am calling for, therefore, is not an insertion of politics into writing center work but rather a critical consciousness and naming of the politics already necessarily at play. When we come to see that writing centers have always already been political—that there is no getting outside politics—we can

DOI: 10.7330/9781607328445.c002

be courageous in articulating a specific political vision that brings our values and practices into greater alignment.

DEFINING AND DEFENDING RADICALISM: OR, THE ETHICS OF LOVE, HOPE, RESISTANCE, JUSTICE, LIBERATION, AND PEACE

To be sure, the term *radical* or *radicalism* is often invoked in lay conversation to refer to a range of strikingly disparate people, activities, or histories, from the Far Right to the Far Left. Nevertheless and of great importance, radicalism in this book should not be understood as synonymous with fascism or terrorism or any other extremist interpretation that values authoritarianism and devalues life. Instead, radicalism is, like every other politics, a set of assumptions and practices based on beliefs about the nature and value of power. Radicalism in this book refers to the belief that (1) truth is a human construction; (2) power is not possessed but exercised, and therefore power is neither inherently good nor bad; and (3) authority resides not in people or entities but in ethically engaged praxis (reflective action). Radicalism is, in its centering of human activity, often (though not always) the politics of revolution. In contrast to liberalism, it is dependent upon the explicit naming of specific values. Further, radicalism is committed to using those values as a basis for creating its ethics.

The value at the center of the radical vision put forth in this book is *love*. Philosophers might never reach consensus on the meaning of this word (indeed, radicalism might interpret love as a potentiality, the realization of which we cannot yet fully know), but I use it to point toward a recognition of the oneness or interconnectedness of all being(s), the reconciliation of false beliefs in a self and an Other, and an honoring of and promotion of life and well-being. Significantly, more than simply a feeling or emotion, love is an activity. It is not a noun, but a verb. The antithesis of violence—which is destructive to vitality and integrity—love is *resistance* against oppression and the creative struggle for *justice, liberation,* and *peace* for all. Love requires *hope* that peace is possible.

The Human Construction of Truth and Injustice

Radicalism is premised on the assumption that truth—whether the conservative notion of an absolute truth, the liberal allowance for multiple relative truths, or even the radical basis in love as a sort of guiding truth—is a human construction. Radicalism draws this conclusion from the belief that all things consist in ideologies. In other words, there is no getting outside ideology; every value, interpretation, conclusion, and social state exists because a human held that value, a human reasoned through that interpretation, a human drew that conclusion, a human built that state. In a Cartesian sense, for the radical to put forward a truth is to put forward a truth as a human being. Though many radicals might identify as atheists, radicalism itself is neither synonymous with atheism nor antithetical to religious or spiritual conviction; rather, radicals concede that belief in, knowledge of, or access to a higher power(s) will necessarily be mediated by human experience—such matters therefore remain in the realm of faith, not absolute truths.

The radical interpretation of truth is a paradoxical sticking point for many radically identified people who struggle to reconcile their own sense of ethics or morality within a framework that by definition would call the absolutism of their ethics into question. In this way, radical politics has been vulnerable to critique. Observing the ways many contemporary radical educators argue forcefully for the righteousness of justice, for example, critics of radicalism find flaws in this seeming disconnect between theory and practice. Education scholar Jennifer Gore criticizes what she sees as internal inconsistencies when she says that given radicalism's "proclaimed allegiance to 'empowerment' and 'freedom,' mainstream educators . . . would be justified in seeing these [radical] discourses as hypocritical or at least inconsistent" (1993, 2).

Certainly, like conservatives and liberals, people who identify as radicals are not immune to a lack of consciousness of their own internalized biases, so Gore's observation here—that an inherent contradiction exists between people's claims of ideological neutrality and their insistence upon the absolute righteousness of their own ethical assumptions—is surely a logical critique. Radicalism an as ideology, however, makes no such claims. Radicalism in fact denies the possibility of neutrality in any position and depends upon naming and deconstructing its own assumptions—assumptions themselves consisting in ideology—in order to engage its vision. But whereas a liberal politics is paralyzed in the face of ideology and chooses, rather than to name itself, to instead devolve into existential crisis, to claim (falsely) neutrality in the face of all beliefs, and to throw its hands in the air in defeat against any hope for action, a radical politics is open to its own theoretical undoing yet committed to and hopeful about human agency in practice. In other words, radicalism does not *reject* ethics or ethical action simply because they are human constructions because to do so would render all human activity moot. Instead, radicalism is explicit in naming its ethics, comfortable with irresolution, and committed to reflective positive change making.

Put differently, when radicalism is understood as the superior position in binary opposition to conservativism or liberalism (e.g., diametrically opposed or absolutely different), radicalism risks performing a totalizing function—the same sort of foundationalism at the center of our critique of conservativism. But if instead we understand radicalism, just as we might any other politics, as a source of idealism, it can serve as a beacon for our ethical intentions. Of course, when we position radicalism as an ideal, we risk condemning our imperfect efforts as perfect failures, which diminishes hope and creates antagonism or even violence among us. That is also not the intent. My answer is to invite ongoing interrogation of the political theory but not at the expense of tangible action in service of justice and peace (which, it's important to note, is radicalism's answer to its own internal contradictions). Likewise, radicalism, in working from love as its foundational value, seeks to disrupt oppression in ways that are humanizing, not violent. I therefore subscribe to the approach "soft on people, tough on systems" in response to ways each of us, myself included, despite our best intentions, will necessarily at times be flawed in our thinking and behavior as we fight for justice. Radical praxis must be forgiving of human imperfection and allow for a range of possibilities, just as it calls on us to do better.

Malachi Larrabee-Garza, community justice activist and partner of Black Lives Matter cofounder Alicia Garza, has spoken in meaningful ways about the risks of engaging in "purity politics," in which people are shamed or banished for the slightest flaws in translating vision into action. Everyone is needed, inconsistencies and imperfections and all, in order to grow a critical mass and radical movement for change.

> So when people look at me and be like, "Oh they ain't down because they work at Starbucks," I be like, "You don't know nothing about their revolutionary potential! You don't know a damn thing!" There's a way Alicia [Garza] and I will say we need everyone in this room, if you're a mechanic, if you're a daycare person, if you're a barista somewhere, if you make pizzas, if you're a school teacher, if you're doing homeless outreach—whatever it is—to own it and claim this movement as yours, and to contribute into it because that's the only way that a flashpoint becomes a tipping point becomes a new reality becomes a cultural shift that we can live within. And so if it's something that's othered or seen as theirs, if BLM is not understood as a call in, if Standing Rock is not understood as a call in, then we will fail. So we won't be loving or laughing or nothing without everyone in this room getting down. ("Malachi" 2016)

With Larrabee-Garza's words in mind, I call on anyone inclined toward change-making work to jump in without inhibition. There is no perfect roadmap for change.

Scholar Charles Mills, in his explication of a political concept he terms "Black Radical Liberalism," tells his readers he is "less concerned with the question of whether any African American political theorists actually self-consciously identified what they were doing under this designation than with the question of whether it stands up to criticism as a plausible way forward" (blog post on *Pea Soup*, February 23, 2015). I find this kind of intention persuasive as a framework for making political claims, so I want to make a similar assertion about the political framework I am offering. My concern is not whether people identify squarely with it or with the other broad categories I offer, or even whether those categories need to be understood in distinctive terms, but rather how useful my description of radicalism can be in supporting us in plotting a new direction for the field.

The particular ethical commitments of radicalism depend upon the people and contexts that constitute it, and the particular version of radicalism for which this book advocates is no different. The discussion that follows is a distillation of the collective works of many radical scholars and activists (most notably Paulo Freire, Henry Giroux, Ira Shor, Donaldo Macedo, Judith Butler, and Patricia Bizzell) whose views on education are particularly relevant to our study of writing centers. As mentioned previously, a key ethical commitment I argue for in this book—that I argue should be a foundation for reconstituting the writing center field—is one of *justice*, or, in the words of Judith Butler, "conceptualizing the possibility of a livable life, and arranging for its institutional support" (2004, 39).

When justice is an ethical framework that animates radicalism, the radical project becomes invested in the study of oppression as a product of human creation. In other words, as with any presumption of truth, oppression is understood not as a natural or intrinsic phenomenon but as something conceived of and enacted by people. Notably, radicalism necessarily assumes that if humans can create unjust systems, they can also change those systems. Radicalism does not assume that change is inevitable or that justice is the natural order of the universe—to do so would be to idealize an absolute truth—but rather that change is *possible* and that justice (as a response to avoidable suffering) is a righteous endeavor.

Distinct from a liberal politics, which often devolves into defeatism, radicalism refuses to succumb to a fatalistic view of society. Whereas liberal educators often lament unjust systems but resort to teaching students to survive within those systems, radicals see the primary goal of education to be to work towards positive social change.

Patricia Bizzell talks from a radical perspective when she observes that "change is possible; indeed, this possibility is implied by the argumentative tack typically taken by the defenders of the status quo, of academic literacy as it is presently constituted" (1988, 239). In other words, if social change were not possible, conservatives would not be working so vehemently to prevent it. In the radical words of Freire, for the "naïve thinker, the important thing is accommodation to this normalized 'today.' For the critic, the important thing is the continuing transformation of reality, in behalf of the continuing humanization of [all people]" (1970, 92). Radical educator Ira Shor similarly captures the function of radical—also referred to as *liberatory* or *emancipatory*—education by saying,

> Liberatory education challenges domination by illuminating reality for what it is, a culture where people have the power to confront manipulation. This critical pedagogy invites people to know what is hidden from us and to know how we cooperate in denying our own freedom. A liberatory class can also unveil the limits of domination in a society where the system presents itself as invulnerable. (Shor and Freire 1987, 174)

The hopefulness inherent in the radical perspective has led it to be referred to by many as a *pedagogy of hope* or a *pedagogy of possibility*.

Angela Hewett and Robert McRuer explain a radical pedagogy succinctly: "Dominant discourses are often naturalized as simply 'common sense' or 'truth,' but a [radical] cultural studies pedagogy insists on interrogating how such discourses function as rhetoric—that is, as nonnatural, constructed discourses intended to work persuasively in particular cultural situations" (2001, 103). Butler characterizes the radical project in a similar way: "To intervene in the name of transformation means precisely to disrupt what has become settled knowledge and knowable reality, and to use, as it were, one's unreality to make an otherwise impossible or illegible claim" (2004, 27). In other words, "The norms themselves can become rattled, display their instability, and become open to resignification" (27).

Although proponents of the sort of radical education theory advocated in this book have been speaking out for over a century around the world, their influence continues to remain marginal in the US academy today. Understandably so! Radicalism as a politics of education is a direct threat to the conservative spaces in which we work because by definition radicalism compels fundamental change.

For the writing center field, a radical politics would compel us to reject the inevitability of our own marginalization, to be courageous in explicitly naming our ethical values and commitments, and to be hopeful about the possibility of our work to effect tangible change within our institutions and the world beyond.

Human Agency and the Negotiation of Power

When it comes to how power is interpreted and valued, Giroux has argued that the radical perspective attempts to retheorize authority in a way existing theories fail to do—by connecting authority to freedom and democracy. While conservatives tend to see authority as positive, and liberals view it as negative, radicals posit that it in fact has no universal meaning; rather, it should be considered dialectically: "In its emancipatory model," says Giroux, "authority exists as a terrain of struggle" (1997, 102). This perspective of authority develops most directly out of Michel Foucault's theories of power, which David Halperin succinctly characterizes as something "not *possessed* but *exercised*."

> Hence, power is not intrinsically, nor is it only, negative: it is not just the power to deny, to suppress, to constrain—the power to say no, you can't. Power is also positive and productive. It produces possibilities of action, of choice—and, ultimately, it produces the conditions for the exercise of freedom (just as freedom constitutes a condition for the exercise of power). Power is therefore not opposed to freedom. And freedom, correspondingly, is not freedom *from* power—it is not a privileged zone outside power, unconstrained by power—but a potentiality internal to power, even an effect of power . . . *The aim of an oppositional politics is therefore not liberation but resistance.* (1995, 17)

Such a conception of power is vital to the radical project, which is often—when power is only understood as negative—critiqued as being overly idealistic. Although critics tend to misunderstand the radical project as desiring an unrealistic utopia, radicals instead do not map out an idealized state. Freire explains most aptly that the "fight is not . . . for a democratic society so perfect it suppresses sexism, racism, and class exploitation once and for all. The fight is for the creation of a society capable of defending itself by punishing with justice and rigor the perpetrators of abuse; it is for a civil society capable of speaking, protesting, and fighting for justice" (1996, 160). In this way, radicals strive for a society that is not a knowable entity but a process of openness; says Butler,

> To live is to live a life politically, in relation to power, in relation to others, in the act of assuming responsibility for a collective future. To assume responsibility for a future, however, is not to know its direction fully in advance, since the future, especially the future with and for others, requires a certain openness and unknowingness; it implies becoming part of a process the outcome of which no one subject can surely predict. (2004, 39)

Because power is understood as something to be exercised rather than possessed, radicalism assumes resistance can be enacted by any person. One does not need to have a formal position of power as the president, the boss, or the teacher to work towards change. The everyday community member, the worker, the student, and even the most marginalized of people can wield agency in the face of oppression. This does not mean that a single person alone can change an entire system, or that resistance will look the same for each person, but that every person can contribute in ways that fundamentally resist the discourses of naturalization that constitute oppressive systems, and that collective resistance can be transformative. Necessary to this process, however, is a critical consciousness-raising (what Freire [1970] in Portuguese coined as *conscientização*), whereby people develop a critical awareness of the ways systems of oppression operate to deny humanity and a reflective action—or *praxis*—in resistance to it.

For Freire (1970), as with many radical educators, this process includes examining the ways people internalize their oppression, or take on self-deprecating beliefs and behaviors that validate the system. This process also involves people in relative positions of privilege working *with*, as opposed to *for*, people targeted by oppression. The process cannot be paternalistic but must be trusting and collaborative. Whereas a liberal politics, which interprets power as negative, often leads privileged educators and students to be paralyzed by guilt, to seek to deny their power, or to assume change can only be made by the people targeted by oppression, a radical politics inspires the person of privilege to recognize and exercise their power in service of resistance to the system—taking risks, making use of their platforms, lifting up silenced voices, changing structures, listening and revising their own practices, holding other privileged people and structures accountable, and channeling their resources. A radical writing center, therefore, might exercise its power by using its platform to create space for amplifying otherwise silenced issues, to share resources or space with marginalized groups or movements on campus, or to advocate for change. Clark and Healy, in proposing a "new ethics" for writing centers several decades ago, similarly argue that "the people who work in writing centers should be confident of their own expertise and insight and should be willing to use their unique position in the academy to challenge the status quo by critiquing institutional ideology and practice" (1996, 43).

Together, argues Freire,

> a revolutionary leadership must accordingly practice *co-intentional* education. Teachers and students (leadership and people), co-intent on reality, are both Subjects, not only in the task of unveiling that reality, and thereby

coming to know it critically, but in the task of re-creating that knowledge. As they attain this knowledge of reality through common reflection and action, they discover themselves as its permanent re-creators. In this way, the presence of the oppressed in the struggle for their liberation will be what it should be: not pseudo-participation, but committed involvement. (1970, 69)

Most important, in order for this joint process of praxis to be authentic, a *dialogue* must occur. Monologues, slogans, and "libertarian propaganda" are rejected as futile objects; rather, "the only effective instrument is a humanizing pedagogy in which the revolutionary leadership establishes a permanent relationship of dialogue with the oppressed" (68).

While Freire's theoretical model is derived from his specific context as an educator in Brazil in the mid-twentieth century, those of us working in schools and writing centers around the world today must complicate this theory in light of the ways teachers (and by extension writing center directors or tutors) are not always members of an undifferentiated privileged class and students are not always, conversely, members of an oppressed group. We know that in fact people's positions within systems of oppression are more complex—and often even more contradictory—than this. In other words, a radical politics compels us to explore the intersectionality of individual identities and systems of oppression: individuals do not exist solely as their race, or their gender, or their sexual orientation, or their immigration status, or their economic status, or their physical ability, or any other marker of social identity. Individuals experience a simultaneous interplay of many identity markers—some of which hold relative positions of privilege over others, and vice versa, within a single individual. In other words, few people are absolute oppressors or in all ways oppressed, though some people are certainly more oppressed than others.

In the classroom, this means that while most educators, for example, exercise a degree of power by virtue of their formal titles, many of those very educators still experience oppression due to other identity markers. Black female professors, for example, are still targeted by misogynoir in ways that have material effects on their careers and lives. For example, their expertise is not always taken for granted by students; they can be exploited by serving, without additional compensation, as de facto advisors for students of color navigating predominantly white institutions that do not support them; they can be harassed by campus police; and so on. In contrast, as Michael Messner (2000) and others have observed, their white male counterparts in those same positions of authority enjoy greater privilege. For example, due to their race and gender, their expertise is generally taken for granted by students; their work is more readily made visible and compensated disproportionately higher than other groups; they often enjoy feeling at home at the institution; and so on.

Likewise, many students, despite their structural position at the bottom of the academic hierarchy, nevertheless can wield power by virtue of their other more privileged identities. By writing harsh course evaluations that accuse instructors of imposing bias, for example, white students can negatively affect the performance reviews of faculty of color who teach courses that compel otherwise resistant students to critically examine issues related to racism or oppression (Messner 2000, 458). Cisgender and heterosexual students can perpetrate the same abuse of power against queer professors who employ critical interrogations of gender and sexuality in their courses. Independent of the course content, students wielding privileged social identities can commit regular microaggressions in the classroom in ways that are violent and alienating to targeted faculty, contributing to a general experience of hostility in the climate of the institution. And so on. A contemporary radical politics would compel us to examine the ways people create discourses around identity and power that fail to bring to light the complexity of actual lived experiences and the systemic, rather than exclusively individualistic, ways oppression operates.

A radical politics therefore demands that we engage oppression and justice at the level of language. In other words, we must change the ways we talk about power. Social identities are addressed more and more frequently in our scholarship and conversations, yet we often struggle with how to engage these issues complexly and risk falling back into simplistic liberal characterizations of the teacher as steward of the institution, the power holder, and the student as the oppressed. The idea of a "peer" tutor—one who supposedly reconciles this dichotomy by sharing a space with fellow students as colearners—fails to account in any real way for the complexities of intersectionality. When the social identities we discuss are taken as matters of difference, but not as theories of oppression, we limit our opportunity to enact real change. Many critical scholars (see for example Barron and Grimm 2002; Denny 2010; DiPardo 1992; Godbee 2005; Green 2016; Smith 2012) and an impressive number of recent peer tutors (see for example Gardner 2016; Moore 2016; Wahlstrom 2013; Wang 2017) do critically engage with the multiple and conflicting social identities inhabited by tutors and students, identities that complicate conceptions of peerness and reveal that the asymmetries of power in the tutor-tutee relationship often involve more than a unidirectional imbalance (i.e., tutor as power-full and student as power-less).

Nevertheless, in the absence of a field-wide radical framework to help them understand the practical implications of these arguments, many well-meaning writing center practitioners fall back on assumptions that dominated our scholarship several decades ago.

Such scholarship exploring peerness assumed wrongly that the primary contradiction tutors must negotiate is the dichotomy between tutor as wielding the power of the institution and tutor as lacking power by virtue of their student status. In these scripts, the students—writers who visit the writing center—were always assumed to be power-less. Accordingly, the primary negotiation of power for tutors was perceived in terms of "loyalty" to the hierarchical values of the institution versus "social allegiance" to fellow students, where knowledge was assumed to be diametrically opposed to process (see for example Trimbur 1987). Acknowledging the difficulty or perceived impossibility in resolving this contradiction, scholars such as John Trimbur proposed admittedly "messy" solutions for "training" tutors that prioritized supporting their "autonomous activity as co-learners . . . outside traditional academic channels" before teaching them disciplinary content such as grammar and theory (1987, 27). His proposal for how to develop training models was radical at the time and continues to be persuasive; indeed, the intention to support tutors in coming to understand teaching, learning, and writing on their own terms rather than merely consuming institutional norms is important. Nevertheless, contemporary radicalism invites us to problematize the very assumptions about power upon which his proposal was built.

This kind of liberal theorization of power implicitly assumes power is a commodity that can be emphasized or deemphasized, used in the present or postponed until later, and that it is therefore the job of the tutor educator to support tutors in first creating a communal space and activities with students divorced from institutional power (the "peer" role) before they go on to consume the negative power generally attributed to teachers by virtue of their knowledge (the "tutor" role). A radical understanding of power helps us see that this construct, however appealing, is a false one. The nature of systemic oppression is such that there is no safe space separate from the institution. As Denny reminds us, "The center, like the margin, has a face and needs interrogation and mapping" (2010, 3). There is no universally neutral identity that allows for people to come together as peers first, institutional participants later. People enter into relationships as three-dimensional human beings already positioned asymmetrically. In other words, power is always already at play—our various social identities position us within existing power structures independent of our awareness or intentions. The radical project does not ask if or how we want to construct our social identities in relationship to others (to do so is beyond our control—such is the nature of oppression) but rather how we will exercise power in service of resistance and liberation. A different model of tutor education, as I have argued elsewhere with Karen Rowan (Greenfield and Rowan 2011a), takes questions about power itself—not peerness—as the starting point for framing tutors' ongoing learning and work.

When a liberal politics fails to sufficiently theorize the power of tutors and students, tutors—viewing power as negative—have no choice but to ignore recognition of their power. This failure to theorize power sufficiently plays out unconsciously in many violent ways against certain students when tutors fail to see their own power; for example, white tutors who posture as colorblind (not having tools to understand possibilities for wielding their power in solidarity and instead retreating into guilt) can retraumatize students of color who are working to give voice to their experiences of racism in their writing. Michelle Johnson's research documents many facets of this phenomenon in detail, analyzing what happens when writing tutors do not have the necessary racial literacy (which includes a critical understanding of power) to engage meaningfully about race (2011).

This failure to theorize power sufficiently can also take the form of tutors being pressured to try to give away their power, which is by definition disempowering to tutors targeted by oppression; for example, trans tutors for whom a struggle for basic human rights, safety, and dignity is often a daily experience may be retraumatized by the expectation that they downplay the authority of their knowledge and experiences as (trans) people, especially in the face of writers expressing transphobia. Regardless of the individual views of the writers with whom they work, students whose general experience of oppression is salient, whose daily experience at school is one in which their intelligence and knowledge is systematically dismissed, may find very little incentive to assume a tutoring position in which they are meant to participate in the erasure of their own expertise. Tutors from targeted groups can find the writing center to be an oppressive environment indeed, one that idealizes the dispossession of their power rather than the recognition and ethical wielding of that power for learning, dialogue, and agency. White directors at PWIs, for example, if experiencing challenges in recruiting tutors of color, could look inward and explore the ways this liberal messaging is implicitly circulating and work to develop a philosophy for their tutors in which tutors are indeed empowered as change agents.

Further, within a liberal framework, when power is not theorized sufficiently and tutors are compelled to hand over their power to writers, writers may interpret their tutors' efforts as patronizing rather than genuinely engaged. On the flipside, writers who are genuinely wrestling with their roles at the institution, navigating a complicated political terrain and making difficult decisions about if and when and how to use their many voices (see for example Green 2016), and seeking support from the writing center in the process may be left without the support they need if the center's staff is not equipped sufficiently to explore that political terrain with students. Independent of the final decisions made by students about their writing choices (certainly, some institutions are more responsive to students' public expressions of agency than others), a radical politics would at minimum critically interrogate the ways power operates by and through everyone.

Notably, whereas a liberal approach to writing centers leads us to refer to tutor peerness as defined by a shared status as students, or complicate peerness only in terms of interpersonal differences, radicalism would question peerness when it comes to the power differences related to intersecting social identities, such as gender or age (Cogie 2001), ability (Gardner 2016), race (Johnson 2011), body size (Smith 2012), nationality and language (Wang 2017), and others. And whereas a liberal approach to writing centers aims to create peerness by falsely minimizing recognition of differences in tutors' and writers' knowledge, experience, and social identities, radical writing centers would be more concerned with bringing those differences to light in ways that affect the tutor-writer relationship, and the writer's navigation of voice, and engaging in transformative dialogue. Peerness, like so many other radical praxes, is not a state but an activity. Put differently, whereas liberal writing center philosophies revere peerness and seek to resolve differences as a desirable antecedent to collaborative learning, radical writing center praxis would not privilege peerness (when defined as sameness) as an inherently positive end goal but rather would interpret the positive potential of peerness to be an activity of shared commitments or an effect of resistance born of radical dialogue. In other words, even across differences in ideologies and social positionings, tutors and students who engage those differences in radical dialogue by definition resist the discourses of naturalization upon which oppression depends. Peerness as a construct, therefore, is less useful to a radical project than solidarity, comradeship, or accompliceship. Radical writing center praxis compels us to think about new language that might better define student labor.

For radicals, dialogue is the crux of pedagogy. It is here that the writing center field already holds tremendous potential for revolutionary work. Important, however, is that a distinction be made between *dialogue* (a radical practice of listening to, learning from, understanding, and changing the self and the world in response to the other) and mere *talking* together or *conversation* (a practice open to signification). Kenneth Bruffee's (1984) "Collaborative Learning and the 'Conversation of Mankind,'" a cornerstone of liberal writing center theory, in which the voice of the tutor becomes, in Kail's words, "intertwined with and a vital part of the student's writing process itself" (2003, 82), is not necessarily intrinsically radical. To the contrary, without further qualification, such a practice could be colonizing. Conversation that does not center a humanizing resonance or agency can easily become, despite its intentions, an act of violence. A radical dialogue, in contrast, is always humanizing.

With the understanding of power described in this section, a writing center with a radical politics would recognize the agency of every person, as well as the center as a collective, to engage in resistance and effect change. It would participate in dialogue with people within, across, and beyond its spaces to develop a more sophisticated and critical awareness of how power and oppression operate around, by, and through it. It would center dialogues that seek to understand relationships more critically, as well as identify each person's different and necessary responsibilities and possibilities within a process of resistance, taking stock of real risks as well as real opportunities. Rather than denying the power of tutors and writers, a radical writing center would seek opportunities to support tutors and writers in identifying the power they wield by virtue of their social identities, as well as opportunities for tutors to exercise their unique agency in the face of real barriers. It would not presume to know all the solutions or demand subversive activity on behalf of students but would rather support students in identifying ways the injustices they face are vulnerable to change. And it would take action courageously, undeterred by the unknown, in a process of continually becoming closer and closer to peace.

The Authority of Resistance

Radicalism does not vest absolute authority in individuals but rather in the self-conscious act of resistance against injustice itself. Radicalism is not distinguished by a singular or supreme method but rather by key values (love and hope) that guide the creation of methods. Specifically, radicalism assumes a comfort in unknowingness: radicals do not claim to know the precise path to justice or liberation or peace, or what any of those outcomes would look like with certainty. Radicalism allows for contradictions and irresolution: radicals are not beholden to certainty but rather to reflective agency. Committed to resistance, radicals are not fearful of condemning injustice.

Thus, in a radical model, schools—and writing centers—are recognized as sites of resistance, and teachers and tutors work together with students to exercise power, to question the naturalized authority of inherited truths, institutional norms, and systems of violence, and to develop—in the words of Giroux—"civic courage." Radicals recognize that all education is inherently political, and it is radical educators' responsibility to make their values and politics known. Accordingly, in radical education, teachers are not simply intellectuals but transformative intellectuals who collaborate with students to struggle for positive social change. Many contemporary United States-based radicals identify democratic socialism as their vision; however, radicalism itself is not prescriptive of a particular governmental or economic system, though it is necessarily critical of many. As Butler insists, "Those who claim that a single political direction is necessitated by virtue of this [radical] commitment will be mistaken" (2004, 39). Radical educators seek to deconstruct and explore their assumptions about the relationships among knowledge, power, and desire, working with students to make meaning from their own experiences and to connect with other social movements outside the classroom or writing center. Such a practice is seen as the ethical responsibility of all persons, even and especially if such students come to the classroom or writing center with a different, uncritical agenda. Put differently, a focus of radical education is to "stimulate students to doubt" (Freire and Macedo 1987, 57).

Freire sums up the radical perspective succinctly when he states, "In order to make education democratic, we must simultaneously make the society within which it exists democratic as well" (Macedo and Bartolomé 2001, 90). This is distinct from a liberal model in which democratizing is often limited to the classroom or the writing center but not explored beyond. The radical writing center, therefore, would understand its work not merely as limited to improving the writing skills of its students but in fact extended to effecting positive social change far beyond its walls.

Many liberal educators fear that this sort of political work is reckless. They fear that to encourage students to exercise their power in the service of social change is irresponsible and somehow setting students up for a rude awakening ("Just because the writing center welcomes students' home languages doesn't mean their next professor will! I can't send them off unprepared!") or imposing something upon them against their will ("It's not my place to tell them they have to be activists!"). These fears, however, are not an accurate reflection of the work radicalism compels but rather a projection of liberal anxiety. Radicalism doesn't advocate unconscious action. It is instead based upon reflective action—praxis. Radical activism is purposeful, informed, measured, and contextualized rather than naïve and idealistic. In the example above, students who go on to use their home language for a class where it isn't welcomed would do so consciously and purposefully, with a critical awareness of its risks and opportunities. Or, they might critically and strategically decide to conform to their professor's expectations in that instance. Radical teaching would not prescribe their writing choices but rather prepare them to question the absolutism of what the academy prescribes for them, and why, and make it possible for them to determine for themselves their unique opportunities for intervention.

Further, to the second example, radicalism does not impose a particular belief or action as the one true faith but instead invites dialogic reflection and action. To separate students from their own decision making is considered an act of violence. Radicalism does not try to make anyone do anything against their will, and it doesn't prescribe the methods of resistance. Defying the teacher or marching at a rally are not the only means to engaging in activism. As radical activist Maya Berenholz writes,

> we don't always think of the artist who paints portraits of activists who inspire her. we don't always think of the dancers who make space together with young folks to connect to their bodies and to each other. we don't always think of the farmer who teaches a workshop on growing greens indoors. we don't always think of the friend who goes to her other friends' events to support them. (2016, 13)

Indeed, just as activism is sometimes big, loud, and visible, it can also be small, subtle, or unseen. In fact, Buddhist monk and human-rights activist Thich Nhat Hanh writes in his book *Being Peace* that bringing peace to the world is a ripple effect that starts simply within one's own ways of being: "If we are peaceful, if we are happy, we can smile and blossom like a flower, and everyone in our family, our entire society, will benefit from our peace" (1987, 13). Indeed, a critically conscious rejection of dominant prescriptions of activism could itself be interpreted as radical praxis. And lest we forget, writing itself is active.

Further, we would be wise to consider the violent political work we perform passively when we do *not* engage in radical praxis.

WHY WRITING CENTERS NEED RADICALISM

I argue that writing centers need radicalism because without it we are not realizing our full potential to be effective and—most important—ethical as a field. To suggest the writing center field is not currently sufficiently either of those things is not to dismiss the very real and very good things the field has accomplished. Certainly, many people have benefited—benefited tremendously—from their experiences with writing centers, myself included. We wouldn't be dedicated to this work otherwise! Rather, the argument here is that while many individual writing centers are committed to radicalism (Catherine Savini's leadership at Westfield State University is one such exciting example), the writing center field as a whole does not unanimously claim transformative justice and peace as its very reason for being. For example, as of 2017 when I am writing this text, the International Writing Centers Association—a key voice for and shaper of the field—features in the "Resources" section of its website a short list of essays that reflect the same narratives that circulate in conversation among directors and tutors at writing center conferences across the country and that inform the practices of many centers. Among the five texts offered as suggested readings for new or prospective writing center professionals are two pieces written over thirty years ago that articulate conservative and liberal conceptual frameworks for writing centers (Harris 1988; Simpson 1985), pieces that explicitly name individualism as a core value and professionalism as a rationale forbidding tutors to challenge authority. In addition to a brief bibliography that hasn't been updated in nearly a decade, the other two texts include thoughtful sample reflections by directors on their experiences in particular institutional contexts—reflections that are instructive in their own right but, when positioned as comprehensive foundational resources to newcomers, reinforce several problematic dominant themes: the debate between product and process (Erard 2006) (rather than social change as a possible mission); a challenge to peerness in terms of interpersonal difference when it comes to age and professional experience (Weber 2016) (rather than social identities marked by power differentials in the context of systems of oppression); and an implicit endorsement of capitalism and conservative practices, such as a spotlight on a writing center located in a bank whose value is derived from its function teaching employees to perform writing skills to suit their employers' expectations (Weber 2016) (rather than exploring a broader liberatory vision). Explicit references to politics in general, or love, justice, peace, or radical politics specifically, are nowhere to be found. This observation is not meant to be a criticism of any of these individual writers nor of the website editor, but rather, when taken together and presented as foundational (to the exclusion of any number of more radically oriented accounts available), they illustrate that our professional organization is communicating a very narrow and specific (and largely uncontroversial) message about the field—one that has not yet embraced radical praxis.

When we tell the history of writing centers and when we talk about the philosophies and pedagogies that guide our work as a field in these ways, we continue to ignore the many people who have been excluded from our centers and professional organizations and who have been harmed by our methods. We ignore the long-term impact of our practices on the lives of people whom we have not served well. And we ignore both the missed opportunities for changing and the implicit participation in enabling some of the most horrific systems of violence within, beyond, and even far beyond our walls around the globe.

A liberal politics of writing centers allows us to argue that working towards justice is simply not everyone's interest or that taking on the task of changing the world is an imposition on individual preferences to simply do writing center work the way we always have, the way we know and love and believe in. Many of us know such an assumption is steeped in privilege, for it is indeed a privilege to reasonably expect exemption from this goal but still feel overwhelmed and unsure about how to change our practices. To be clear: nobody *wants* to have to do revolutionary work, and no one finds it easy. As my brilliant former student-turned-colleague Keshia Pendigrast beautifully expressed, "Nobody *wants* to be a feminist. Rather, people *have to* be feminists because gender oppression leaves no other option." (Keshia would rather spend her time scuba diving than be forced to advocate for the rights and freedoms from violence that her home country denies her.) But the conservative and liberal paradigms for writing centers, ones that allow people to opt out of radical humanizing work, enable people to oppress and kill one another.

I say this because we live in a world suffering from staggering violence fueled by the cumulative effective of our local actions and enabled by our inaction. Whereas conservatives might argue that such violence is simply human nature or even that suffering is a necessary part of life, and liberals might argue that it is terrible but will never change, radicals argue that violence (and the rhetorics of violence) is created by people for specific cultural purposes and is therefore not inevitable. According to the World Health Organization (2016a), 35 percent of women worldwide—that's more than one in three—experience interpersonal violence in their lifetime. In some parts of the world, the rate is much higher; in Tanzania, for example, the rate of violence against women by an intimate partner is reported at 71 percent. In the United States, it is estimated that one in five women has experienced rape or attempted rape in their lifetime (National Sexual Violence Research Center 2015). Native American women are raped at twice that frequency (RAINN 2016). Women with disabilities experience domestic violence and sexual assault at a 40 percent higher rate than women without disabilities (American Psychological Association 2016). Trans women of color are estimated to be the victims of hate violence at a greater frequency than any other population in the United States (Terry 2015). And when these various and other targeted social identities coalesce, some women are so vulnerable to abuse it is unimaginable. Sickeningly, almost half those who experience sexual violence are children (RAINN 2016). In the Democratic Republic of Congo, reports (Adetunji, *Guardian*, May 12, 2011) estimate that forty-eight women are raped every hour—that's more than 1,152 women every day—more than 12 percent of the population. Forty-eight. Every. Hour. Grotesquely, children and even babies are also targeted.

Indeed, rape is not only an act of interpersonal violence fueled and enabled by patriarchal societies but has been and continues to be used as a strategic tool of war. This is why the astronomical violence of rape we see in the Democratic Republic of Congo is not an anomaly nor merely "collateral damage" but rather is comparable to what is routinely perpetrated in many areas of armed conflict, including present day Syria (Wolfe 2013), just as it was before in Bosnia and Herzegovina, Croatia, Peru, Rwanda, Bangladesh, Cambodia, Cyprus, Haiti, Liberia, Somalia, and Uganda (UNICEF 1996), and in the U.S. war in Vietnam before that (Turse 2013), and when the United States invaded France during WWII before that (Schuessler, *New York Times*, May 20, 2013), and during the European colonization of the Americas before that (Amnesty 2007). The statistic of violence towards Native American women cited earlier comes into greater focus when we recognize that the majority of present-day perpetrators are nonnative men (Amnesty 2007), continuing a legacy of settler-colonial violence specific to the ongoing occupation of this land. Indeed, weapons of both imperialism and capitalism, rape and slavery continue to be tools of an underground yet rampant global marketplace where many more than the reported tens of thousands of people are victims of human trafficking—modern-day slavery consisting of sexual exploitation, forced or bonded labor, domestic servitude and forced marriage, organ removal, and the exploitation of children in begging, the sex trade, and warfare (Costa 2009). In the United States, where thousands of cases of human trafficking are reported annually, slavery also continues out in the open as the for-profit prison industrial complex takes advantage of the caveat written into the thirteenth amendment of the constitution, which makes allowances for slavery and involuntary servitude "as a punishment for crime"; that the United States ~~enslaves~~ imprisons more Black people today (NAACP 2016) than were freed at the signing of Lincoln's 1863 Emancipation Proclamation (Gates 2014) should come as no surprise, though it certainly should shock.

We live in a world where at least sixty-seven countries are currently engaged in some known form of war, and where a combined 711 drug cartels, militias/guerillas, and terrorist, separatist, or anarchic groups are involved ("List of Ongoing Conflicts" 2016), statistics that are themselves subject to debate, as they woefully underrepresent United States involvement in conflicts abroad and fail to recognize, for example, the state-sponsored domestic terrorism described by present-day colonized peoples of the Americas and African diaspora. Conservative estimates of upwards of two million deaths have been attributed to the US "war on terror" begun in 2001 (Lazare 2015). In the United States, the Centers for Disease Control and Prevention estimates that roughly fifty-six thousand people per year suffer violent deaths (CDC 2015), including almost thirty-three thousand deaths by guns ("Gun Violence" 2014). The recent rise of hate groups in the United States (the Southern Poverty Law Center documented 917 active groups in 2016), including the Ku Klux Klan, is a frightening reminder of how vulnerable we can be to hateful ideologies, especially when such ideologies are systematized into our policing and criminal-justice system. In the United States, Black adults and children are killed by police officers at alarmingly high rates. For shopping at Walmart (John Crawford). For standing on the sidewalk (Eric Garner). For walking down the street (Michael Brown, Rekia Boyd). For playing at the park (Tamir Rice). For sleeping on Grandma's couch (Aiyana Stanley Jones). And rarely is the perpetrator indicted for, not to mention convicted of, the crime. Xenophobia plays out in other violent ways as Muslims, for example, are shot for being terrorists, which they aren't (Giridharadas 2014), and Sikhs are violently assaulted for being Muslim, which they aren't (Kaplan, *Washington Post,* September 10, 2015).

In Connecticut, a young man can enter an elementary school and murder twenty-six young children and educators with military-grade guns while the world reels in horror, and then numbness takes over as an average of one school shooting per week continues across the United States ("185 School" 2016). Abroad, terrorists can enter a school in Peshawar, Pakistan, and massacre 148 people, mostly children (Saifi and Botelho 2014). Young Pakistani girls are shot on school buses for claiming their rights to education, and most of their attackers are acquitted (Wescott 2015); their first and only woman prime minister (Benazir Bhutto) is assassinated just a few years earlier, and innocent civilian families (comprising 90 percent of those killed) in Pakistan have their bodies exploded into pieces by bombs dropped by US drones (Fang, *Huffington Post*, October 15, 2015). This same atrocity extends into Yemen, Somalia, and Afghanistan. Outspoken female critics like politician Malalai Joya survive repeated assassination attempts by Afghani warlords ("Malalai" 2009). Youth in Saudi Arabia risk beheadings for nonviolent protests (Benjamin 2016). Queer activists in Bangladesh are hacked to death for promoting LGBT acceptance ("Editor" 2016).

Worldwide, at present, nearly sixty million people have been forced to leave their homes to escape violence, a number that is dramatically on the rise (Graham 2015). Many have been dispossessed due to colonization/occupation/gentrification. In the United States, there are an estimated 46.7 million people living in poverty (United States Census Bureau 2015). Worldwide, that estimate is 1.3 billion, most of whom are children and 22,000 of whom die each day as a result. Eight hundred and five million people suffer from a lack of access to food, resulting in three million deaths per year. More than 750 million people lack access to clean drinking water, leading to 2,300 deaths each day. Lack of access to healthcare results in the preventable deaths of two million children each year and countless more adults ("11 Facts" 2016; UNICEF 2015).

In India, where poverty is rampant, many of the country's 4.6 million women sterilized each year are coerced into the usually dangerous, sometimes-deadly procedure with the promise of meager compensation, as are the health workers who perform them (MacAskill 2013). In Slovakia, racially targeted Romani are similarly coerced or forced to be sterilized (Center 2016a), while hospitals in Chile routinely sterilize HIV-positive women without their knowledge or consent (Center 2016b). Indeed, the rights of women to have autonomy over their own bodies is threatened around the world, from countless women who lack access to reproductive health decisions to more than two hundred million girls spanning more than thirty countries, including the United States, who have experienced forced female genital mutilation (World Health Organization 2016b).

This disregard for life manifests wholesale and intersects with other forms of violence as the Amazonian rainforest is razed to make room for commercial agriculture and cattle ranching. Animals suffer unconscionable abuses during their unnaturally short and exploited lives on factory farms around the world, representing a gross distortion of generations of subsistence-living practices of indigenous communities guided by a profound reverence for the circle of life. In the United States alone, more than nine billion animals are raised and slaughtered each year for human consumption, the waste from which causes alarming rates of air and water pollution ("Factory" 2016), wreaking havoc on the environment. From fracking that rapes the earth and pollutes our water, to the massive amounts of garbage dumped into our oceans, to human-made ocean dead zones, to global warming, the violence humans are inflicting on one another, on animals, and on the very planet that sustains us is nothing short of a global crisis of the most profound order that implicates us all. This list of atrocities could go on for volumes. It is neither representative nor, frighteningly, even remotely exhaustive of the violence human beings are perpetrating around the world.

It is understandable that we could read such a list and be completely overwhelmed. Without a radical framework, it also makes sense that we could read such a list and think, "Yes, those things are terrible! But what do those problems have to do with writing centers? Writing centers don't exist to solve those sorts of problems! Writing centers exist to help students become better writers! Writing—not peace and justice—is my area of expertise! I do classical rhetoric." Or "I do research methods." Or "I'm just a collaborative-learning enthusiast." To bolster our hope and courage and to see ourselves as people capable of intervening, however, we can begin by resisting conceptualizations of writing center work as internally logical and inherently good, as an idealized space separate from the world around us. After all, writing cannot at once be meaningful and meaningless in its relationship to the world. We can also learn to grapple with our own relationships to and participation in these systems. After all, our work with students cannot at once be meaningful and meaningless in its relationship to the world. A radical politics helps us understand there is no space or position outside a totalizing system. Rather, our writing centers stand in relationship to the systems of our institutions, which are themselves part of a larger web of systems beyond the academy, and thus we all exercise power in service of or in resistance to the violence such systems perpetuate. Who we teach, what we teach, how we teach, where we teach, and why we teach are all necessarily informed by our places within these systems and in turn have an effect on the perpetuation or dissolution of those systems. If the field grabs hold of radicalism and reorients itself towards such a vision, rendering radicalism the norm rather than the exception, those of us who feel less equipped to take on these critical analyses, less familiar with models of change making, and less certain about how to engage such a vision in writing centers in relationship to our individual research and teaching interests will find a more abundant—indeed ubiquitous—community of resources to support us.

Even more specifically, as writing educators, we know language is both constituted by and a creator of ideology. The language we use, the language we teach, and the values we implicitly promote through our writing centers shape our larger cultures. How we interact with one another—how we communicate—creates conditions either liberatory or oppressive. What we do with our words either promotes peace or incites violence. Our failure to speak and our failure to act enable existing violence to continue. We do not live in a vacuum such that the perpetrators of abuse are acting somewhere far away from us and our work. Violence is perpetrated in the writing center, as it is across our schools, as it is across the globe.

When Boquet, invoking the work of Mary Rose O'Reilley and O'Reilley's mentor Ihab Hassan, invites the writing center field to ask if it is possible to do our work so that people stop killing each other (Boquet 2014, 24), the shock we may feel at such a stark juxtaposition of activities—tutoring writing and saving lives—reveals how difficult it can be to recognize how our work is inextricably mingled with the larger workings of the world. Do we want our centers to play a central role in facilitating violence? Of course not! So part of our work will be to develop language in our missions, in our publications, in our discourses that clearly and pointedly articulates our rejection of participation in violent practices and our unwavering commitment to be facilitators of justice and peace. If we are reenergized by a sense of hopefulness and possibility, we can be creative about how we employ language to those ends.

THE PROMISE AND RISKS OF RADICAL WRITING CENTERS

Trimbur makes the optimistic claim that "social justice and the democratization of higher education have always been parts of the mission of writing centers" (2000, 30). Grimm has argued convincingly, however, that because "so many writing centers were developed by people influenced by the liberal sympathies of the late 1960s and early 1970s," writing centers are in fact "particularly implicated" in a *defensive reaction* to social change. Believing in education as progressive and liberating, writing centers have sought to help create college access for previously excluded populations by teaching them "to be more like us" rather than rethinking education itself (1999, 12). When the field lacks a common language for defining its mission in social-change terms, those of us committed to such work are left to navigate uncharted territory as we try to communicate a mission within and outside our individual centers.

This failure of the field to articulate a radical mission, and to fully support the development of writing centers through a radical framework, is what would enable a conservative tutor, such as a recent outspoken undergraduate at a small liberal arts college writing center, to be understandably offended by what he described as unwarranted criticism from his director that he was not contributing to the "safe space" of the writing center (Glick, *Claremont Independent*, February 26, 2016). Resigning from his job with the rationale that "the writing center's mission is to teach writing, not ideology" and publishing an open letter to explain his grievances in an independent conservative student newspaper (of which he was the editor in chief), this former tutor made a familiar argument in favor of an "apolitical mission." While liberal readers might rightly scoff at his mocking suggestion that he "hadn't realized the writing instruction would be delivered with a side of ideology and that the ideology was not only mandatory but also more important than the actual teaching of writing," his critique is not necessarily off base. Indeed, in his letter he appeals to the language the writing center field has defended for decades—what Grutsch McKinney has identified as a "grand narrative" of writing center work (2013, 3) in favor simply of providing one-to-one consultations with writers. As Grutsch McKinney has reminded us, "Writing center work is complex, but the storying of writing center work is not" (3). The "cognitive dissonance" that necessarily emerges "between the work we do and the work we talk about" (4) was both jarring to this tutor and simultaneously baffling to many in the field "for whom the telling has become so naturalized, so transparent, that we no longer recognize our tellings and retellings as one of many possible representations" (4). To be told, as this tutor interpreted it, that he must consume and prioritize particular arguments about racism, capitalism, and heteropatriarchy—arguments with which he disagreed and about which he saw no connection to tutoring writing—in order to perform his job, was indeed an aberration.

From the student's expression of grievance alone, we can see ways both the student and the writing center field were at fault in this dispute. A radical politics makes clear that there is no value-neutral work and that in order for our work to be ethical, we must be courageous to name and enact those values. When the fundamental value of the writing center is love, and tutors are unwilling to explore the ways their words and behaviors may be dehumanizing to others, such tutors have no business working in a writing center (or anywhere else that involves collaborations with different people). I do not know the director's side of the story (though I am inclined to be sympathetic to that director and applaud their efforts as I read between the lines of the disgruntled student's letter), but I can indeed affirm that if the student was unwilling to be reflective about the kind of environment he was creating for students, the director was justified in requiring a change or terminating his position. Writing centers should be confident in taking a stand against implicit violence and saying, "No, if you are not committed to reflecting upon how your behaviors affect other people's safety, you cannot work here."

At the same time, the writing center field cannot continue to talk about its work as though an apolitical approach were indeed possible. If questions of social identity and power are not lenses through which tutors come to learn about writing and writing center work but rather special topics introduced later in their learning (if at all), tutors such as the one in the story above will be justified in their resistance to what appears to be an imposition of ideology, failing to see the connection to their work. Radicalism is dependent upon agency. It cannot be imposed, only engaged. Radicalism does not say, "You must believe this conclusion." Instead, it invites questioning about assumptions. Radically inclined directors have a hard time with this in practice because our field does not yet provide a foundation for it. As a result, many writing center directors teach their tutors "topics" widely favored by radical scholars (such as antiracism, antisexism, antiheterosexism, etc.) but do not know how to teach the assumptions about ideology and power that necessarily underlay these arguments. This student's failure to understand that *he too* brought a distinct ideology into the center and failure to articulate the values and assumptions central to that ideology were shortcomings of both his own thinking and of the field he entered that was unable to be an abundant resource for him in developing a more sophisticated, critical reading of political dissonance. What resulted was, I can only assume, a battle of wills over issues, not a radical dialogue about different philosophies of learning, communicating, and community building. That writing center may very well be better off without him (I wouldn't be inclined to employ him in my center!). But he has a fair claim to make about the field's false advertisement.

Despite my firm critique, all hope is not lost in making good on the radical potential of writing centers. Indeed, because writing centers have reached a ubiquitous status across institutions of higher education in the United States (and increasingly in both primary and secondary schools) and are emerging in numerous countries across the globe, the field holds a mighty collective potential for cultivating significant transformative change. Significantly, many of our philosophical persuasions hold potential for revolutionary work if only we can critically examine them through a radical framework rather than remain beholden to received wisdom.

Though daunting, a truly radical politics must be open to its own undoing. This means there are risks involved. Adversaries will make themselves known, for sure. Resources may be taken away. Our centers themselves may crumble in the face of opposition. We may lose our jobs. It may bring an end to the field as we know it. But a radical politics compels us to be courageous in facing the unknown. Others in the field have made a similar call; Frankie Condon has encouraged us to "risk uncertainty and failure" (2007, 31) and to "extend ourselves beyond what has been said and done—beyond the known" (32). For when we face the known—a system in which we are complicit in perpetuating injustice and violence—we can see that the status quo is unequivocally unacceptable. Change is necessary. This is not a call for an end to writing centers! But it is a call to put an end to our inaccurate claims of neutrality and to hold ourselves accountable.

As we struggle to bring our theories and practices into greater alignment, we must recognize our individual paths will look very different. Our positions of relative privilege or oppression within and beyond our institutions mean the personal challenges, risks, and costs will differ significantly among us. The consequences of enacting an overtly radical politics are most dangerous to those who are targeted by the systems the radical project is resisting. Inherent in that danger is the promise of transformation, as the systems depend on the complacency of those they subjugate in order to persist. In other words, resistance and change are possible. Writing center scholars, directors, tutors, and students who inhabit positions of relative privilege have an ethical commitment to use their power in service of positive change.

Jamaican writer Marlon James, critiquing the ways well-meaning people adopt a passive approach towards racial justice, makes an important distinction between being "non-racist" and "anti-racist." To be nonracist, he explains, means to adhere to a moral stance and life code for dealing with all the injustice in the world "by not doing a damn thing": "I don't sing the 'N' word." "I don't burn crosses." "I'm not a skinhead." Meanwhile, injustices continue. To be antiracist, he offers, is to get active, to hold people accountable, and to recognize that injustices in the world are to an extent our fault (2016). Many conservative and liberal writing centers might imagine themselves to be *non*-oppressive in the ways most people who work within them, I will generously assume, are well-intentioned and do not seek to cause harm (I say *imagine* because we know systemic oppression operates by and through us, regardless of our intentions). The radical writing center, in contrast, is an *anti*-oppressive space, one that actively seeks to understand and dismantle oppressive systems. Important, however, to the theory of radicalism advocated in this book is a politics rooted not merely in opposition but also in hopefulness. As such, while radicalism operates squarely *against* injustice, it also operates purposefully *for* justice, love, peace, and other humanizing activities. *Against* and *for* are mutually dependent. In other words, the radical writing center seeks to build, not only dismantle.

In the primarily liberal politics of the contemporary writing center, many directors and tutors are willing to acknowledge oppression exists but do not know how to take steps towards action that would bring about transformative change. Freire argues that our critical investigation of oppression "cannot be purely intellectual but must involve action; nor can it be limited to mere activism, but must include serious reflection: only then will it be a praxis" (1970, 65). The following chapters offer a starting point for developing radical praxes in writing centers.

3

MAKING A BETTER WORLD
Rearticulating a **Raison d'Être** *for Writing Centers*

We have to get over this whole writing thing.
—Brian Fallon

This book is a call for a paradigm change for writing centers. As such, rather than offering a how-to guide structured by a familiar rubric that moves from theory to practice or that provides a pragmatic offering of strategies in terms of institutional positioning, recruitment and hiring, tutor education, tutoring practice, assessment, and so forth, I am suggesting instead that we start from ground level and rebuild the writing center field anew, imagining radical possibilities for our work unencumbered by the trappings of the past. The next three chapters bring the reader through the process of building that radical writing center field, proposing new responses to foundational questions that ground every discipline: *Why? What? How?* Specifically, I ask, *Why* should we do radical writing center work? *What* is radical writing center work? *How* should we do radical writing center work?

This chapter takes on the first of those questions and explores *why* we should do radical writing center work. In other words, in a radical paradigm, what is the writing center's *raison d'être*—our most fundamental reason for being—and how do we articulate that vision? While the radical project is by nature dialogic and hopeful, not static or merely reactive, the liberal writing center field so often crafts the language it uses to describe itself in defense against perceived misunderstandings that we rarely collectively pause to map out a positive vision of the future. To engage in ethical practices, we need to get clear on what, exactly, we want writing centers to *achieve*.

A REASON FOR BEING
The conservative writing center takes its ethical impact for granted by measuring very specific outcomes that cater to existing institutional

DOI: 10.7330/9781607328445.c003

interests (e.g., average grades yielded by visitors, attrition rates of visi-tors, postgraduation jobs of tutors, etc.). The liberal writing center takes its ethical impact for granted by mistaking objectives for outcomes (e.g., if a lot of students are coming to the writing center, we are doing good work in the world). A radical politics, in contrast, compels us to ask why those outcomes matter, whom or what those outcomes best serve, and whether different outcomes might be more just or more clearly con-nected to resisting oppression or creating peace.

Better Writers?

Despite our varied institutional contexts, the work of many centers is strikingly similar: the common commitment to North's ideal that "in a writing center the object is to make sure that writers, and not neces-sarily their texts, are what get changed by instruction" (1984, 438) is so ingrained in the field's discourse that it fails to be questioned. Indeed, this mantra is nothing short of a doctrine to which many a writing center has clung with religious zeal since his game-changing argument more than three decades ago, even despite North's own objections some time later (1994). This mission statement is deeply troubling, as is argued in the first chapter of this book, in its failure to articulate any ethical com-mitment with respect to its work. *What* is a better writer? To what *ends* are these changed, better writers being produced?

We can see, as Bawarshi and Pelkowski have interpreted, the colo-nialist ideology motivating this agenda, as the "basic assumption for North is that changed writers are improved writers because changed writers are writers who can better function within academic discourses and the university" (1999, 45). Certainly, a writing center might resist this interpretation and instead explicitly define better writer in more transformative terms. Although an improvement, the compulsion to define the aims of our work at the level of the individual writer—rather than at the level of the larger systems in which we operate—serves to deny the culpability of those systems and perpetuates a myth that through mere grit alone a single student can somehow transcend oppression. I argue, as do other radical scholars—most notably, Grimm (1999)—that the aim of better writers is insufficient at best, and unethical at worst, as a mission statement for writing centers. In rejecting this statement, I do not suggest a return to privileging the *text* over the writer but rather a commitment to being more critical in our examination of our sociopolitical contexts and more courageous in our ambition to reorient our view about who or what we are trying to make "better." In many ways, this means in fact redefining our relationship to texts and writers.

At the National Conference on Peer Tutoring in Writing a number of years ago, keynote speaker Brian Fallon (2011) made an important argument about the central role empathy plays in the relationships peer tutors form with their students (echoing a sentiment Noreen Lape [2008] promoted several years prior). This quality, this skill, he argued, is more important than the technical knowledge of writing or writing processes tutors may impart to their mentees. In fact, in an offhand remark, he offered a gem of a sentiment: "We have to get over this whole writing thing." Indeed, despite the field's efforts to promote processes over products, to focus on the writers rather than the writing, our failure to articulate an ethical end goal for these processes, for the development of these people, perpetuates false claims about the inherent righteousness of people and processes that remain open, in fact, to infinite significations. Writing can't be an ethical end goal and neither can the ability to write well when we do not articulate the work such writers and writing do in the world. What is the impact of such people and texts? Who is harmed and who is healed in the process? What oppressive systems are resisted and what opportunities for liberation are created by their texts? So as Fallon suggested, we must all get over this whole writing thing and instead, I argue, we must all get really into this whole justice and peace thing. Doing so doesn't eliminate writing, nor even marginalize it really, but rather gives us a lens through which to more courageously make meaning with and in relationship to it.

A Better World

Clark and Healy make the radical assertion that ethical writing centers should "offer a broad, encompassing vision," one that "will look past individual texts and writers to consider the whole range of literate practices in the academy" (1996, 43). With an eye towards the "larger discourse communities" in which students operate, Clark and Healy emphasize the classroom as an important realm for which the writing center "ought to show some concern" (43). Grimm, in her postmodern critique of the writing center, similarly argues that instead of focusing on individual students as the sites of instruction and change—which ignores systemic injustices—our centers should adopt a more radical commitment to creating "better institutions" (2011, 87). Not merely broadening the scope of our work, Grimm in fact redirects our attention to the ways asymmetries of power influence institutionalized practices, calling on the writing center community to intervene at the source. If the institution supports teaching practices and grading criteria, for example, that perpetuate racist or colonizing assumptions about language, it is the institution—not the student—who has the ethical imperative to change. The writing center, she suggests, has an obligation to facilitate such change.

In agreement with these scholars, I argue that the further we go in our interrogation of injustice, the more clearly we will be led not only through the oppressive norms and policies of our institutions but to the many intersecting systems that interplay with our institutions. Radicalism assumes there is no position outside a system: the institution does not operate in isolation. Consequently, we might continue to revise Clark and Healy's implied "better classrooms" and Grimm's "better institutions" to encompass a better society and ultimately a better world. To do so is not to succumb to a false sense of our own capabilities (it is not to suggest a single center can at once change the entire world) but rather to recognize that our centers are not separate from the world and that the work in our centers has a collective influence in ways both small and large on the world within and around us.

Radical activist adrienne maree brown, in her groundbreaking work *Emergent Strategy*, observes that the "crisis is everywhere, massive massive massive" and yet "we are small" (2017, 3). Nevertheless, she is purposeful in her perspective on how we might harness our power, like a fractal: "But emergence notices the way small actions and connections create complex systems, patterns that become ecosystems and societies. Emergence is our inheritance as a part of this universe; it is how we change. Emergent strategy is how we intentionally change in ways that grow our capacity to embody the just and liberated worlds we long for" (3). While writing might be our explicit object of study, we imbue our study with meaning when we ask what good this study will do in the world. The imperative to examine our work through an ethical framework is not exclusive to writing centers. Any field or human activity that does not understand justice and peace to be the logical ends of its work is, from a radical perspective, fundamentally unethical.

The notion of a better world, while expanding recognition of the scope of our influence, nevertheless remains open to signification. Accordingly, it becomes critical that the language of love, justice, and peace be made explicit, both in terms of how we describe our work to ourselves within the field and how we talk about our work with others. In a pragmatic sense, that means that the words *justice* and *peace* themselves be regularly invoked as everyday considerations in writing centers, not only as special interest topics. It also means that a vocabulary comprising a range of related concepts related to resistance (e.g., antiviolence, anti-oppression, decolonization, antipatriarchy, antiracism, antisexism, anti-cissexism, antiheterosexism, anticlassism, etc.) and peace (radical love, radical engagement, community care, space holding, etc.) and other contemporary ethical imperatives be made familiar, par for the course, redundant. This approach is not about being "politically correct" or reifying sanctioned "social justice jargon." To the contrary, as our ideas and understandings deepen, so too must our language evolve with us. But if we cannot as a field come together to articulate with a modicum of clarity an ethical intention, we cannot hope for our collective work to make good on the radical promise. Certainly, we may never reach con-sensus on a specific reading of the world, but an explicit and ongoing investment in dialogue about our ethics—and in fact a redefinition of the field as invested in a critical collective examination of the ethics of language production—would be revolutionary in practice.

REFLECTIONS ON THE CONUNDRUMS OF RADICAL WRITING CENTER MISSIONS: A CASE STUDY

In theory, of course, this all sounds quite lovely. In practice, the institu-tional politics become, let's say, a bit more complicated. I recall giving a presentation years ago at the National Conference on Peer Tutoring in Writing on translating Paulo Freire's radical education theory into the writing center context and suggested tutors be recruited and hired based less on their writing skills and more for their willingness to explore the revolutionary potential of dialogue. An audience member, representing the concerns of many writing center directors, demanded I translate this ideal into practical terms: "How do you actually communicate that publicly in your institution when your funding depends on maintaining the status quo?" When we talk publicly about this kind of critical con-sciousness and revolutionary change, our institutions become justifiably fearful, and that fear can translate into material repercussions for our centers and the people in them. What institution can reasonably be expected to welcome a writing center that openly purports to want to aid students in subverting the institution's power?

As we engage this question, however, we must be careful not to be defeated by a liberal assumption that the institution and the institu-tion's exercise of power are fixed phenomena. Whereas the liberal writing center worries about how to construct a mission statement for the writing center in a way that enables the center to thrive within the very institution it is encouraging students to challenge, a radical politics assumes a different premise. A radical writing center does not want to thrive within an oppressive institution because to do so by definition means complicity in that oppression. A radical politics compels us to engage the world dialectically, to see the world not as a fixed entity but as a changeable process. A radical writing center therefore seeks to identify its opportunities for agency and instead asks how to negotiate institutional and societal change rather than coexist with oppressive policies.

One practice, perhaps the one to which liberal writing center activists are most accustomed, for dealing with what can been seen as two conflicting agendas is to connect the writing center's revolutionary ambitions to the sympathetic yet safe language of the institution's mission—the language of leadership, or civic engagement, or critical thinking, or the like. William J. Macauley Jr., in his chapter "Connecting Writing Center Assessment to Your Institution's Mission," makes clear that he does not argue for the "whole-sale appropriation of writing center work . . . to accommodate institutional flag-waving" (Schendel and Macauley 2012, 60). Instead, he builds a case in favor of "mining institutional statements about mission, vision, and or strategic planning for language that can be useful in writing center assessment" (59). His rationale, which resonates with many directors, is that when writing center assessment is not "using the language of the agenda of the institution . . . it is much more vulnerable to resource reductions, absorptions of other institutional entities, and even the possibility of elimination" (59). Mary Lou Odom cites this approach explicitly when describing her journey to defend her particular writing center, which otherwise risked losing its "Center" status (and all the funding, resources, and opportunities that attended such a designation) despite years of successful operation at her institution. "We cannot ignore the importance that local arguments hold," Odom (2016, 28) affirms, for individual writing centers and directors to demonstrate a center's worth in terms of an institution's goals, plans, and initiatives. The practical value of this approach is significant, and Macauley in fact calls on directors to be "generous" in seeing that our institutions can provide a "great deal of information, direction, and prioritizing" (Schendel and Macauley 2012, 60).

At the same time, Macauley goes on to make an important clarification: within our centers we must not be so shortsighted as to limit our work to this but rather must continue our creative pursuits. Even nudging us to explore our subversive potential, he argues that because the ideas available in institutional statements of mission, vision, or strategic planning "are often so broad, [writing center directors] can find concepts that reflect the values of the institution that do not jeopardize the center's values or purpose" (Schendel and Macauley 2012, 62). He posits that this strategy helps to make visible shared interests between the writing center and the institution as well as to position the writing center to challenge the status quo by inviting the institution—through the writing center's assessment practices—to consider ways its stated aims are not yet being realized (62–63).

While certainly practical and enticing, a strategy such as this presents a quandary for radical writing center directors. Appealing to institutional language risks limiting the center's radical potential if the institution prioritizes different ideals or especially if the compatible language of the institution can be generalized so broadly as to theoretically encompass the writing center's radical ambitions while not in fact clearly naming them. In the latter case, a writing center could engage in purposeful linguistic manipulation by publicly appeasing its skeptics while continuing in private to strategize with tutors about how to radically negotiate their power, ask problem-posing questions, encourage students to consider the sociopolitical implications of their writing, and point students in directions of transforming the classroom, the school, the world! But there's something deeply unsettling about operating in this way because it risks neglecting the radical agenda of engaging in transparent and transformative collaborative dialogue—of challenging the institution to achieve *more* (or something *different* from) its stated aims, especially if those aims do not unequivocally include the promotion of justice and peace.

What follows is a case study from my earlier years as a writing center director attempting to temper my radical vision within the liberal language of the institution. I explore the ways this strategy broke down, both practically and theoretically, and seek to make meaning from the experience by way of a radical dialogue with a former student who helped me to better theorize the politics of institutional language and inspired me to engage in more overtly radical practice.

For a number of years I directed a writing and speaking center at an institution that had a long and impressive history of promoting women's pioneering education. The founder's oft-quoted words enticing students to act boldly were frequently invoked on campus in an effort to inspire women to be empowered as leaders during their college careers and beyond. Like many selective liberal arts colleges with traditions rooted in important and idealistic missions of global citizenship, social service, and academic excellence, our college's mission celebrated women's leadership as its raison d'être. Of its many initiatives, the college had founded an interdisciplinary leadership center as a way to provide resources and opportunities for students to learn how to translate their idealism, passion, and curiosity into actual leadership. The relatively young writing and speaking center I directed had been strategically housed within the leadership center in an effort to situate the goals of developing strong communication and critical thinking skills within the context of leadership. Because of this strategic position, we sought to develop a mission for the program that was both consistent with contemporary writing center philosophy and appealing to the discourses already at play in the larger campus community; in our program, we said that a better writer meant a better *leader*.

This desire to define writing ability through the lens of leadership suggested a number of advantages. While the phrase *better writer* might connote any number of meanings, including the sort of colonized subject identified by Bawarshi and Pelkowski (1999) and others, we intended the phrase *better leader* to invoke more specific qualities—in particular, inspirational change maker. In contrast to privileging a narrow conception of leadership as based on a formal role, title, or position of power (known in the literature as *positional leadership*), we intended to invoke a version of leadership in which the individual, through their demonstration of inspirational qualities such as integrity, trustworthiness, vision, and passion (known in the literature as *transformational leadership*), motivates others to make change. In this way, we imagined that strong leaders are skilled rhetoricians: they are careful listeners, strategic and persuasive arguers, multilingual communicators, and proficient navigators of multiple discourses and contexts. They are powerful critical thinkers: reflective, insightful, and creative. They are strong collaborators: able to negotiate across difference, learn from others, and inspire others to make change in the world. And they are courageous: they claim their own agency, claim their own voices, challenge assumptions, demand justice, and take action. Significantly, the passion and humility with which they approach any endeavor inspires others similarly to engage purposefully in their own lives. Believing in leadership as embodying these kinds of radical qualities, my colleagues and I drafted a mission statement for our program: "to empower leaders who think critically and creatively and who write and speak persuasively."

The mission of empowering leaders through the development of their speaking and writing allowed us to tap into potential opportunities for engaging with speaking- and writing-related activities across campus in a way we might otherwise have missed. For example, we were able to offer workshops on writing and speaking (telling your story in an application essay, making a strong first impression, overcoming public-speaking anxiety) as part of the leadership center's annual student conference. We were able to provide peer mentors to help a group of high-school students invited to campus as part of a leadership program to craft and hone speeches about creative initiatives they were seeking to develop to change the world. We were invited to participate in an international women's education conference where student delegates from women's institutions around the globe came to our campus to collaborate with other women students to explore their leadership potential—our program was one of the first campus entities considered by the conference organizers to engage these students in the leadership potential of our work. We had students who found their passion for peer mentoring through the lens of helping empower other women leaders to find their voices and express themselves with confidence. And we were able more clearly to demonstrate to our own student staff the transformative potential of their work with their peers. Indeed, through the context of leadership, the act of writing was recontextualized—it was a way to understand writing not as a technical or isolated skill but as a vehicle for purposeful engagement with the world.

More important, invoking this assumedly shared commitment to leadership with other faculty and staff on campus helped create a firmer foundation upon which to build relationships, communicate goals, recruit students, advertise resources, and maneuver strategically and diplomatically through politically difficult interactions. It was a way for our work to be received with legitimacy by the faculty; as we were not housed in an academic department, this mission gave us a way to demonstrate that we had a robust connection to the work of the college. Indeed, our program's supporters grew in number each semester. We had allies across the disciplines in departments, student organizations, and administrative offices. We had a thriving center with a visiting body of students that grew dramatically each semester. We had faculty from the humanities, social sciences, natural sciences, and the arts requesting to work with our classroom-based student mentors. And being a person relatively new to a position in a program with a history of its own prior to my arrival, that mission of leadership was a powerful tool for faculty outreach and campus relations on which I could rely to redirect otherwise challenging disagreements or misperceptions.

For example, early on in my first semester on the job, I found myself in an uncomfortable exchange with two tenured faculty members (my directorship position was classified as staff) who had both sent students to our writing and speaking center and had worked with our program's classroom-based mentors long before I ever arrived on campus. Both these faculty members had been long-time supporters of the program, and yet both were quite vocal in their frustration over my newly instituted requirement that all students complete the requisite peer-mentor education course prior to being able to work as a peer mentor. Both believed the hired mentors were already strong writers and that the mentoring course was therefore a waste of their time. While one professor was patient in the discussion, the other was significantly more frustrated. Finding myself rather trapped and outnumbered, and calling upon common writing center narratives to explain how the course was focused on exploring collaborative learning, interpersonal dynamics, question asking, and the negotiation of difference—not on teaching basic writing or proofreading skills—it wasn't until I redirected our conversation to the mission of leadership that I was most confident with a definable and defensible goal. If faculty are focused on the idea of writing as merely a technical process or skill, it is difficult to argue about the role of a peer mentor as anything other than someone who provides a remedial service; if a larger mission such as leadership is invoked, suddenly the purpose of writing, the value of writing, the possibility of writing—and, perhaps most important, the significance of mentorship—takes on greater meaning. In the moment with the two faculty I've just described, nevertheless, I had to explain what leadership skills I had in mind and how the work of speaking and writing tied into them. Not incidentally, the buzzword *leadership* was not enough to win them over, but it did create a moment of calm and finally a reluctant nodding of (one of) the heads, "Ah, yes, well, putting it that way, it does make sense."

I believe most faculty *want* students to be critical and creative thinkers who engage with material deliberately and who offer the world something new in return, even if the faculty don't realize that the particularity of some of their assignments might be, for example, culturally biased or in some other way at odds with their larger ethical views. I believe most faculty *want* students to find their own voices, to develop a personal passion for a subject, and to push their own thinking in return, even if the faculty's good intentions have prevented them from thinking through their grading criteria to recognize their assimilationist function. Most faculty across the disciplines, like us in our writing centers, I believe, simply don't know how to transform our practices to more fully realize our ethical ideals in the face of what feel like competing imperatives. The mission of leadership allowed me to appeal to my colleagues in a way both nonthreatening (without the rhetoric of words like *revolution* or *resistance*) and accurate, insofar as my own definitions were concerned, about to what ends my program was teaching writing, speaking, and critical thinking.

Despite these successes, being committed to this mission in theory didn't mean we had somehow transcended the sort of political challenges with which most writing centers and programs grapple. The misunderstandings that had North shaking his fists back in 1984 could still be found on our campus. We had faculty who didn't understand the role of a peer mentor. We had faculty who didn't understand why a peer-mentor education course was necessary to prepare them. We had faculty who were convinced a student couldn't possibly help another student as well as a professor could, whereas others expected more from the peer mentors than any actual faculty member could reasonably achieve. And we had a few faculty who were downright hostile. In general, nevertheless, by situating the work of our program within the stated leadership objectives of our institution, we seemed to have garnered a relatively stable place for our work in the eyes of the administration and, by extension (though differently, perhaps), the faculty. But let's not get too comfortable just yet . . .

Just as I was beginning to think that leadership might be the ticket or, more broadly, that connecting the language of the writing center to the language of the institution might be how the radical project reconciles its own threat, my radical practice of engaging in transformative dialogue with my own student staff forced me to completely upend my assumptions. One student in particular, a brilliant undergraduate peer mentor named Megan Durling, rather than subscribing to my suggestion of leadership as inherently right and good, engaged me in a good deal of problem posing. What began as a conference presentation together turned into many years of conversation and collaborative writing long after her graduation from college. What follows is, in Megan's own words when she was still a student, her radical critique of my appeal to institutional rhetoric.

The Limits of Institutional Rhetoric

by Megan Durling

Before we suggest that all writing centers align their mission statements with those of their home institutions, let us take a moment's pause to consider the implications of adopting the terms and appearance of an institution we seek to change: "He who dictates and formulates the words and phrases we use, he who is master of the press and radio, is master of the mind . . . Such is the Pavlovian device: repeat mechanically your assumptions and suggestions, diminish the opportunity of communicating dissent and opposition. This is the simple formula for political conditioning of the masses" (Meerloo 1956, 47). The antitotalitarian words of Dutch medical doctor and psychoanalyst Joost Meerloo may seem a harsh, even paranoid, invocation for the purpose of this discussion. However, they do shed light on a subtle dynamic hiding behind the act of appealing to institutional powers with "nonthreatening" language to gain funding, institutional legitimacy, or the like. But let us save that juicy bit for last, as there are a few stops along the way before we get there.

To convey why the invocation of an institution's language is in fact a contentious move for programs with a counterhegemonic agenda, we will explain how doing so resulted in certain theoretical and practical quandaries for us. To begin, let us revisit the intentions and assumptions of our writing and speaking program administrators in framing our program's mission statement in terms of *leadership*. As Laura previously indicated, from a writing center administrator's perspective, *leadership* might seem to offer a unique opportunity to accomplish three goals. First, the term *leadership* promises to provide a vehicle for publicizing the program's counterhegemonic agenda, fulfilling that longed-for goal among social justice-driven writing centers of demonstrating program ideals transparently. Second, the articulation of *leadership* to suit our agenda opens up discursive space to teach students a reimagined version of leadership, one that reaches beyond conventional notions idolizing authority and prestige. Finally, exploiting such a seemingly popular term allows the program to appeal to all stakeholders through institutionally sanctioned language. It is this final goal that is most telling, revealing crucial assumptions that, if proven false, have significant implications for the attainment of our goals. In particular, the attempt to appeal to the campus community through the institution's discourse rests on the assumption that a particular definition of *leadership* is shared by all, and that such a definition is *safe*, accepted—even celebrated—by all parties on campus. However, as anecdotal evidence now suggests, the term *leadership* is a bit more complicated than anticipated, existing as a highly contentious and politicized object of debate outside of—and perhaps incited by—our institutional discourse.

Shortly before I began working on this piece, I was talking with a student, Amelia (pseudonym), as part of a project for our program's annual newsletter. Wanting to learn about her experiences in the writing and speaking center, I asked, "Do you think any of the skills you have picked up through your visits to the writing and speaking center have made you a better leader?" At first she looked at me puzzled. After a moment, she said, "Well, I suppose if I *wanted* to be a leader, being able to speak, argue, and write would help me get there. But I don't really want or feel like I need to be some big leader. I love to dance. That's my major, and that's what I do."

As I continued these conversations, other students claimed, "Leadership is just another buzzword thrown around on this campus," and many of them said they did not even know what leadership *really* is. While some pointed to the ambiguity or emptiness of the word, others echoed Amelia's response: a rejection of leadership as a "big" position of power. For these students, and some faculty as well, the term we had adopted was nothing more than a buzzword used by the institution to attract parents of prospective students and outside funding and one whose conventional usage evoked images that were, in fact, antithetical to the very ideals of the program. Despite our program's desire to help students discover diverse definitions of the term, questions like "Why do I need to be a leader?" and "Is it possible for everyone to be a leader?" in addition to outright condemnations of leadership as "elitist," "hierarchical," and "authoritarian" pointed to the pervasiveness of the notion on campus that leadership is defined by formal positions of authority—and to the fact that such a notion was not celebrated by everyone.

Looking at the admissions and publicity practices of most colleges, it is easy to see why this understanding of leadership—promoted in powerful, if unspoken, ways—is so inescapable among students. Like other competitive institutions of higher education, our college selected for students who embodied the very type of leadership we sought to redefine. This institutionalized preference was apparent in the college-application process, which asked specifically about formal positions within high-school clubs, organizations, sports, or other extracurricular activities. It was apparent in grant and internship applications that sought similar qualifications. It was apparent on college websites, at campus events, and in other venues of college publicity that trumpeted alumna leaders who were at the top of their fields, managing big-name businesses and nonprofit organizations, teaching at elite educational institutions, writing for top-notch publications, and so on. Indeed, college-admission policies selected for prospective students who exhibited these quantifiable characteristics of leadership. The notion that leadership meant formal positions of power was implicit everywhere and was reproduced, in large part, by the institution itself.

As my conversations with students suggest, however, the version of leadership implicitly and explicitly marketed on campus was an often uncomfortable and undesirable one for students, and one that was in

fact at odds with the type of leadership our program intended to foster. Consequently, the question we then faced concerned whether our
rhetorical maneuver had accomplished our intended goals—indeed,
whether a mission statement could ever serve such goals while employing an institutional discourse like *leadership*. If *leadership* (or any other
term) is in fact a contentious term on campus, what are the implications
of adopting such a mantra for a writing center? By using the discourse
of *leadership*, we invoked the connotations of that buzzword, despite
our intentions to redefine it with the students who walked through our
doors. Indeed, because our explicit mission statement neither clearly
rejected its dominant associations nor offered reimagined possibilities
for the term, *leadership* assumed its conventional meaning by default.
Through this mismatched appeal, we may have been failing to reach
the very students whom we might have welcomed most eagerly: those
invested in progressive understandings of leadership and those seeking
a place for counterhegemonic work within the academy.

Furthermore, by resting on the institution's discourse, the potential to achieve our ultimate goal of making our private agenda public
was threatened. If a program cannot openly invest a term with new
meaning, adopting that term—in this case, along with undesirable
connotations—prevents such a program from achieving the goal of
transparency. Instead, the writing center sacrifices its private agenda
(at least rhetorically) for institutional appeasement. Indeed, this is precisely the notion that fellow writing center staff expressed when asked
whether *leadership* encompassed our true aspirations in the writing
center. In these discussions, student staff argued that *leadership* seemed
like an effective way to appeal to and gain credibility from the academic
institution, but it did not allow for the full representation of our goals.
As one coworker put it, the term *leadership* masked what we *really* aim
to do in the writing center. As I suspect, this is precisely why Laura was
able to console skeptical faculty members as she explained, in terms of
leadership, the purpose of educating course mentors: for these faculty,
leadership did not likely conjure up our controversial ideals of fostering
multiple literacies and encouraging students to challenge academic
standards. Instead, *leadership* diverted their attention from these more
threatening issues, rhetorically displacing a counterhegemonic agenda
with vague yet familiar institutional discourse. This is the essence of the
buzzword, a term so variably co-opted, stretched, and deployed it virtually loses all discernable meaning. Like a vessel, it is repeatedly emptied
out and refilled to suit the context and audience, all the while maintaining its outward appearance. As such a vessel, the term *leadership* might

be able to house both our public and private agendas in the writing center. However, a word that can readily mystify or otherwise obscure our counterhegemonic aims does not allow us to achieve the goal of being transparent with the program's private agenda. Instead, those private aims remain perpetually unknown to the audience, lost amidst competing definitions; all we see for certain is the fuzzy, friendly mascot of Leadership, a safe institutional icon capable of public diplomacy, but a costume nonetheless.

All this points, perhaps, to a more fundamental problem: Is it even possible to attach the full meaning of a counterhegemonic agenda to a paradoxically hegemonic discourse to unify our public and private agendas through institutional rhetoric? Can we effectively rearticulate such language without explicitly refuting its current connotations and substituting them with our own? And given the direct contradiction between the conventional and reimagined versions of some of the terms we select, is it even practical to attempt such a rearticulation? In other words, are there inherent limitations in working with institutionally sanctioned language to achieve counterhegemonic goals?

Our quandary thus returns us to a question that is all too familiar among writing center activists: can one work effectively for institutional change while operating within institutional boundaries? For certain, the situation our program faced demonstrates that language poses a serious challenge in this struggle. As I argue below, it is no coincidence that counterhegemonic programs such as ours ultimately resemble the broader institution in discursive practice: indeed, the control of language is a crucial way through which the institution suppresses counterhegemonic activity such as that of the writing center.

Writing center scholars are familiar with assertions about the inextricable relationship between language and humans' perceptions of reality. Applying this relationship to the effects of propaganda in totalitarian regimes, Meerloo explains, "Man learns to think in words and in the speech figures given him, and these gradually condition his entire outlook on life and on the world" (1956, 46). In other words, the limitations of language are not only determined by broader language systems and their grammatical, syntactical, and other constructs; the language that shapes our perception of reality is also determined by *political systems* and the way people in power manipulate and deploy language.

Of course, the rhetorical practices and indoctrination strategies of an educational institution are a far cry from those of a totalitarian state. However, it should go without saying among writing center activists that institutions of higher education are political structures with a vested interest in shaping language practices: our jobs would not exist if this were not true. But institutions control more than just the language standards students are expected to uphold within academia; they also determine the range of acceptable language that can be used by their workers, including writing center staff and administrators. In the context of this power structure, language becomes *a tool of governance* the institution uses to serve its own interests of order and self-preservation, in service of and laden with the ideologies we seek to undermine. However, as Meerloo suggests in his bold statement quoted at the beginning of this essay, the power that "dictates the words and phrases we use" controls more than simply what we say; dialectically, those words and phrases come to shape our understandings and affect material reality—what we are able to *do* in the writing center. It is thus in large part through the control of language that sites of power such as educational institutions have a hand in shaping our reality: by constraining discourse, institutions suppress counterhegemonic activities like those of the writing center, and it is in part through the adoption of institutionally sanctioned language that we get folded back into the hegemonic order.

Radical Possibilities

Megan's sharp critique above, for me, made clear the futility of appealing exclusively to the liberal rhetoric of the institution when attempting to engage in radical work. Indeed, I felt so persuaded by her arguments that it was easy to adopt them as my own. Rather than being defeated by the recognition, however, I emboldened my commitment not only to envisioning the writing center as a counterhegemonic force but also to claiming language on my own terms. Of importance, it was through the very act of problem-posing dialogue with Megan and with others that my radical hopefulness about the change potential of writing centers was bolstered. Indeed, it is in this radical investment in dialogue, rather than in any sort of absolute certainty about the ideal mission statement or the ideal set of practices for writing centers, where we can find hope and courage in negotiating the very real and tenuous risks we will face when we come out of the protective cover of a feigned neutrality and instead name our radical ethics publicly.

To begin, when language itself is engaged as a terrain of struggle, writing centers have the extraordinary potential to bring our values and practices into alignment: we model radical praxis. In practice that means we talk with our tutors, for example, about our mission statements not as neutral vehicles for conveying clear messages to audiences but as sites of complex negotiations of power and meaning. That also means our mission statements remain in process, negotiated and renegotiated as our own critical understanding and that of our students continue to deepen.

Recall that radical educator Freire (1996) interprets liberation not as an idealized end point (or in our case, the resolution between a radical writing center and the oppressive practices of its institutional context) but rather as residing in the act of resistance itself, in the conscious process of exercising agency by denaturalizing fixed assumptions. Rather than frantically seeking an immediate solution to result in a perfect mission statement that is simultaneously counterhegemonic, transparent, and embraced by the institution (to do so is by definition paradoxical), engaging in the process of naming the agency of the writing center in the face of domination is itself revolutionary.

By way of example, after dialoguing with Megan about the problems inherent in invoking the language of leadership in the center's mission statement, I brought our questions to the entire student staff, giving them space to submit both anonymous written input on the mission statement as well as to have an open discussion about it at several staff meetings. Indeed, students were overwhelmingly critical of the language of the existing statement, as well as forthcoming with ideas for different language and concepts to highlight—language that resonated well with the kind of work already taking place in the program, as well as my own vision for its future. Equipped with notes from the discussion and a hefty stack of written feedback, I organized a retreat for the center's administrative staff and that of the broader leadership center. At the retreat, the administrative staff reviewed the students' feedback and spent time in discussion seeking to articulate a new vision for the center. Walking out of that retreat, we had committed to stop using the old mission statement and had a draft of a new statement with language that seemed to more fully express our ideals. Once the semester began, we continued our discussions and invited our newest community members—students currently enrolled in the preparatory peer-mentor education course who had not yet begun to work—to weigh in on the language we were developing. The revised statement that emerged read as follows: "[The writing and speaking program] aims to support students in growing a critical awareness of the need for women's voices in the public sphere; in cultivating courage and agency for using their voices to effect change large and small; and in mastering tools and strategies for doing so creatively and effectively." We also began to construct an addendum to explicate the philosophy driving these aims, to be more transparent in our intended meaning:

Guiding [the writing and speaking center's] efforts is a belief that leadership is a measure of any person's ability to inspire and positively influence the people and world around her, not an automatic effect of a formal position or title; that learning is a social process strengthened through collaboration and community; that communities thrive when all members can navigate multiple discourses; that education cannot be divorced from equity and justice; and that speaking, writing, and people matter.

I intended throughout the following semester to further edit that articulation into a concise statement and to collaborate with my students while doing so. I imagined that in the near future, the statement would need to be revisited yet again to account for new challenges, new views, new needs, and new voices in the program and at the college. That process, which was itself meant to be transparent, responsive, participatory, collaborative, bold, purposeful, and—most important—dialectical, seemed to us at the time to be a revolution in practice.

Such work, however, is not immune to consequence. When engaging in radical work explicitly, our institutions will not always be supportive. We might find great champions among our deans and provosts and presidents, or we might find ourselves alone and in battles that ultimately risk costing us our jobs. Indeed, I eventually moved on from that particular job, having reached the limits of what I believed my philosophy could achieve in that space and inspired to bring my work to a larger and more vulnerable community. We may be tempted to read my leaving as a failure of radicalism, or at least as proof that my vision of radicalism is merely idealistic and woefully impractical for those who do not have the privilege to take such risks with their livelihoods. But I argue that it is our conscious engagement with such tension—not just in the conditions that welcome it—where hope for radical resistance resides.

For those privileged folks who can take such risks, as well as those who cannot, we must remember institutions do change. The scope of that change may be limited, however, if our vision of the future depends on a fixed notion of what our individual work in relationship to it will look like. When we look to history for examples of how change happens, both within US academic institutions and social systems across the globe, we observe that there is no single blueprint for change. Change is often motivated through mass demonstrations, occupations, and protests that remove the process of change from the bureaucratic structures that typically limit it. Change also happens through the comings and goings of different people across the boundaries of the institution—leaving it slightly changed for the members of the next generation who enter it and engage the outside world differently having themselves been changed while there. Change renders the past unrecognizable; radical resistance transforms the very topography of society and the institutions that once comprised it.

Consequently, the end of a center, or a job, or a set of practices as we once knew them, if such ends are the resulting products of a radical process of resistance, cannot be understood as failure. Likewise, the maintenance of a center that quietly works to make the world just a little bit better, in the small but meaningful ways it can while trying to keep its doors open in the face of oppressive institutional pressure, cannot be understood as a perfect failure either. Indeed, as Lynn Shelley (2014) persuasively writes, consciously engaging in practices that demonstrate that the students in our writing centers *matter* (paying them attention, caring what happens to them, being proud of their achievements and saddened by their failures, helping them feel needed, and appreciating their efforts) can have a profoundly important impact on all of us, particularly marginalized people. We might still read these experiences as containing elements of radical success, if those efforts are made in conscious resistance to oppression, because the dialogues that take place along the way will still resonate in the hearts of those who learned from them after they leave these spaces. The model of courage and ethical commitment that comprised the radical practices we sought to enact will inspire the future actions of those who bore witness to it. That revolutionary process is a training ground for future revolutionaries, who will take the work far beyond the walls of the institution and work to transform others. "We are volcanoes," says Ursula K. Le Guin (1986). Writing of what happens when women radically offer their experiences as human truth, she observes, "All the maps change. There are new mountains." So too is a radical writing center a volcano; bursting with power, it may one day lie dormant or its lava may flow slowly and continuously, but the terrain in the wake of its eruption will forever be different.

For some, a center whose mission is so compromised due to institutional pressures that it is violently contributing to the oppression its stewards may in theory wish to dismantle may be better off shut down. For others, that thought is a bit too scary, or quite frankly out of the question—we must grapple with the ways our individual identities afford some of us the privilege to take risks with our jobs and others not. For those who cannot, Macauley's (Schendel and Macauley 2012) and Odom's (2016) strategy may be precisely what it takes to survive in order to engage the center's radical vision in other ways. Regardless of how we as individuals must negotiate our unique circumstances, the radical project reminds us to question why we perceive the system as invulnerable and to recognize the agency we do have for change.

In my own experience, my paths across systems next led me out into the community and then back into a different college where my global vision for radical dialogue seemed to have a better chance to flourish. Inspired by my past experiences, I forged new terrain in these spaces, more boldly and more explicitly than before. The community-based organization I started, Women's Voices Worldwide, Inc., drew on the lessons I learned from my time in the academy but was reconfigured for a broader audience of students, an expanded understanding of communication itself, and a desire to change the contexts in which marginalized speakers struggle. I crafted a mission of "promoting social justice around the globe by educating women and girls to be powerful speakers in all areas of personal, academic, professional, and civic life" and, through a collaborative dialogue with my colleagues, articulated a vision of "a world transformed by the complete personal, social, and political liberation of every woman." Of importance, that work called not only for women to speak courageously but for people of all genders to listen differently to women and others of marginalized gender identities.

Forever changed by my time in the community, my reentrance into the academy brought with it an even bolder commitment to explicitly naming my politics. In deep collaboration with the students in my new college program, which I named the Transformative Speaking Program, we took our cues not from institutionally sanctioned language but from our own values, observations, and visions to articulate a statement of purpose. We began this process within the same year protests were erupting in Ferguson, Missouri, catalyzed by Darren Wilson's murder of Michael Brown, and our own institution, despite the college's recent and very vocal stated intention to be "anti-racist," was dealing with (or struggling to deal with) its own failures at responding meaningfully to ongoing concerns expressed by students, staff, and faculty about racism, sexual assault, transphobia, and other forms of violence experienced on campus. Critical of the culture of the college as one where people routinely failed to listen to each other, tended towards silencing each other, and defaulted to practices of "calling out" rather than investing in relationships and shared learning, my program's student staff forged our first mission statement: to "promote radical dialogue to change the world." Over the years, as we observed how people responded to, resonated with, questioned, or misunderstood that statement, we have added the explanatory language of aiming to "cultivate a culture of ethical communication on campus and beyond, one that is both disruptive to systems of oppression and humanizing."

CONCLUSION

A radical writing center praxis, aiming to create, as best as our limited language can describe, some notion of a better world risks expanding into a project so large the idea of writing itself risks getting lost. Just how much, exactly, do we want to get over this whole writing thing? While the radical project does, implicitly, invite an interrogation of disciplinarity itself, it does not require that we leave writing behind. Indeed, as an object of study and a means of engaging dialogue, writing becomes a significant medium for radical praxis. As a field, therefore, we must articulate in more critical and complex ways a philosophy of writing, one that allows students (and others) to not merely collaborate at the level of some abstract notion of process but to fundamentally interrogate how language can be used, as Megan writes, as a tool of governance and, simultaneously, as a tool for reconstituting our reality and exercising agency. These theories of writing, and of discourse, abound in our sister fields of composition and rhetoric, communications, literary criticism, cultural studies, and others, but as a field we must grab hold of them more firmly and articulate a vision for how writing centers can wield such study towards ethical ends.

In the process, I caution my revolutionary peers not to internalize the dilemma in which our rhetoric has rendered us speechless. After all, our inability to name our own revolution is not a shortcoming of our writing centers; rather, this silencing is an effect of the very systems we seek to change. So I offer that a necessary condition for this work is a dedication to resilience—we must courageously move forward in our counterhegemonic ambitions and be willing to embrace, for the time being, our discomfort in a liminal space. Necessarily, when we engage in the dialectical process of naming and creating and renaming and recreating our work, the many possibilities for our everyday radical practices emerge much more clearly and powerfully.

4

LOVE-INSPIRED PRAXIS
Towards a Radical Redefinition of Writing Centers

Yet the writing center is most interesting to me for its post-disciplinary possibilities, for the contradictions it embraces, for its tendency to go off-task. And I would like to argue . . . that we would do well to think of the future of writing centers in excessive terms. —Elizabeth Boquet

The previous chapter began the project of building a new, radical writing center field by proposing the creation of a better world—resisting systems of violence and creating conditions of peace—as an ethical political vision for our work. When we reorient our purpose away from individual writers and towards collective peacemaking, we must necessarily also reorient ourselves and all we do. Indeed, if we seek to align our practices with this radical vision, such a change will render much of our old work unrecognizable. So how will we come to recognize our new work as writing center work? Can we even call it that? This chapter begins a reorientation process by exploring radical possibilities for redefining writing centers. Specifically, I ask, *What* is a radical writing center? In other words, What exactly would it look like? What would happen there? Who would be involved? What kinds of learning would result? Just what specifically would emerge to replace the old "idea of a writing center"?

This task of crafting a new definition, however reasonable our desires to achieve some kind of clarity may be, proves a bit sticky when approached through a radical lens. The stickiness has to do with the ways radicalism understands definition—and the process of crafting definition—itself. As will become clearer as the chapter unfolds, despite any preliminary definitions I might offer of a radical writing center, a larger argument of the chapter is in fact a metacommentary on the process of definition itself. To clarify: a fundamental quality of conservativism, in its belief in firm truths, is to seek certainty in definitions—to encounter a thing and name what it is, to interpret it through a positivistic framework, and to

DOI: 10.7330/9781607328445.c004

evaluate it in absolute terms. Conservativism's fear of the unknown, the unrecognizable, the unnamable is rooted in what Hayden White (1982) has termed the "sublime," a terror that arises in the face of an incoherence out of our control. Radicalism, in contrast, embraces comfort in unknowingness, problematizing received definitions—frameworks, boundaries, languages, limits—whose perceived fixedness thwarts efforts to imagine and enact a better world. When Butler (2004, 27) proposes that radical problem posing enables us to make otherwise "illegible" claims, she disarms the sublime and in so doing rewrites the sublime out of existence, as the unnamable is no longer something to fear but is in fact a source of opportunity to transform dehumanizing conditions and to recreate the world. In suggesting that to transcend the fixedness of definitions creates space for new experiences to come into being, she points to the ways we need not remain tethered to the limiting language of the past. In simpler terms, definition creates limits. In resisting the limits of definition, we create opportunity for change.

At the same time, a radical politics does not throw definitions entirely out the window by celebrating anything and everything as a desirable or ethical description or meaning. Such relativism is more indicative of liberalism, which is paralyzed in the face of paradox. The paradox of course is this: in recognizing the limits of definitions, we must nevertheless rely on some notions of coherence—however fleeting they may be—in order to use language to come to know the world around us, to give voice to it, and to recreate it. We must have some sense of what we are talking about in order to talk about it, even if the "it" remains elusive. The radical project therefore does not aim to get entirely outside definitions but rather to challenge their fixedness or inevitability, to question the history of definitions and the agenda such definitions serve, to engage the tension that emerges among competing definitions, and to venture forth into uncharted territory. The radical project is skeptical of conclusions that proclaim "Aha! Now we know what it is!" in favor of questions that explore: Why do we think this is what it is? What might be missing here? What could be possible beyond what we think we know? So radicalism seeks not to define but to redefine and to find potential in the spaces between and beyond what is (re)defined. This process is not merely an intellectual exercise but an intentional form of love-driven, iterative practice meant to bring us all closer and closer to peace. In that sense, in radical terms, there are no absolutes to be named; there is only praxis.

What does this have to do with writing centers? The conservative currents within the discipline have guided the field to define writing centers in concrete, knowable terms. These definitions limit both our ability to recognize and talk about the diversity of ways writing centers are actually conceived and our ability to talk about and enact what could be that has not yet been imagined, that has not yet been tried. The fixedness of definitions precludes the realization of our radical potential. A number of critical writing center scholars have explored the reductive and stifling effects of such fixed definitions. Most recently, Grutsch McKinney, using the framework of narrative theory, problematized the dominant definition that writing centers are "comfortable, iconoclastic places where all students go to get one-to-one tutoring on their writing" (2013, 3) despite the diversity of values, practices, and visions actually at play in real writing centers. Similarly, but through a different and more explicitly radical framework, Boquet examines the historical tension in writing centers as a discipline that has defined itself un-self-consciously and defensively in terms of both distinct *spaces* and *methods* (1999, 464), naming our fidelity to these distinctions as inadvertently preventing the realization of our radical potential. In doing so, she makes a bold call for the field to explode these definitions and explore the "way in which the writing center exceeds its space, despite the university's best efforts to contain it; the way in which the writing center exceeds its method" (478).

Motivated by the vision of creating a better world, how do we define writing center work in new terms? Can a radical writing center even be defined? This notion of excess, of going beyond the fixedness of definition, offers an important conceptual framework for engaging in the process of seeking a radical (re)definition of writing centers, so it is in that tradition that the following chapter develops. I explore four (somewhat arbitrary though nevertheless common) descriptive lenses through which a discipline might seek to define itself. I offer radical readings of writing center work through those lenses while simultaneously pushing back at the limits of those same lenses, inviting us to engage the tensions at the edges of the limits in order to locate different radical possibilities. Ultimately, it is in the engagement with the tension itself—not in the conclusions we might draw—where I locate the radical writing center.

RADICAL SPACES

If we were inclined to use the conceptual framework or the language of *space* to map out a plan for building a radical writing center, how might we identify and describe that center? Many conservative and liberal writing centers, as the above-mentioned scholars have examined, define themselves in local terms—labs, centers, and other physical areas on campus separate from traditional classrooms where resources for writers are offered. Understood in this way, a writing center is defined fundamentally as a special *place to which one goes*, usually to talk about or find support with one's writing. A radical writing center, in contrast, cannot easily be defined in terms of space because spaces have fixed, knowable boundaries. Spaces are finite, with insides and outsides, insiders and outsiders. Radicalism, as a politics, is critical of such absolutes and of the inequities those boundaries frequently facilitate.

At the same time, a radical writing center is not *not* a space. All human activity happens in the world, in context, so the task of a radical writing center is not to get outside space but to maintain a critical relationship with space, one understood as always in process or rather under construction. A radical writing center therefore questions the ways humans create spaces—as physical sites and ideological categories—and resists the ways people exercise power to maintain exclusive control over how spaces are configured, how walls are erected to keep out the undesirable, and how myths are circulated to enforce the perception that such walls are natural and permanently impenetrable.

A radical politics reminds us there is no such thing as being outside a system. Even those most subjugated by a system are not, in fact, outsiders but rather are necessarily exploited insiders, the backs upon whom the dominant classes depend to build their violent empires. A radical writing center, therefore, challenges the temptation to imagine we exist outside and apart from the rest of the world. The writing center is the world, and while we may try to recreate a better world within our walls on a campus, we cannot assume that simply because we wish to be immune from injustice we can at once rid ourselves of our social identities, be cured of our implicit biases, or erase the asymmetries in power that shape our lives outside the writing center as if they do not affect how we must negotiate our relationships within it. Likewise, when we step out of the writing center, there will be consequences for our activities within it. What happens in the writing center does not stay in the writing center—it is not Las Vegas, as it were. We cannot assume we are self-contained.

Despite how strongly we might desire to, and should try to, make it so, a writing center (or any space) can never be a completely "safe space." The 2015 massacre by a white supremacist of nine Black worshippers attending a Bible study at the historic Emanuel African Methodist Episcopal Church in Charleston, South Carolina, one of the oldest Black churches in the South, made horrifically visible the reality that even spaces designed to be sanctuaries for targeted groups are still vulnerable to violence when the broader violent contexts in which they are constructed require the need for sanctuaries in the first place. The 2016 massacre by a racist homophobe/transmisogynist of forty-nine people on Latinx Night at the Pulse gay bar and dance club in Orlando, Florida, was another sobering reminder of the vulnerability of space. The shooter in the latter case, for example, was not an outsider but was in fact a frequenter of the club, who many speculate had internalized the very oppression clubgoers sought to escape—society's hatred towards LGBT people of color—to such an extent that he saw no alternative but to eradicate them/himself. Indeed, the temptation to find a scapegoat to explain away such violence (naming radical Islam, for example) rather than recognizing the homegrown ideologies that cultivate it is a conservative rhetorical move to eschew the sublime. A writing center may seem like a far cry from a Black church or a gay night club, but the rhetoric that circulates in conservative and liberal discourses about the function of a center as distinct from and therefore not implicated in/by the oppression that circles around and through it makes the comparisons meaningful.

Sloan's investigation of the writing center as what Mary Louise Pratt coined a "contact zone" (Sloan 2004) more accurately describes the conditions of the writing center in the way it makes clear that various systems and differences necessarily collide and are negotiated there. Without assuming a natural outcome of such negotiations, a radical writing center would critically examine how power and hierarchy operate within the writing center and how each of us is limited and constituted by it. Likewise, a radical writing center would critically explore the transformative potential of spaces as sites of resistance to negotiate what happens in and across—and therefore how we come to understand the work of—the space.

If we understand that the notion of a distinct, self-contained space is an illusion, a human construction, and that the physical walls we erect therefore obscure our ability to contend with the systems of oppression that necessarily transcend them, the radical writing center opens up countless possibilities for redefining its work. In one sense, in seeking some semblance of coherence in our understanding of space, we are compelled to question, in favor of more universal designs, the ways dominant definitions of space reinforce the systems of oppression that cultivate those definitions. Rather than reinforcing an idealized space in relationship to the rest of the institution—see, for example, Grutsch McKinney's (2013) apt critique of the metaphors of "home" that guide the interior designs of many writing centers—a radical writing center would ask how the narratives and practices associated with finite space itself perpetuate exclusionary or oppressive practices. It would explore opportunities to challenge assumptions about the inevitability of those practices and to reimagine them. What assumptions about writing, about people, about learning does the design of the space support? Who benefits from these assumptions? Who is disadvantaged by them? Who stands to gain by presenting the value of the space as self-evident? What alternatives might be imagined? In practice, therefore, a radical writing center space is not static but rather always changing in a dialectical process in conjunction with its interrogation of power. These problem-posing questions require us to move beyond a liberal, inclusive approach to space, an approach that limits its change to discrete accommodations for visitors deemed atypical. Instead, it asks us to reimagine the space entirely so all engage differently and meaningfully within it and across it and so the boundaries of the space become illegible. To make boundaries illegible, though, brings us back to the radical paradox of definitions. To radically define space, therefore, as Boquet compels us, is to exceed it.

What does it mean, in a radical sense, to exceed space? To move in the direction of an answer, consider the ways a writing center I directed years ago, by virtue of its construction and conceptualization as a finite physical space, was unwittingly complicit in some of the very same systems of oppression I intended the work of the center to resist. The philosophies of the center were intended to be empowering and change making. Discussions of institutionalized power, systems of oppression—racism especially—and language politics were regular topics of conversation in the center. The ratio of peer mentors of color, multilingual mentors, and international student mentors in relation to their white, monolingual, domestic counterparts far exceeded that of the general population of the school. Nevertheless, I came to learn that a number of Black students, whose languages and social identities were both overtly and covertly under attack on the campus, were finding writing resources and camaraderie in working with several Black peer mentors . . . *outside* the writing center space and our processes. They had arranged the sessions outside the formal scheduling processes, not via WCOnline or by calling our receptionists. The mentors were not submitting the online session report forms we required of all mentoring staff for our data collection, and the students were not submitting the anonymous online feedback forms that asked all visitors to reflect on their experiences. The mentors were not reporting the time spent conducting these sessions on their work logs and thus were not getting paid for their time. Indeed, as the director, I was entirely oblivious that these sessions were happening.

Finally, one of the mentors who had been leading these sessions came to me in hopes of bringing about some kind of change. She shared with me that the students had expressed being so fearful of the judgment they might encounter in the center that they would not step foot inside. It didn't matter that I intended the space to be radical and empowering. It didn't matter that there were Black students available as mentors in the space. It didn't even matter that we offered, via a sign on the door, a by-request "accommodation" of meeting with students outside the space if it were otherwise inaccessible to them. What mattered was that the students' experiences were informed by the racially hostile climate on campus and in society at large and that the writing center was situated within that world, no matter how sincerely we tried to separate ourselves from it. What mattered was that for many Black students, the act of being seen entering and working within the space (defined by a highly visible entrance and wall of windows) carried with it a poignant meaning that it did not for white students, whose challenges with writing were by and large viewed by the institution and society as individual and educable, not pathological or symptomatic of a biological or cultural deficiency. Despite the radical understandings of identity and literacy the peer mentors sought to engage, the meanings of the center were open to signification by the context in which it was erected, a context in which Black students were systematically judged for their language practices and assumed to be academically underprepared or incompetent. What mattered was that the risk of psychic violence posed by potential encounters with other students—whether the mentors or fellow student visitors—in the space was too great for some students preparing for the necessarily vulnerable process that talking about one's ideas and writing usually is.

A conservative writing center, in this kind of situation, would shut down the "underground" sessions or would remain ignorant of or disinterested in them. A liberal writing center would try to convince students to come out from underground and have more trust in the space as it is presently constructed, encouraging students to sit confidently and visibly at an open table amidst other groups of conversing writers—imposing that idealized forum as a prerequisite for participation. A liberal writing center might even try to make minor accommodations such as allowing some tutors to meet with students in a different designated location or in the center outside regular open hours, or cite—in defeat—a lack of material resources to renovate or move into what it imagines a more welcoming space to be. A liberal writing center might say it empathizes with students—and sincerely mean it—but focus its energy on trying to create a "safe space" in the center for all who visit.

A radical writing center would, in contrast, come to terms with the ways it can never be a completely safe space and come to understand the complex ways power still operates within and through it. A radical writing center would problematize how the space itself reproduces the physical conditions of oppression, as it did in the above scenario, and imagine new ways to both redefine space and exceed space. A radical writing center would not only explore new configurations but would also recognize no single configuration will ever achieve a perfect ideal because such an assumption strips it of its temporal sociopolitical context. Instead, the problematizing of space as the source of self-definition for the writing center and the resulting transformation of activities as an iterative process would become its radical praxis.

Put differently, a radical writing center would question the assumption that its activities be reduced to space, necessarily problematizing the limited understanding of work extending from it and reimagining its very practices. In the above case, for example, as a starting point, I expanded my understanding of the limits of our space, which were defined in part by the protocols designed for a location that implicitly privileged white student visitors, and paid the mentors for conducting these sessions, both retroactively and moving forward, symbolically and materially recognizing their work as valued labor. Through small-group conversations with some of these mentors and students who met with me in my office outside the center to share their experiences, I made substantial changes in response to what I learned, including making changes they requested to the center's schedule, offering phone appointments, and starting the process of advocating that the center itself be moved to a different location on campus that was still central but more physically accessible yet not so strikingly visible. While I believed these choices to be an important use of my power as the director to make meaningful changes, the work of resistance—the exercise of agency by the students—is what made the writing center radical. It did not depend exclusively on my response. In such terms, the "underground" sessions described in the above scenario did not, as I originally described, take place *outside* the writing center. Those students, rather, were *redefining* the writing center itself. They exceeded the limits of its conservative space by recreating its practices on their own terms. By wielding their agency in resistance to the dominant construction of our space and protocols, they reinvented and reenacted a radical writing center outside the walls that sought to contain and control it.

A radical politics also compels us to exceed the limits of space by understanding the power of our work as residing not merely within some kind of location, to instead see the writing center as operating across systems by exploring possibilities for intervening in the systems limiting us. In the case of the "underground" writing center, the students' experiences reinforced our ethical imperative to be a transformative force within the larger culture of the institution. As such, for example, we began to facilitate larger community conversations (in the English Department's reading room) with faculty and staff across the disciplines about the history and politics of standardized language instruction generally and Black Englishes specifically; hosted student panels for faculty (in an auditorium in the science building) so faculty could learn more about the experiences of multilingual students in their classrooms; and served as guest speakers in classes to discuss the intersections of anti-Black racism and assumptions about language. By exceeding our space, we in fact redefined our work itself in both theory and practice from individualized student instruction to collective institutional transformation.

When writing centers exceed our spaces and are defined more by our work across systems than by our work in locale, questions arise as to how to understand and negotiate our various relationships to others across campus. Most notably, our relationship to the curriculum becomes particularly significant. Whereas North (1984) once argued for an implicitly liberal ambivalence to the curriculum, others have mistakenly suggested that if "we locate writing center origins in the extracurriculum, we then set the precedent for a counter-hegemonic model of writing center operations, one which attempts to wrest authority out of the hands of the institution and place it in the hands of the students. (See, for example, the work of Marilyn Cooper and John Trimbur)" (Boquet 1999, 466). Despite the radical intentions animating such an assertion, the assertion depends on a liberal theorization of power as a commodity to be possessed rather than exercised and therefore an interpretation of empowerment as a gift the writing center gives to students by supposedly removing them and their work from the systems that oppress them. Radicalism tells us power does not simply get removed from one hand and put into another but rather gets exercised and negotiated across relationships. This liberal model fails to recognize that despite what we may desire, we are always insiders of intersecting systems, and therefore we always in fact stand in some relationship to the curriculum.

In other words, a radical politics reminds us that, in an academic institution, *there is no extracurriculum*. Everything is always in relationship, so the distinction itself (supporting or working independently from the curriculum) becomes less useful than what we make of that relationship—how we negotiate it, what meaning we make of it, what we seek to do with it, and how we remain open to redefining it. Seeking to be outside the curriculum—where inside is presumed to be bad and outside is presumed to be good—ignores our potential not simply to be unfettered by it but to be a force in transforming it for the better because we cannot transform anything we don't stand in some relationship to. Being wholly outside the curriculum, as though such a thing were possible, would prevent us from having a positive influence on it. A radical writing center, therefore, is not extracurricular but consciously and purposefully intercurricular.

This exceeding of space compels a radical writing center to see the curriculum as merely one of many systems to which it is inextricably tied and therefore to see the physical and conceptual walls of other campus entities (from libraries to academic departments to students groups) not as boundaries separating our work but as ideologically constituted in implicit relationship to the writing center—from resistant, to disinterested, to heavily invested. As such, these imagined boundaries are at once deeply problematic and bursting with potential for renegotiation and transformation. Perhaps this is where Kail's (2009) call to abandon the rhetoric of marginalization is most important—when we understand ourselves as a distinct and separate space, our work is subject to the power other imagined spaces might impose upon us. When we understand the writing center as exceeding space, our consciousness of our ability to exercise agency across the institution grows as well. Indeed, we can choose to recognize our universal relevance or even our centrality.

A logical progression of this argument leads us to acknowledge that the walls of the institution itself create the appearance of a self-contained space rather than a temporal site of discourse and practice at the intersection of many systems. These systems inform and limit the institution's work, and simultaneously the institution informs the work of those systems. A radical writing center, therefore, defines its work not merely by what it achieves on campus but by what it achieves in the world beyond. Or more accurately, a radical writing center understands that the school *is* the world beyond.

The relatively recent emergence of community writing centers offers a compelling opportunity for investigating the influence of our work beyond the walls of the school. While the physical locations and communities directly served might be different from those of a campus writing center, exploring the tensions among the ways our practices are defined differently in spatial terms may make visible the negotiations of power conservative and liberal writing centers are quick to gloss over, and as such they offer valuable sites of inquiry (see Tiffany Rousculp's *Rhetoric of Respect* [2014] for an important exploration of one such community center). Certainly, community writing centers are not inherently radical. The same paternalistic models of "empowerment" in a traditional writing center can be just as devastating, if not more so, in a community context. But this shift in location, and all the attendant shifts that come with it, provides a new opportunity to think about how writing centers resist injustice and create conditions of peace when the institution is different but the social systems are not. A radical politics does not prescribe that every campus writing center become a community writing center. Rather, when spaces shift, so too do communities and practices (which I discuss explicitly later in the chapter). Exploring community writing center models offers us the opportunity to complicate our understanding of what community means. Accordingly, redefining community can be understood itself as a way to exceed space.

As we get closer to a definition of a radical writing center space, we find ourselves perpetually negotiating boundaries. Boundaries, as limits, as clearly delineated markers of within and without, serve a function. The radical writing center asks who created these boundaries. What functions do these boundaries serve? Who is best served by these boundaries? Who is harmed? How can we, individually and collectively, resist these boundaries when necessary in service of justice? Most important, when we define ourselves both literally and ideologically only in spatial terms, what radical possibilities are lost?

RADICAL METHODS

If we were inclined to use the conceptual framework or language of methodology to map out a plan for building a radical writing center, how might we identify and describe that center? The language of methodology is indeed widespread in writing centers, as we often define our work by a particular set of practices meant to distinguish ourselves from common classroom pedagogies. These practices are described readily in contemporary liberal writing centers in terms of their student-centered, collaborative, and conversation-based nature. A radical writing center, however, is not defined by methods because methods are fixed, knowable practices based on fixed assumptions about writing, learning, people, and power. At the same time, a radical writing center is not *not* a set of methods. All human activity is practice, so the task of a radical writing center is not to avoid methods and remain in the realm of theory but to maintain a critical relationship with methods in which methods are always engaged in a process of transformative interrogation or ethical reinvention. A radical writing center questions the ways humans privilege certain methods. A radical writing center resists the ways people exercise power to create and maintain control over those methods and how discourse operates to reinforce the perception of the superiority, inevitability, universality, and necessity of those methods. Accordingly, a radical writing center is not defined by its methods but by its praxes.

One way oppressive writing center methods are perpetuated is through assumptions about the implicit value of student centeredness and the centering of individualized instruction that emerges as a result. This is not to suggest that valuing students and offering one-on-one conversations with them is a bad thing—to the contrary! Rather, a radical politics compels us to question the origins of these dominant methods by asking who is supported and who is disadvantaged by them, and why. Grimm (1999) puts forth a convincing implicitly radical critique of the culture of individualism that pervades our academic institutions by foregrounding the ways this culture places the responsibility on individual students to survive unjust systems rather than on the systems to become more just.

A culture of individualism is what enables liberal educators to absolve themselves of responsibility for changing the unjust contexts in which their students find themselves and instead puts the entire onus on the individual students to somehow figure out how to survive within the existing systems. In the education system broadly, we see this phenomenon resisted by radical scholars who, like Andre Perry (2016) in his article "Black and Brown Boys Don't Need to Learn Grit; They Need Schools to Stop Being Racist," argue convincingly that "students are ready for systems and institutions to change" and that schools must "stop adjusting youths to injustice." Indeed, the idealization of "grit"—a cultivated quality to tough it out and persevere in the face of obstacles—has been rightly critiqued for its pathologization of students who live in poverty and for its air of eugenics (Strauss, *Washington Post*, May 10, 2016). A culture of individualism is what enables even critical scholars like Bawarshi and Pelkowski to conclude their postcolonial critique of dominant writing center theory not with a call to action for the writing center to change the institution or for the writing center field to change the world but a call to help individual students learn how to critically "use and be used by" (1999, 44) the assumedly invulnerable institution, even though they recognize it to be unjust.

A radical writing center does not necessarily stop offering individualized instruction (though it might) but rather exceeds individualized student instruction as its sole method of educating for change. A radical writing center recognizes that everyone who stands in relationship to it has both the agency and the ethical responsibility to work towards change. That means individual students who want to improve their writing are not the only ones with work to do. Classroom teachers, administrators, staff, students who never step foot into our physical space, and even alumni and members of the surrounding community can be engaged by the writing center in a process of resistance.

This expanded vision of whom the writing center seeks to reach means teachers can be engaged to think differently about the educational spaces they facilitate, the lessons they teach about language use, and the ways they respond to student writers and speakers. This means the student body can be engaged to think differently about the climate on campus and about how social norms, assumptions about difference, and other cultural practices affect their experiences and their relationships with one another, particularly in terms of their discourses. This means administrators and staff can be engaged to think differently about hiring practices, workplace norms, and protocols perpetuated by prejudiced assumptions about language differences, communication practices, and power differentials. This means peer tutors and directors themselves can be continually engaged to challenge their own assumptions and revise their practices based on what they learn from others. While not every person is inclined to be an activist in the sense of holding up picket signs or attending a rally, the writing center can facilitate the intentional engagement of people across campus looking to make change, through letter writing, art installations, sharing of resources, holding of space for otherwise silenced voices, hosting dialogues, or making simple subtle changes to everyday behaviors.

Indeed, the specific methods that emerge will be varied and not prescriptive. They could come in the form of group discussions, workshops, seminars, institutes, collaborative projects, shared research, writing circles, or other such community activities that invite more than just single students to participate in reflective practices in thinking together about language, learning, and power in service of transformative change. Our institutional contexts will certainly influence the degree to which we can overtly facilitate such forums. Many years ago I tutored in a center, for example, where the director refused my proposal for the writing center to host a discussion about students' experiences speaking Black Englishes at the university because she said she was under too much pressure from the larger writing program in which we were housed to "emphasize grammar." My pushback on this was unsuccessful. Instead, I took it upon myself to initiate such conversations about language use and power in less formal spaces with smaller groups of my writing center colleagues and in my individual sessions with writers. More important than the methods chosen, therefore, is whom the methods intend to engage and to what ends.

Significantly, a radical method would not simply put the onus of being a better writer or speaker on the student, but—in service of making a better world—would demand the same accountability of fellow students and teachers to be better *readers* and *listeners*. Recognizing writing, speaking, and even rhetoric broadly not simply as unidirectional but rather as necessarily part of a mutually constituted process, writing centers can support the kind of education that equally emphasizes the strategies, opportunities, and ethical imperatives necessary for the *audience*. The teaching of writing as rhetoric in which the writer or speaker carries the sole responsibility for the communicative act positions the audience to exercise power in a way that privileges the implicit biases of the reader or listener, including their assumptions about the person's race, gender, age, and body, as well as discourse patterns, language use, accent, and other markers—regardless of the writer or speaker's actual communicative competency. Accordingly, writing centers (and the teachers with whom they work) can also help students and teachers be good audiences. Doing so goes beyond developing active or even critical listening or reading skills to instead becoming empathetic, self-reflective, and indeed radical readers and listeners open to change. People can consider what it means to reject a speaker based on what they look like or the language variety they speak, what it means to hear only the difference and not the message, what it means to form opinions about the speaker's ethos based solely on unfounded linguistic assumptions, and how to share responsibility by participating reciprocally in a communicative act. Grimm's leadership at Michigan Technological Institute, where she offered seminars to the campus community on understanding accented English as a counterpart to the courses the university offered to international students on accent reduction, is an example of radical work. I explore this shift in responsibility in greater detail in the final section of this chapter.

In group gatherings or individual tutorials, a radical writing center would call into question the dominance of any single method for teaching and learning. In particular, a radical writing center would call into question the dominance of "nondirective" tutoring, often employed through Socratic or Rogerian questioning, as the sole ideal for engaging student communicators. Grimm, for example, shows that approaches in the classroom and writing center that expect (standardized) English-language learners to be responsive to open-ended questioning rather than explicit instruction as an educational tool "enact the belief that what is expected is natural behavior rather than culturally specific performance" (1999, 31). In other words, "nondirective" questioning is often a liberal approach when based on the false assumption that knowledge of standardized English is an innate resource of all writers when it in fact requires specific knowledge that must be taught to many speakers and writers. Grimm argues accordingly,

> Many modernist assumptions about individual autonomy get in the way of providing authentic support to the students who come to writing centers. The collaborative talk of the writing center always has to be carefully qualified so that it doesn't appear that writing center tutors are telling students what to think. Writing center tutors are often trained to take a "hands-off" approach so that they do not appear to be doing the work for students, undermining individual autonomy or responsibility. Writing center tutors are supposed to use a nondirective pedagogy to help students "discover" what they want to say. (31)

Fearing oppressing their students, liberal educators often overcompensate by providing insufficient direction. Within the context of standardized English, students who do desire to learn a dominant language variety nevertheless often fail to do so in the classrooms of liberal teachers who refuse to participate in what they misinterpret as an oppressive practice. Liberal writing center tutors, who are similarly taught to fear imposing on students by appropriating their texts, likewise are encouraged to employ practices that fail to provide necessary direction. The concept of "directive" tutoring is widely rejected by writing center practitioners as a legitimate means of engaging with writers, even in the face of several decades of scholarship that calls this dismissal into question (e.g., Blau and Hall 2002; Grimm 1999; Shamoon and Burns 1995; Sloan 2003; Thompson 2009).

A radical writing center less fearful of directive tutoring and more critical of nondirective tutoring would courageously examining how power operates in the writing center. Specifically, the productive role of the authoritative educator is mistakenly confused in liberal writing center work for authoritarian practices. Whereas Freire observes that in a "banking" model "the teacher confuses the authority of knowledge with his or her own professional authority, which she and he sets [sic] in opposition to the freedom of the students" (1970, 73), writing center tutors are frequently so fearful of abusing their own professional authority that they unnecessarily deny the authority of their knowledge, including their familiarity with language patterns, academic writing conventions, or effective revision strategies, for example. Unable to differentiate between direction (being explicit and transparent about perceptions, opportunities, strategies, and stakes) and oppression (demanding passive consumption and adoption of dominant practices and beliefs), writing center tutors risk retreating into an indeterminate set of practices in which they are expected to be nondirective, but in reality their guidance is often direction-*less*. Such a refusal to recognize tutors' authority and share their knowledge in fact serves to perpetuate oppression through a willful maintaining of inequity in access to resources and decision making.

In questioning the absolutism of nondirective tutoring, a radical politics does not require that we turn the binary on its head and privilege directive tutoring in its stead. Rather, a radical politics compels us to *engage the problem of the binary itself.* Who benefits when tutoring approaches are reduced to binary terms? Who benefits from this particularly binary? Who is disadvantaged? How might the binary be resisted? A radical interrogation would invite us to explore the ways a liberal framing of directive (assumed to mean telling the student the answers) as bad and nondirective (assumed to mean leaving it up to the student to figure things out on their own) as good enables writing center educators to avoid coming to terms with their own power, avoiding guilt and absolving themselves of their responsibility. Rather than adopting a do-everything or do-nothing approach, radical writing center educators can develop methods that more critically dive into rather than turn away from the negotiation intrinsic to *collaboration*—approaching the liberatory process as a shared endeavor. To do so means we can expand our awareness of different kinds of conversations and the kinds of radical listening, trusting, reflecting, and discomfort on behalf of all parties that necessarily attends change-making work. This also means we question the absolutism of conversation itself, recognizing the ways many people (introverts, especially) do their most creative work not in conversation with others but happily snuggled under covers alone in their rooms (see, for example, Cain 2012). How can writing centers tap into the radical potential of multiple methods of knowing and doing?

A radical writing center would question the absolutism of any singular method upon which a traditional writing center might construct its identity. Submitting papers for review before a session even begins, requiring students to read their papers aloud, always talking about argument and organization before sentence mechanics (indeed, the decontextualized conception of HOCs and LOCs altogether), making rules about never writing on the students' texts—all privilege particular students, particular ideas, and particular systems. See Grimm (2011), for example, for a detailed critique of dominant methods through an antiracism framework or Brian DiNuzzo (2014) for a story of a tutor whose initial impulse to adhere to his writing center's strict prescribed methodologies "sent the session tumbling toward disaster" when he was working with a visually impaired writer who needed something very different. A radical writing center does not unilaterally reject all the dominant methods but questions their origins and effects, their absolutism, their presumed neutrality, their centrality. A radical writing center invites tutors and students to collaboratively and consciously identify and negotiate the methods that best serve their aims.

A necessary corollary to resisting the dominance of a singular method is that the notion of a typical versus atypical writing center session, and therefore person, is destabilized. In contemporary discourses, assumptions about normal sessions (which implicitly involve US-born, white, standardized-English-speaking, cisgender, straight, etc. students and tutors) serve to alienate people who do not embody dominant social identities and whose ways of engaging in the writing center are necessarily different as well. As other scholars have noted (Greenfield and Rowan 2011a; Kiedaisch and Dinitz 2007; McDonald 2005), students and tutors who do not fit the norm are either completely erased from writing center discourses or relegated to the sidelines as aberrations to be dealt with through some mysterious and unmanageable means. When a distinct set of methods necessarily though rarely acknowledged as privileging a distinct population of people maintains its dominance, so too do the people those methods best serve. Simply devising different methods for different people does nothing to upend the power structure that renders some different and some standard to begin with. This separate-but-equal mentality is objectifying and dehumanizing.

The field's fetishization of multilingual students is one of the most strikingly visible manifestations of our conservative fidelity to a standard identity and set of methods in the writing center. The "problem" of how to "deal" with ESL students or international students (often falsely imagined as synonymous) persists as a special topic of interest in our writing center publications, conferences, and other forums, never to be resolved. The premise itself, of course, is flawed. It assumes some students and tutors are neutral in terms of language, culture, identity, and education whereas others ("ESL students") are defined by an essential and limited experience. A radical politics reminds us that we all stand in some kind of relationship to each other—indeed that our experiences are mutually constituted—but that our experiences differ because we are positioned differently within the systems of power in which we all operate (globally and locally). In other words, standard practices regarding language use, textual production, and academic conventions and the means by which they are produced are not naturally occurring phenomena or even merely cultural practices requiring an informant for outsiders but rather problematic norms that serve to maintain existing social inequities. These norms, therefore, stand to be interrogated and engaged differently, not merely by students presumed falsely to be "outside" the system but equally so by students who feel very much at home within it. A radical politics reminds us we are all responsible for resisting these systems, and therefore the standardized methods stand to be resisted as well.

All this is not to say that we ignore the unique differences and needs presented as meaningful by individual tutors and students but that we as an entire field should not profile entire populations of people and scramble to find accommodations for them. Rather, the need for accommodations should be read as a resounding alarm that the standard is deeply flawed. To perpetuate the myth that there are people called *ESL students* who need something different from an indeterminate norm is to perpetuate a system of inequity that maintains the dominance of one group and the subjugation of another. Rather than devoting all the field's efforts to how to adapt writing center tutoring to the needs of ESL students (which we see in countless presentations, articles, and books), a radical writing center would problematize the internalization of superiority and dominance it tacitly teaches tutors and students who are read as "native" English speakers. A radical writing center would study the relationships between language and power and challenge the dominant practices that are failing all our students in their development of *conscientização* and therefore failing in the larger project of global liberation.

Finally, methods that require tutors (and even students) to feign neutrality towards students' ideas are necessarily called into question by a radical politics in favor of methods that are humanizing and consciously transformative. During a session on microaggressions at a recent Northeast Writing Centers Association conference, an undergraduate tutor asked earnestly how he should handle working with students whose writing expressed opposition to marriage equality when he, as a gay man, was made deeply uncomfortable by helping those students. He was fearful of staying quiet and having to endure the violence of the students' views, fearful of the guilt that would come from not saying anything, fearful of the students' response to the tutor outing himself, and fearful of the director's response if she were to deem his personal interjection as somehow unprofessional. Was it appropriate, he wanted to know, to voice disagreement?

The questions this student posed were important and ones a radical politics would readily engage. The climate of his center and the apparent philosophy of his director, implicit in his uncertainty of her response and the appropriateness of engaging in personal/political discussion on the job, were decidedly not radical. While a radical politics would not presume a clear answer to the questions he posed (he might have exercised his agency in any number of ways that differ from session to session and tutor to tutor), it would provide the conditions for exploring them and the support for grappling, however imperfectly, with them in practice. In a radical writing center, no tutor wonders whether it is appropriate to discuss the personal/political implications of writing and speaking. They know that to do so is essential to the mission of the writing center and therefore an everyday activity of their job. For a tutor to wonder whether it is okay to engage the personal/political in a radical writing center would be as odd as it would be to wonder whether it is okay to talk about writing in a conservative or liberal writing center.

Accordingly, in a radical writing center, notions of tutor "professionalism" can shift from meaning disinterested, objective, and impersonal (tools of production in a capitalist system) to instead reliable and accountable (humans in relationship to community and committed to its vision). This shift enables directors to be able to depend on their staff to be at work and to do their best without imposing an unrealistic and often violent imperative that tutors somehow check their humanity at the door to their job. A radical writing center does not merely *allow* tutors to engage critically with the content of student work or the ideas that circulate across the space—particularly when the arguments and rhetoric are offensive and violent—but in fact *expects* that collectively tutors will do so in ways that exercise their agency.

Sometimes that exercise looks like calling students out (bearing witness and testifying to an injustice by interrupting violent rhetoric/behavior to assert one's own humanity or that of others). Sometimes that exercise looks like calling students in (reaching out to the student to challenge their thinking in a way that seeks to promote further dialogue and preserve the relationship). Sometimes that exercise looks like asking questions. Sometimes that exercise looks like walking out of the session. Sometimes that exercise looks like remaining silent on the issue in order to survive the interaction and then seeking relief elsewhere afterwards. Sometimes it looks like another tutor intervening when the tutor in the session is too vulnerable to do so. Sometimes it looks like something else. But it never looks like only one of those things all the time. And it never looks like a single person navigating the questions and the practices alone. There is no idealized method to promote. Indeed, a radical staff keeps the conversation open about how to engage others in radical praxis. They also continue to engage with their own radical discomfort and change; no staff, no matter how self-conscious or radically inclined, is infallible to perpetrating injustice. A radical writing center would explore ways for students beyond the center to call out/call in/differently engage the tutors themselves, and the tutors one another, and the tutors the director, and so on.

In sum, a radical writing center is not defined by a single, static set of methods. It does not prescribe what happens in sessions. It does not recognize a typical session, a typical tutor, or a typical student. It might not even consist of sessions, or even of tutors and students. Rather than liberally pronouncing that anything goes, however, a radical writing center defines itself in part through its critical examination of methods. This examination goes beyond cognitive or pragmatic lenses to include sociopolitical lenses. A radical writing center remains open to changing and being changed by its methods. It remains open to the unknown.

In creating radical methods, we will continue to circle back to the question of language. A radical approach to methods necessarily compels us to question the terminology used to describe the doing of those methods and the people who engage those methods. Given the dominant language of *tutors, writers, students,* and *tutoring,* we might ask, Who benefits from the use of these terms? What methods do these terms readily enable, and which methods get shut out? Whom does this language benefit and whom does it disadvantage? If the dominant conservative and liberal paradigms of writing centers have given rise to such language, this language necessarily limits our imagination in conceptualizing different kinds of activities. How might we define writing center work differently if we don't conceive of it as tutoring but rather use language that more readily points towards culture building, shared resistance, and liberation? Certainly, terms such as *consultants* and *clients* would be called into question in a radical writing center for their capitalist connotations, their invocation of the marketplace, where knowledge is commoditized for profit and people are reduced to products and consumers. Indeed, when writing center work is conceived as a service, the benefit is assumed to be unidirectional, limiting both the reciprocal and communal transformation possible in working towards justice. A radical project problematizes the objectification of people and change making in this way and seeks opportunities for humanization. Rather than defining itself in terms of entrepreneurial values, a radical writing center would be more curious about definitions that evoke movement building, community organizing, or peace making.

The field already boasts a range of synonyms for *tutor*—words such as *mentors, coaches, assistants,* and *fellows* abound. But the radical writing center asks us to interrogate the relationship between language and function, resisting the naturalization of a role itself and reimagining possibilities for different kinds of being that give way to different kinds of activities that more readily promote peace. How might we name a community that works in solidarity to better the world, a community filled with contradictions and inequities yet negotiating hopefully for change? Would we be *facilitators, negotiators, comrades, accomplices, promoters of peace?* Is there language to describe our collective, rather than individual, identities, such that one might say something like "I am part of the radical writing center movement" rather than "I work at the writing center"? What if we did away with labels that describe a fixed role all together? What if we were simply Carmen, or Fangzhou, or Quin? How might the methods of engagement, consciousness-raising, shared learning, and exercise of agency emerge differently if the language itself were different, and how might we continue to reimagine both in an ongoing dialectical process?

RADICAL COMMUNITIES

If we were inclined to use the conceptual framework or language of communities to map out a plan for building a radical writing center, how might we identify and describe that center? In *The Everyday Writing Center* (2007), coauthors Anne Ellen Geller, Michele Eodice, Frankie Condon, Meg Carroll, and Elizabeth Boquet implicitly explode the limits of the space/method dichotomy for defining writing centers by arguing for a radical understanding of the human and relational nature of writing center work. To them, the radical potential of writing centers rests within the complex potential of a field defined by a "community of practice." Building upon the work of Etienne Wenger, they put forth a convincing analysis of the nature and practices of such a community that offers a fruitful foundation for radical engagement. Their interpretation and application of Wenger is key, as they remind us "much of Wenger's understanding of a community of practice involves exploring the relationship between identity and social organization" (90). In other words, to understand our work as a radical community of practice is to go beyond the notion that we are simply a group of people engaged in a shared endeavor and instead to examine the sociopolitical contexts continually reshaping who we are, how we come together, and what we do.

Perhaps the most promising radical definition of writing centers yet to emerge in the field, Geller et al.'s community of practice must be engaged with the same values and political underpinnings that animated these authors, however, in order for it to operate as a transformative frame for the field. Put differently, we must be wary of the ways their vision risks being appropriated and reduced to an empty writing center catch phrase, the sort of vessel Durling critiques—a phrase variously emptied and filled according to our various political aims. We cannot assume every group of people or every set of shared activities is radical in intent or effect. Indeed, a conservative or liberal writing center could happily operate by calling itself a *community of practice*, reducing its meaning simply to a static and finite group of people engaged in prescriptive or laissez-faire methodologies. Such is not Geller et al.'s vision.

A liberal reading of communities of practice risks the same sort of defeated relativism that plagues its anthropological cousin culture. When culture is understood as a group of people with shared meaning making, inherently (or relatively) good in its own right, culture becomes reified and used as an excuse to justify all sorts of violent traditions and norms. Given this openness to signification, a radical writing center is not simply a community. A community can be a finite group of people, small and knowable to one another through a shared culture, such as a writing center's student staff, or large and "imagined" (Anderson 1991), such as a nation or, I argue, a disciplinary field. Implicit in such a concept of community is a fixed nature—some people who are in and some people who are out, fixed criteria for gaining entrance, and fixed criteria for remaining an outsider. In essence, a community stays coherent because it is, by definition, exclusionary. As Shannon Carter writes, "A liberal-democracy that values both plurality and equality creates 'the people' by articulating an 'us' that can only exist through a simultaneous articulation of a 'them'" (2009, 137). Exclusivity belies the radical project, so radicalism cannot be defined by community. At the same time, a radical writing center is not *not* a community. Whether conscious or not, all human activity takes place in relationship to others—other individuals, other groups, and other webs of groups—so the task of a radical writing center is not to somehow resist community but to maintain a critical understanding of and engagement with it. Grimm, also drawing on Wenger, calls for an implicitly radical approach to community.

> A closed community becomes defensive and creates structures that lead to stratification, disconnectedness, dogmatism, narcissism, marginality, factionalism, and imperialism . . . The key to maintaining vital learning communities is keeping membership open, recruiting new members and paying attention to the creativity that occurs at the boundaries, particularly to the nexus where communities overlap and members reconcile their membership in multiple communities. (2011, 91)

When writing centers take this approach to community, Grimm interprets, then "the scope of their practice and their function within the university changes in significant ways" (91). These changes are how radical writing centers stand poised to exceed the limits of definition community imposes. To be a community of practice in a radical sense depends not only on asking questions about who comprises the community, how the community is formed, and what the community practices are but also on diving purposefully into the tensions that emerge at the boundaries, in fact redefining and relocating the community and its practices there. In this way, boundaries themselves are at once central and ephemeral—exceeding the limits of within and without, rendering old definitions moot and plunging forward purposefully into the unknown.

A radical writing center is always critically conscious of the ways power can be used to structure communities inequitably and works to resist those structures and instead continually transform them in service of liberation. This transformation goes beyond simply changing who is in and who is out but rather redefines the very culture and practices that provide an excuse for where the boundaries are drawn, for naming who counts and who doesn't, who finds the work relevant and who doesn't, and whom the work supports and whom it oppresses.

A radical writing center questions the ways humans exercise power to create the appearance of insiders and outsiders and thus to separate people from a recognition of their own agency. A radical writing center resists the limitations of the community as presently constructed, refusing to accept as natural the criteria that serve to label some as inherently more worthy and others as less deserving, and works to redefine the community itself. Accordingly, a radical writing center is not defined by the community that imagines itself to constitute it (its director and staff, for example, or "native English speakers") or the community it imagines it serves (the student body, for example, or "ESL students") but rather by the critical and collaborative exercise of power *across* communities that both explodes our false beliefs about what divides us (our belief in an *us* and a *them*) and transforms the human-made structures themselves that limit us in material ways. A radical writing center is conscious of, engaged with, and constituted by hybridity.

For these reasons, the liberal rhetoric of "inclusion and diversity" has no place in a radical writing center. Despite the good intentions from which such rhetoric might emerge, these concepts reinforce the fixedness of existing systems of power, merely nominally and futilely shuffling around its actors. As Ellen Berrey (2015) argues in "Diversity is for White People: A Big Lie Behind a Well-Intended Word," "Diversity is how we talk about race when we can't talk about race." It becomes a stand-in for serious interrogation of systemic inequities, ultimately centering whiteness (e.g., how does diversity help everyone?) and sustaining the tokenization and marginalization of people of color in practice. Diversity on its own does nothing to transform systems. A liberal writing center at a predominantly white institution, concerned about racial diversity, for example, implicitly already constituted by whiteness (and many other compulsory/normative social identities), asks only, How can we make our community more diverse? How can we recruit more tutors of color? How can we get more writers of color into the space? A liberal writing center fails to ask, In what ways is our work inherently colonizing and white supremacist? In what ways can we engage in decolonization and antiracist praxis? A radical writing center would engage questions of diversity beyond only race to explore the intersectionality of many social systems and the various needs for conscious and active intervention.

The attending liberal act of inclusion likewise depends on a fixed system and a liberal understanding of power—one in which gatekeepers possess the power to determine who enters and participates and who does not. If the community has the power to include, it also has the power to exclude. Because in a liberal model the exchange is not imagined as transferring power to those perceived as outsiders but rather paternalistically inviting those outsiders to participate in the activities controlled by the insiders, inclusion is not an empowering or transformative exchange but rather dependent upon assimilation and accommodation. The liberal writing center asks only, How can we make our centers (or the writing center field) more inclusive? How can we be more accommodating to "others"? The liberal writing center fails to ask, How can we disrupt assumptions about who "we" and "others" are? How can our centers be agents of change in our institutions (or the academy and society at large)? What might shared leadership look like? How can we see ourselves in the work of resistance already happening on the boundaries?

In everyday terms, to understand writing centers as radical communities of practice, we must call into question the fixed means by which we determine formal entrance into our spaces and what we do in those spaces. For example, what implicit biases influence our hiring of tutors? A conservative or liberal writing center might focus its application and interview questions on potential tutors' facility with standardized English grammar, dominant conventions for structuring arguments, and sanctioned processes—practices that reinforce existing inequitable power structures. A radical writing center might instead assess a student's willingness and interest in initiating critical conversations about identity, power, and discourse, in reflecting critically on their own identity, and in engaging meaningfully across differences. A liberal writing center might focus its tutor education on reading and responding to texts and disembodied tutoring methods, ignoring or relegating discussions of race, gender, learning disabilities, or English-language learning to an isolated conversation shaped by individual differences near the end of the term (see Greenfield and Rowan's [2011a] critique of this approach). A radical writing center might instead consider the foundational lenses it uses to frame its discussions of texts and mentoring, integrating questions about racism, ableism, compulsory heteronormativity, and other intersecting forms of oppression as indivisible from writing center practices. A liberal writing center would reduce oppression to special-interest topics to be dealt with outside the daily life of its work. A radical writing center would recommit daily to reflective and transformative change making.

On a larger scale, professional organizations such as the IWCA or its regional affiliates might think differently about how they talk about and come to understand who participates in their networks. A conservative field fails to notice or be concerned with the dominance of white people, for example, at its conferences and on its committees. A liberal writing center field fails to notice and listen to the people of color who are in fact there and focuses instead paternalistically on how to better include underrepresented writing centers such as HBCUs by extending more invitations and offering a few token scholarships. A radical writing center field would trust the leadership of people of color and turn the lens inward and ask in what ways its philosophies and practices are white supremacist and therefore by definition dehumanizing.

Karen Keaton Jackson, director of the Writing Studio and university writing program at North Carolina Central University, as part of a series of posts to *The Writing Center Journal* blog, observes, "Though colleagues at HBCUs were center stage of conversations about Composition and literacy instruction in the past, our voices no longer are heard consistently at conferences or in the scholarship; we must ask why, and then consider what is lost" (March 1, 2016). In addition to naming funding and time as significant barriers to participation, Keaton Jackson in her next post on May 17, 2016, shares the words of several fellow writing center professionals at HBCUs to shed some light on the many "reasons for our loud silence." Dr. Hope Jackson, former writing center director and SWCA 2009 Conference host at North Carolina A&T State University, gave a particularly telling response: "Honestly, [the reason for our absence is] whiteness and the white paradigm. Race studies are included when they benefit self-interests, not collective ones. We've been conveniently 'overlooked.'" Mr. Robert Randolf, instructor and current writing center director at that same institution similarly observes, "Racial issues are still seen as supplementary scholarship, something to be added once the 'real' research has been done—an afterthought." The striking absence of discussion of oppression (not only racism but any kind) and the relegation of such discussions to the margins of special-interest groups rather than the centering of such discussions in the daily life of the dominant professional organizations demonstrate that the field is not yet, indeed, radical in nature.

Keaton Jackson (*Writing Center Journal* blog post, March 22, 2016) goes on to identify a number of ways writing center professionals at HBCUs have sought to develop communities of practice through their own initiative, such as the creation of the North Carolina HBCU Writing Center Consortium launched in 2012 by Dr. Dwedor Ford, which included ten of the eleven HBCUs in North Carolina. The consortium provides an ongoing forum for organizing, engaging in professional development, and sharing ideas about pedagogies and best practices. Accordingly, a radical professional organization would learn from the ways otherwise marginalized groups consciously create and participate in activities beyond the limits of the dominant organization as an act of radical resistance. In another post (May 17, 2016), Keaton Jackson cites Dr. Kendra Mitchell, an expert on multilingualism and writing centers at HBCUs: in Mitchell's view, radical professional organizations would get curious about the "'contributions these institutions have to offer.'" In other words, radical writing center work is already happening, even if such work is not recognized by or cannot be contained by the dominant organizations.

The efforts towards inclusivity made recently by some of the dominant organizations are an encouraging move forward but are limited in potential without a radical framework to support them. The well-intentioned liberal conference theme, such as the 2016 National Conference on Peer Tutoring in Writing's "It's for Everyone: The

Inclusive Writing Center," is one such example. The implicit conception of a coherent "It" to which all people are already naturally inclined suggests a liberal desire for justice but is thwarted by a struggle to come to terms with the ways the writing center field is not, in fact, within the current paradigm, for everyone. Indeed, the phrase Inclusive Writing Center betrays the conference's good intentions. When *writing center* needs to be modified by the adjective *inclusive*, it suggests inclusivity cannot yet be taken for granted—it is not an essential part of the definition of writing center. Radical praxis compels us to question that very definition. A radical reorientation of such a conference title might instead begin with the difficult acknowledgment that conservative and liberal writing centers by definition are exclusionary and would invite interrogation as to why. This shift in orientation is significant. When we begin from a place of radical questioning, from posing as a problem the assumptions of standard practice, we are able to denaturalize fixed assumptions about writing center work in order to fundamentally reinvent it in ways that may be more just and universally liberating. When we start with the assumption that the writing center is already for everyone, our imaginations become limited to seeking accommodations for the different people whose needs are somehow dissonant from the norm. The "It" is never called into question or fundamentally changed.

Ultimately, a radical community of practice is by definition a changing community—one that extends beyond understandings of inclusion and exclusion and rather is always negotiating its boundaries, understanding that there is no outside the community, that all are in fact part of the community because all the world is touched by its work. It is not a community with fixed practices or fixed gatekeepers that manage the difference that enters. It is, again, a dialectic—as the boundaries of communities are negotiated so too are its practices and spaces. It is in the attendant shifts in practice and space where the radical writing center exceeds its definition as community. These negotiations give way to new negotiations of boundaries and so on, in continued reflective resistance to injustice and towards a relentless vision of peace.

RADICAL DISCIPLINARITY

Finally, if we were inclined to use the conceptual framework or language of disciplinarity to map out a plan for building a radical writing center, how might we identify and describe that center? In other words, what is the radical writing center's object of study? On one hand, if radical writing centers seek ethical transformation, emerge from hybridity, and do not retain a fixed, knowable structure, the object of our study itself cannot be entirely knowable or finite. In other words, to define our work with certainty as a discipline concentrated on writing or the tutoring of writing or any other finite concept would necessarily, through its naming as a clearly delineated branch of knowledge, reinscribe a conservative agenda. A radical writing center, therefore, cannot be defined by an object of study—it is not a discipline.

At the same time, a radical writing center is not *not* invested in a particular study. We need some semblance of coherence, however impermanent or divergent, that motivates us into conversation, that locates our inquiry, and that grounds and facilitates our ethical change making. A radical commitment, however, requires that such study does not presuppose answers, which means it cannot remain faithful to a single disciplinary approach, nor can it remain closed off to following what its radical investigation reveals. A radical writing center can go beyond disciplinary boundaries, for example, by collaborating across disciplines. Geller makes a convincing case for cross-disciplinary dialogue, one that compels those of us whose "education as rhetoricians" otherwise reinforces "how not to yield if we have strong beliefs" to forego our "defensiveness" and "lack of curiosity" by "suspend[ing] our judgment of others" and believing our colleagues across the disciplines do in fact have important insights to offer about writing and the teaching of writing (2009, 30).

A radical writing center would also go beyond disciplinary boundaries by exceeding traditional notions of disciplinarity itself (Boquet 1999). To do so does not mean our scope grows so broad we get lost, become all things to all people, and devolve into a vague and diluted version of our former work but rather that we are open to reconceptualizing, recontextualizing, reorganizing, restructuring, and reinventing our practices and ourselves with respect to that work, and more important, to understanding differently what that work even is or could be. In other words, writing cannot always mean the same things, hold the same significance, and be centered in our analyses in the same ways as our work progresses. In order to understand writing through a critical political framework, we come to see that writing is inextricably interdefined by its larger contexts and relationships—the systems and discourses of oppression that shape and are shaped by it. Radical disciplinarity, in this way, is responsive to heteroglossia (Bakhtin 1981) writ large, in which history and power in particular motivate our inquiry not only into texts but also into relationships, and the shifts in meaning we decipher are met with shifts in disciplinary lenses and practices.

The object of study, therefore, for a radical writing center could be understood not as an object at all but as a negotiation of objects—the interplay of writing, of discourse, of people, of systems across time and space. Through a radical lens, such work would include the study of how power is negotiated with respect to communication (in all its various modes and forms, including but not exclusively writing), rhetoric (in all its various uses and practices), and language (in all its varieties, constructions, and connotations) by communities (people who are privileged or subjugated by dominant practices and those who reinforce or resist them) and individuals embodied in real sociopolitical and historical contexts. To guide its research and practices, a liberal writing center discipline would ask, what makes good writing and how do we best teach it? A radical writing center discipline, in contrast, would ask, How and why is oppression perpetuated by and constituted in discourse, in writing? How and why are dominant discourses and conventions of writing presented to us as natural, neutral, and unchangeable? How can writing be used as a tool of resistance and/or how can writing itself be resisted? How can people imagine new ways of coming together in community to create conditions for peace, and what role would (or wouldn't) writing and learning play in that process?

When writing centers examine writing as a politically situated practice, we come to see that our opportunities for radical resistance necessarily compel us to engage in related questions about other modes of communication—to exceed disciplinarity by finding potential in the tension at the (imagined) boundaries. Specifically, speaking centers, which are gaining momentum as emerging arms of increasingly numerous writing centers (or, in a handful of cases, are emerging as their own entities), when engaged critically, have the potential to represent a radical interpretation of writing center work, as the lens of speech raises new kinds of questions about identity, embodiment, context, and voice. Multimedia centers, which incorporate visual rhetoric and digital literacies; multilingual centers, which work with students across a range of languages (not simply English or not English at all); centers that explore ASL and other signed languages; and centers that critically engage entirely different forms of voice and expression from the visual arts to mathematics all represent radical potential (though they are certainly not intrinsically radical) in their expanded engagement with discourse through a range of perspectives. Further, as radical writing center praxis compels us to go beyond changing merely individual students to changing the discourse contexts students enter, an explicit object of study will necessarily include the negotiation of writers and readers, of content and context, of words and the world. In other words, radical writing centers would examine radical listening, radical reading, radical viewing, and radical engagement.

To these latter ends, a radical writing center does not assume that the process by which a text is produced (North 1984) is the most significant lens for the study of writing. Rather, as is referenced earlier in the chapter, a radical writing center asks why the focus on the responsibilities of the writer, and not the reader, is taken for granted in dominant academic (and other) discourses. Such questioning might lead on one hand to a critical examination of cultural assumptions about communication, revealing the ways dominant Western rhetorical conventions expect the speaker or writer to adapt to the needs of the audience rather than the other way around. But rather than remaining in the liberal and primarily theoretical realm of contrastive rhetoric, a radical approach would compel us to ask further what systems of injustice are preserved in a particular sociopolitical historical context when the onus for accommodation rests squarely on the writer or speaker. Who is privileged in such systems? Who is disadvantaged? What agenda is maintained? Who has more platforms to speak and who doesn't? Who is taken more seriously and who isn't? Which modes of expression are valued and which are condemned?

When the audience bears no responsibility for the communicative exchange, listeners are enabled to summarily reject the speaker and the speaker's ideas under the guise of critiquing their rhetoric or language. In a highly racialized contemporary climate that promotes "colorblind" rhetoric, for example, the ability for a listener to hide their racial biases behind a seemingly mundane distaste for the speaker's communication practices is a vile and dangerous mechanism by which white people silence people of color, avoid grappling meaningfully with pressing issues of justice, and perpetuate racial inequities. A critical look at the history of discourse in the United States, for example, when it comes to race and gender reveals that the systematic violence and devaluing of Black women's lives is both reflected in and reconstituted by dominant white male discourse patterns. Beyond even the systematic stigmatization of Black speech patterns, which has been widely discussed in the literature, consider the ways in which Black women, even when adopting dominant discourse patterns ("following the rules"), are nevertheless routinely denied platforms to speak out about racism. Consider the ways, paradoxically, Black women are condemned for creating their own platforms or their own rules.

Even a cursory review of history makes the patterns abundantly clear. Born a slave in 1862 in Mississippi, Ida B. Wells-Barnett became an outspoken antilynching activist. A journalist, publisher, teacher, and organizer, Wells-Barnett's courageous use of voice came at a cost. In 1891 she was fired from her teaching job in Memphis, Tennessee, for being a vocal critic of the conditions of the Blacks-only school. She received threats while touring the South as a journalist collecting information about lynchings. Her newspaper office was destroyed by an angry mob who threatened her with death if she were to return to it. Indeed, her message that "lynching is a color-line murder . . . that requires a national remedy" and that "lawmakers must be made to know that human life is sacred" (1909) was repeatedly the target of white supremacists who sought to destroy her and her platform to speak.

A half-century later, Fanny Lou Hamer, an outspoken Black racial justice and voting-rights activist, found herself like countless others being shut out of opportunities to give voice to her experience of racial violence. In 1964 she testified before Congress about her experience and that of many fellow Black citizens being intimidated, threatened, falsely imprisoned, and relentlessly and brutally assaulted nearly to death by police officers when trying to register to vote in Mississippi. Fearful of the sympathy she might garner from the many people watching the live televised broadcast of her testimony, President Lyndon Johnson called an impromptu news conference right at the moment she sat down at the microphone to speak, compelling the broadcast to cut out immediately. His announcement? That it was the nine-month anniversary of the day Governor Connelly had been (nonfatally) shot. When he concluded his absurd press conference and the broadcast returned to Congress, Hamer had finished her remarks ("Fanny Lou" 2014). In her words: "Our lives be threatened *daily*, because we want to live as decent human beings in America" ("Audio" 2010). The state knew the importance of her words and used its power to take away her platform, seeking to silence her and her message.

Another half-century later, leaders of the contemporary Black Lives Matter movement, motivated by the urgency of the need to end state-sanctioned violence towards Black bodies and acutely aware of the lack of platforms for Black women to speak out and be taken seriously, have resorted to time-tested protest strategies of interrupting public forums to demand their message be heard. The systems of racism that allow listeners to swiftly condemn their tactics and shout "boo" at Black women who take the microphone and name racial injustices separate us from our humanity. A liberal approach to listening professes to value racial equality (meanwhile doing nothing to create it) while refusing to engage with the speakers' message. The liberal listener claims to be willing to take the speaker seriously if only she will speak more calmly, more politely, when it is her turn. A liberal listener fails to recognize that the speaker's turn is never granted.

Instead, a radical listener is courageous enough to allow her heart to break as she resonates with the pain in the hoarse and desperate voice of Black Lives Matter cofounder Patrisse Cullors, for example, who was with a group of activists who interrupted a Democratic presidential primary campaign town hall gathering in 2015:

> First of all, it's not like we like shutting shit down, but we have to. We are tired of being interrupted. The governor [O'Malley] is going to be able to speak. We know that he's been here. We also know that Senator Bernie Sanders is back there. We appreciate you listening to us and the audience holding space for us. But let me be clear. *Every single day* folks are *dying*. Not being able to take another *breath*. We are in a state of emergency! We are in a state of emergency! And if you don't feel that emergency, you are not human! (Roguski 2015)

A radical listener trusts a young Black Lives Matter activist Marissa Johnson, who takes the microphone at a presidential primary rally in Seattle and speaks courageously through her tears as white audience members shout angrily for her to be quiet: "We are going to honor all of the Black lives lost this year, and we are going to honor the fact that I have to fight through all of these people to say *my life matters*! But I have to get up here in front of a bunch of screaming, white racists to say that my life fucking matters!" ("Bernie Sanders" 2015) A radical listener understands that there is a context of violence speakers are negotiating and is willing to set aside the discomfort that comes from witnessing the breaking of public norms of etiquette to take in the deep urgency of the message itself. A radical listener is transformed by the experience and listens differently in the future, is inspired to be more courageous in their own speaking, and pursues opportunities to wield their own agency to make change and to create and protect platforms for otherwise silenced voices. Actor and activist Jesse Williams has offered a pointed critique of listeners who are quick to condemn those who protest against oppression: "The burden of the brutalized is not to comfort the bystander. That's not our job, all right—stop with all that. If you have a critique for the resistance, for our resistance, then you better have an established record of critique of our oppression. If you have no interest in equal rights for Black people then do not make suggestions to those who do. Sit down" (Williams 2016).

Radical speaking programs by definition must be critical of oppression, which means they must simultaneously be radical listening programs, inviting not just students but also people at all levels of the institution to reexamine their assumptions about the various ways in which listeners silence speakers. Such programs would explore, for example, how racial bias influences how listeners devalue speakers who use stigmatized language varieties despite the value of their ideas and how such biases influence listeners' ability to be willing to understand the speaker's meaning even when the speaker employs standardized conventions (Gilyard 1991). Such programs would explore opportunities for listeners to resist this phenomenon rather than focusing merely on how the speaker must change to appease the listener, which, as the research implies, is impossible in practice to do.

Such programs would also explore, for example, the ways assumptions about gender influence listeners' responses to women. Research shows that in spaces where women are not the majority, women are more likely to be interrupted, challenged, dismissed, or labeled negatively than are men when they speak, and that as a result, women in fact speak up less often. Radical programs would explore opportunities for listeners to protect platforms for women to speak, to question whose ideas they challenge more readily and who is given a free pass, and to intervene at moments of gendered discursive violence rather than merely compelling women to change their speaking practices to warrant a more meaningful response. As the research shows (see, for example, Eagly and Carli 2007), women are in fact in a bind when it comes to their speech. To assert themselves with authority is to risk criticism and loss of material opportunities; to adopt a more passive approach is to risk losing the ability to influence their surroundings. A radical speaking center would support women in developing critically conscious strategies for navigating an acknowledged oppressive system while resisting the internalization of that system (doubting the value of one's own voice and silencing the self), all the while putting the greater onus of responsibility on the collective for changing the very conditions that silence women. Of importance, the above are merely illustrative examples; radical speaking centers would explore a wide range of intersecting systems of oppression and seek opportunities to intervene.

Radical writing centers, likewise, must simultaneously be radical reading centers. To read radically is not simply to be an astute close reader, able to identify, analyze, and critique the nuance of a writer's argument and structure. Rather, a radical reader is one who reads beyond the page, seeking to understand what the writer intended. A radical reader is one who seeks to consider how the writer's experiences in their broader sociopolitical context is influencing their experience as a writer—what they feel empowered to share and what they must protect and how they are wrestling with (or oblivious to) the pressures to perform a particular discourse. A radical reader is one who is highly self-reflective, committed to examining their own implicit biases and assumptions that influence how they value or interpret the text and challenging themselves to read differently in order to engage with it in a more humanizing way. A radical reader is open to challenging their own beliefs and desires and to changing their behaviors as a result of what they learn. A radical reader sees their role as audience as equally responsible for the success of the writing and of peace in society.

Given such a holistic approach, a radical writing center, defined by its object of study as a negotiation among writing and the contextualizing forces that create its meaning, must necessarily recognize as key the negotiation of an explicit relationship to the institution's curriculum. If we want to transform systems of injustice facilitated by fixed discourse norms, we must transform the discourse itself. That means we must be able to work with other educators to increase understanding about how power dynamics and identity politics are going to influence their students' choices—in writing, speaking, listening, convening—differently. We must be a purposeful part of a process of supporting educators at our institutions to construct writing assignments, create classroom dynamics, and facilitate discussions in ways that support student agency and require accountability from the audience—the other students and the professor. We must engage with educators about how to advise students and respond to and evaluate student work—papers, speeches, class discussion, participation—in ways that are ethical and transformative. And we must do this work open to the possibility that these very frameworks themselves—assignments, classrooms, students, teachers, evaluation, and so on are all constructs of our particular sociopolitical moment, whose limits we might resist even as a starting point for entering into a practice. Radical writing center praxis does not require that writing center directors be experts in all fields. It does require that directors have a foundational understanding of key concepts related to systemic oppression and can provide leadership in facilitating examinations of oppression with respect to interpersonal relationships, educational practices, and discourse conventions. The interdisciplinary scope of the radical lens invites new kinds of important cross-disciplinary collaborations, in which the boundaries among disciplines are purposefully blurred. Radical writing centers exceed disciplinarity by resisting the notion of centeredness itself; rather, the work is defined by its negotiation of boundaries.

5

RADICAL WRITING CENTER PRACTICES
Stories, Resonance, Shared Leadership, and the Sustenance of Life

What if revolution isn't a product, some distant promised land, but the relationships that we have right now?

—Kai Cheng Thom

Return us to silence, joy, song

—Becky Thompson

In an effort to initiate a process of building a radical writing center discipline, previous chapters explore foundational questions about *why* we should do this work (vision) and *what* this work could be (definition). This final chapter moves us forward in the process to ask *how* we can do radical writing center work (pedagogy). As I hope to have shown, radical praxis requires that theory and practice be mutually constituted. We cannot simply articulate a theory and then translate that theory into practice; rather, our practices inform our theories, which inform our practices, which inform our theories in an ongoing dynamic process. Concluding the book, therefore, with an explicit attention to practice is not meant to suggest this process is now finished. To the contrary, the practices explored in this chapter necessarily initiate a new process of inquiry into radicalism itself. For this reason, this chapter frequently echoes topics and questions raised in previous chapters but points even more explicitly to turning ideas into action. My sincere desire is that this book not be received as merely an intellectual exercise but that it prompts significant, tangible changes to the work we do. Accordingly, here I foreground a set of broad practices intended to clarify and make both tangible and feasible everyday opportunities for radical writing center work.

Radical education theorists insist radical education is not a prescriptive method. Rather, specific pedagogies, informed by a radical politics,

DOI: 10.7330/9781607328445.c005

must be created in context. Accordingly, this book does not presume to suggest the right, or even best, way to enact a radical praxis. At the same time, to leave the work in the realm of theory, only to return to our liberal practices, defeats our radical intentions. As such, this chapter offers a series of examples of ways we might rethink what is possible for our work given the radical questions explored. These practices are not prescriptive or exhaustive or perfect but are rather examples intended to spark new and different ideas and to encourage more creativity in grounding our ethical commitments in tangible activities.

I am hopeful readers uncertain about some of the ideas offered here—perhaps agreeing with an idea in theory but uncomfortable with the changes necessary to leap into practice—will use their skepticism as an opportunity for radically questioning their own assumptions. What conservative or liberal beliefs are informing that skepticism? What privileges allow us to question the viability of a specific radical approach? What allegiances to existing systems of oppression are informing our doubts? Beyond this nudging into radical courage, it is my profound hope that readers will in fact challenge the unspoken limits of the ideas I myself offer below and will be even bolder, even more visionary, than I am. Collectively, I call on all of us to radically transform the field so dramatically that even the ideas here become obsolete.

CULTURES OF RADICAL ENGAGEMENT

Radicalism, in its understanding of injustice as human-made social structures, compels us to explore alternative possibilities for coming together in community. In 2016, I had the opportunity to learn from Lucien Demaris and Cedar Landsman, educational activists, healers, and community builders who work out of the Relational Center, an organization that supports transformative culture through the nurturing of deep relationships ("Who We Are"), and who lead Relational Uprising, "a training and coaching institute that supports inspired activists and organizers engaged in frontline movement building to cultivate interdependent relational culture" ("Our Mission"). Community partners who have worked with Relational Uprising include Schaghticoke First Nations, TightShift Laboring Cooperative, Momentum, the Peace Poets, Ayni Institute, Healing Justice, Movimiento Cosecha, IfNotNow, Sunrise Movement, and Real Food Challenge, among others. Demaris and Landsman visited my current institution, Hampshire College, through their partnership with the college's Ethics and the Common Good Project (an affiliated program through which my speaking program receives its grant funding) for a weeklong residency (2016a) and a follow up training day (2016b), and it was through participating in these spaces that I encountered their work and from which I gleaned the ideas I will describe here.[1] Demaris and Landsman, in collaboration with Mark Fairfield, the director of the Leadership Institute at the Relational Center, have created a powerful theory and practice for what they call "cultures of radical engagement" that I believe holds mighty potential for writing center people to rethink how we tell our stories and how we come together in and create community.

Their work is rooted purposefully in ecology, tracing the necessity of supportive human relationships as interconnected to the story of life on Earth. The ecosphere, which consists of earthly conditions (sunlight, gravity, land, water), structure (decentralized and holistic shapes of individual organisms and entire ecosystems), and culture (mutualistic, diverse, alive), has a story to tell. That story, from the emergence of the very first cells of life (4.6 billion years ago) to the emergence of the first humans in Africa (200,000 years ago) to today has been a progression from conditions, to vitality, to sensitivity, to emotionality, to vulnerability, to the ability to tell life's story. That story is one of profound interconnection. Citing recent shifts in perspective from the "survival of the fittest" models of evolution that focus on individual genes to relational models that focus on the survival of the ecosystem as a whole, Demaris and Landsman (2016a) point out that life (from bacteria, to plants, to animals) in fact persists where there is greater diversity, density, and connection. It is not competition but rather support that allows life to thrive. Indeed, periods of mass extinctions have been marked by the absence of these conditions.

Unfortunately, the most recent chapter in the story of human life, they argue convincingly, is one of separation—separation from nature and the body, separation from a diversity of voices, and separation from one another. The separation from nature and the body, they observe, has been enacted through the human story of "dominance over nature," which asserts the power of humans over the entire ecosphere; we can see the disastrous effects of this story in our collective exploitation and destruction of the natural resources necessary to sustain life. The separation from a diversity of voices, they go on to observe, is evident in the human story of "civilizations" that asserts the power of individuals or groups over others; we can see the disastrous effects of this story in our fracturing into nations and tribes, in our isolation from diverse cultures and peoples, in our battles and wars across imagined boundaries and interests, in the reigns of individual leaders or kings, in the valuing of one way of being over another. The separation from one another, they observe finally, is apparent in the human story of "self-sufficiency," which alienates us from and makes us suspicious of one another and denies the power of relationships; we can see the disastrous effects of this story, ultimately, in our failure to contribute to and draw on the support of our communities and to see our collective survival as mutually dependent.

In response, Demaris and Landsman (2016a) argue, it is vital (critical to life) that we tell new stories—stories of connection that promote healing and support. These stories are ones of interdependence and shared leadership, mutualism and strengthening of bonds, and bridge building across difference. The stakes, for Demaris and Landsman, are nothing short of the survival of life on the planet. And key to this radical, humanizing process of storytelling are radical listening and *resonance*. Resonance is the locus of connection, the moment of empathy felt deep in the body by the listener and shared with the storyteller. As a sort of "relational meditation," it is a gift to humanity that opens up the possibility for love. Demaris and Landsman emphasize that resonance is not asking questions, making meaning, giving advice, or telling your own story in response to what you hear. It is simply an expression of the moments you felt "right there with" the storyteller.

When individuals come together, share their stories of challenge and support, and communicate resonance, powerful humanizing connections are formed. When communities come together and collectively tell their stories, we begin to create cultures of radical engagement. Demaris and Landsman (2016a) propose that such cultures aim to decentralize and share leadership in order to sustain everyone ("you lead me"), to strengthen bonds and share collective resonance ("you move me"), and to build bridges for radical diversity and accessibility ("you change me").

Inspired by Demaris and Landman's vision, how might we reimagine writing centers to be incubators of cultures of radical engagement? What would a writing center community look like if we approached our work through radical storytelling and resonance? How might writing centers contribute to the very sustenance of life on the planet? Below I explore possibilities for translating the above qualities of radical relational culture into tangible writing center practices.

"You Lead Me"

Demaris and Landsman (2016a) propose that in a culture of radical engagement, people share leadership, decentralize agency, and learn collectively. How might these activities be cultivated in a writing center?

Shared Leadership in Tutor Education

One starting point for such cultivation might be through our peer-tutor education models. Popular training models (often brief and intensive prior to the beginning of work) focus on the consumption of prescribed concepts and the successful performance of prescribed methods. These training models, however conversation based they might be, assume peer-tutoring knowledge to be primarily conclusive and finite: directors are the leaders passing on their received wisdom to the tutors, their followers. Slogans such as "a good tutor makes the student do all the work" or "the ultimate aim of a tutorial is an independent writer," as Grimm (2011) critiques, commonly serve as the imposed assumptions that lead to similarly prescriptive and unquestioned tutoring rules, such as always have the student read the paper aloud, focus on HOCs before LOCs, or never write on the student's paper. Serving as stewards of the discipline in this kind of model, directors provide little opportunity to foster a radical culture. When leadership is decentralized and learning is shared, what alternative models might emerge?

To begin, as I have argued elsewhere with Karen Rowan (Greenfield and Rowan 2011a), a simple yet necessary step is to shift our language from tutor training, which is finite and knowable, to tutor education, which carries potential for understanding tutoring as a process that requires life-long study, reflection, collaboration, and reinvention. We might even think more radically than this, describing this formative work in terms of tutor community building, organizing, or mobilizing. While not all directors have the opportunity to create full-fledged credit-bearing courses as part of their programs, all have the opportunity to think radically about what foundational questions support a life-long learning process and how ongoing education might purposefully be infused throughout tutors' careers with the center and beyond. Be it through formal ongoing education workshops, discussion groups, buddy systems, staff meetings, wikis, or social events, how might education be integrated into the regular life of the center?

For this ongoing education to be radical, tutors must be understood as shared leaders in the learning process. This means they are supported in learning not only from the director but also from others on campus and one another, and most important, the director (and other administrators) are learning from the tutors at the same time. Together, directors and tutors ask questions about language, about writing, about speaking, about listening, about discourse, about power, about their experiences, and about writing center lore itself, and together they uncover new answers and ask new questions. In the process, the director's understanding of writing center work, both its assumptions and practices, is changed. Necessarily, the tutors, through their critical examination of the field, recreate the field itself. Directors who continue to teach the same tutor-education syllabus year after year (whether in a semester-long course or some other model), with the same progression of logic, the same set of readings, and the same activities with little variation enact a conservative model, one that disconnects students from their agency, as the director is not changed through a reciprocal process. This initiation into a static field not only disconnects students from their work with each other but ultimately disconnects directors from their own agency as well and stagnates the field as a whole. Radical education requires regular revision.

For example, for many years I taught a tutor-education course in which the first several sets of assignments included readings by foundational writing center scholars whose work continues to be a driving force in the field—Bruffee (1984), North (1984), Harris (1995), and the like. Later assignments sought to present counterpoints to the arguments in those texts, moving the questions in what I intended to be more radical directions—Grimm (1999), Bawarshi and Pelkowski (1999), Denny (2005), Victor Villanueva (2006), Geller et al. (2007), and the like. Indeed, in my mind, Bawarshi and Pelkowski's "Postcolonialism and the Idea of a Writing Center" represented the definitive radical text—challenging North's vision for the field as inherently colonialist. And for many semesters I taught it as such, inviting and encouraging students to see this text as holding the key for our transformative work together—until one semester, an unusually savvy group of students (shout out to Fangzhou, Bryan, Kira, Ajmal, Googie, Quin, Ben, and Brittany!) immediately called the text into question. Despite being convinced by the authors' postcolonial critique of assimilationist practices, they were perplexed by what they read to be the authors' ultimately defeatist conclusions. They wanted to know, Why are the authors advocating not that students subvert or reject or resist academic discourse but instead that students "self-consciously . . . use and be used by" (Bawarshi and Pelkowski 1999, 44) the institution's discourse? What exactly does that mean? Is that a cop-out? Indeed, as I came to see when reading the text anew through their eyes, Bawarshi and Pelkowski, despite critiquing the institution, implicitly assume the institution is unchangeable. Nowhere do they explore student agency in a process of *de*colonization; rather, their postcolonial solutions are explicitly rooted in the dominant discourse. Their conclusions, as such, are decidedly liberal: develop a consciousness of injustice but adapt your practices (however purposefully) to the existing structures. This radical critique not only compelled me to change where I positioned the text on the syllabus and how I invited discussion of the text in future semesters but indeed sharpened my own ability to analyze writing center discourse with respect to political ideologies. Without those students, I wouldn't be able to articulate my radical vision with the precision I can now. Because of the ways I have differently framed the discussion leading up to that text—providing a vocabulary and grounding in a range of political theories—subsequent generations of tutors (or mentors, per the language in my program, so I will use *tutor* and *mentor* interchangeably for the remainder of the chapter) continue to raise the same critique of the text before I even propose it to them.

So rather than structuring syllabi around predetermined writing center answers we want students to reach, we can structure our syllabi around genuine questions we want students to explore. These can be questions we ourselves are working to understand, which means our questions each semester will likely change. Some of the questions guiding my mentor education course this semester, for example, have been, What is ethical peer mentorship? What should a speaking program's role be in relationship to institutional oppressions? How should a speaking program articulate its mission? How can a speaking program ensure its values are in alignment with its practices? What does it mean for a speaking program to be transformative? What do you think of the Transformative Speaking Program's mission of "promoting radical dialogue to change the world"? I am also transparent about my purposes: the peer-mentoring education course title is Revolution through Collaboration.

Not every institution will be supportive of the education models we seek to use, and not all students will be responsive to the radical questions we pose. Directors will need to continue to be savvy in negotiating their practices in light of specific institutional contexts and stakes. Rather than assuming there is only one correct method of enacting radical education, directors can in their own ways explore unique opportunities to invite their students to have agency in their learning process and in speaking back to the dominant discourses of the field, and directors can challenge themselves to be open to having their own assumptions questioned and to continually revising how they themselves conceive of writing center work and perform its practices.

Shared Scholarship and Professional Leadership

When student mentors are supported in a culture of shared learning, one in which they are revisioning and recreating the field itself, a radical writing center praxis also creates opportunity for them to exercise their agency in ways that influence the field beyond the immediate space of the campus. Student mentors can be supported in participating in the professional work of the field, building relationships, sharing their voices, and making meaning across the broader community. This means supporting students in activities such as publishing their writing and presenting at conferences. The field already does a remarkably good job at encouraging student participation and indeed even centering student voices. Forums such as the yearly National Conference on Peer Tutoring in Writing (and its joint meetings with the International Writing Centers Association), the *Dangling Modifier* online journal, the "Tutor's Column" within *WLN: A Journal of Writing Center Scholarship*, special undergraduate research issues of *The Writing Center Journal*, the PeerCentered collaborative online spaces, and the student essay contests held by the Northeast Writing Centers Association, among others, are notable opportunities for students to offer their voices in the field and collaborate with one another.

Beyond these student-focused spaces, however, a culture of radical engagement calls for collaboration across our differences, for students, directors, and other professional writing center scholars to share in the learning process scholarly production enables. In other words, if directors and other scholars are not learning from what the students are sharing, our work ceases to be radical. I recall overhearing a respected, seasoned writing center scholar make a patronizing comment about bringing new students to writing center conferences and watching them grapple with the same questions generations of new students grapple with each year. Implicit in his comment was the resignation that there was a standard process for encountering writing center work and that he, so many years later in his career, had nothing new to learn by engaging with novices. I remember being quite put off by his comments but later feeling a prick of shame as I found myself similarly disengaged at writing center conferences by what had started to become a familiar exploration of the same old writing center questions. How do you find an effective balance between directive and nondirective tutoring? How do you tutor ESL students? How do you mentor a science writer?

What I have come to see is that my distaste for the aforementioned scholar's comment as well as my own shame for relating to it both provided opportunities for radical reinvention. First, a radical approach *should* compel us to be critical of condescension towards students and of assumptions that we have nothing to learn from them. In a radical model, writing center conferences and other interactive forums should be gatherings where directors are engaged and learning from the student presenters to the same degree students are learning from more experienced professionals. That is a vision for which we must continue to strive. At the same time, the conservative and liberal models dominating contemporary scholarship are necessarily leaving us stuck, circulating the same values, assumption, mantras, and methods with little opportunity for new possibilities to emerge. In the absence of a radical paradigm, generations and generations of novice mentors will indeed continue to engage with the same old set of questions, and generations and generations of seasoned scholars will continue to look on from a distance with little new to learn. This is not a critique of novice mentors who engage earnestly and rigorously with the questions put before them but rather is a challenge to seasoned directors and scholars charged with mentoring them. If students' learning processes do not contribute to our own learning, we are missing something as a field.

What happens instead when we work with students to cocreate our questions and to pursue scholarship that intrigues and excites us both? What radical questions might we pose? Rather than rearticulating the familiar, what if we questioned the directive versus nondirective binary itself, or introduced questions of collaboration in terms of radical dialogue without ever using the language of that old construct at all? What if we questioned the premise that ESL writers are somehow atypical and instead problematized the ways monolingual English speakers are made central and normative in writing center discourse? What if we challenged the assumption that science writers require fundamentally different (or fundamentally the same) tutoring approaches, asking instead in what ways the sciences are implicated in systemic oppression and how science writers might intervene?

Critical to the culture of radical-engagement framework is that we tell stories of support. Stories of support enable us to resist notions of self-sufficiency and to draw attention to the value of community connections and interdependency. Such stories are also a source of hope. Here is one of mine: collaborations with students have been central in my career, and I have sought to bring groups of students, including students who are newly enrolled in my mentor-education courses (not yet having conducted a single mentoring session) with me to conferences every semester I have had funding to do so. One year I brought a group of students to IWCA/NCPTW, where two of them (shout out to Ariel and Julia!) encountered the idea of a high-school writing center in a session they attended. Over dinner that evening, they excitedly but reluctantly shared their interest in seeing whether they might build a relationship with a local high school and help start a writing center there. To their surprise (they later shared), I reached my hand across the table and shook their hands: "Let's do it." With my mentorship, they went on to build a beautiful partnership between our college and a local high school, setting up a center that went on to flourish even after they had graduated and left the area. In subsequent conversations, they shared with me that that moment of support at the dinner table had been a critical moment in their sense of belonging in our community, in their sense of worth and capabilities as new mentors, and in their vision for their future. They did not know it at the time, but that same moment was equally important for me. Their courage in creating a vision and taking the steps to bring it to life served as a source of inspiration to me when I made the leap to temporarily leave academia and start a community-based nonprofit organization. If my students could have the courage and capabilities to build something new, why couldn't I? This moment of shared learning grew into shared leadership and ultimately shared agency.

Shared Leadership in Program Development

If students are true collaborators in learning about the field, recreating the field, and recreating the field's discourses, it only makes sense that radical writing center praxis would entail students' active participation in leading the work of the centers on their home campuses. To do so would mean students share responsibility for defining the program's philosophy, devising its pedagogies, and creating its everyday structures, protocols, and practices. Part of this work would mean, as explored in previous chapters, being collaborators in creating, interpreting, and revising the mission statement of the center and the language the center uses to talk about its work. Beyond shaping the language, however, students can participate in shaping (and revising) the very work of the center.

Staff meetings can be one forum where leadership is shared through dialogue and collaboration with the director. Directors can share with students key questions around programming and invite students not simply to weigh in on possibilities but also to critically examine together the motivations, barriers, rationales, and stakes related to various choices, particularly in the context of the program's radical mission. For example, several years ago as my students were in the midst of developing language for our mission statement ("to promote radical dialogue to change the world"), we received a series of requests from faculty in our college's social entrepreneurship program for peer mentors to lead several speaking workshops and trainings for their students. In particular, they were interested in a workshop on speaking for women (one professor had noticed that in her male-majority classes the women were mostly quiet) and in providing a training for our mentors in business pitch making (their program was hiring professional consultants to lead this training, which the peer mentors would then use to train students). Without giving it much thought beyond feeling pleased that faculty knew who we were and were interested in our resources, I agreed.

At our next staff meeting when I excitedly shared the opportunity with the students and asked who wanted to help facilitate, I was met with an uncomfortable silence. "I don't want to do it," one student finally said. The rest remained quiet with their eyes fixed on the table. "Okay, let's talk about this," I responded. "What's going through your minds right now?" The student courageously shared that if we were truly to be committed to our mission, then passively supporting the work of social entrepreneurship would be hypocritical. To their minds, social entrepreneurship is a deeply flawed (liberal, defeatist) activity that paternalistically makes money off injustice and that perpetuates the very capitalist systems at the root of the problem such ventures purport to solve. Another student thought that with our limited resources we should be focusing on supporting students who are marginalized by oppressive systems, not helping already-privileged students develop skills for making a profit. They argued that our integrity was at stake—this was a defining moment testing whether we were going to live our stated values or just pay lip service to them.

Other students shared that they didn't know very much about social entrepreneurship and wondered whether it was possible or even ideal for the entire staff to take a position on it. What would be the political cost of alienating the social entrepreneurship program? Would we jeopardize our own work by refusing a relationship with them? Weren't we an interdisciplinary program meant to support the entire campus? Was it right to pick and choose the people with whom we work? Others asked in contrast what the cost would be of collaborating with them. Who would we implicitly alienate by creating that relationship? Students feared that the very students our program sought to reach, ones whose voices were often marginalized and ones interested in social change, challenging the status quo, community organizing, protesting, and dialoguing would be turned off by that partnership, putting our other relationships in jeopardy. What were we to do?

Ultimately, we decided together that if our mission promoted "radical dialogue," we could not make a decision without first engaging in such dialogue with the potential partners themselves. Accordingly, we invited one of the requesting faculty members to join us at our next staff meeting with the hope of gathering more information about what social entrepreneurship meant, what values were informing their work, and what their vision was for how our program would support it. We also hoped to share more about our work and philosophy and decide together whether there were points of resonance that would make for a viable partnership. To our delight, they readily agreed to talk with us.

I had been a little nervous that the conversation would turn out to be antagonistic, but the students and I talked beforehand about needing to be welcoming and open to listening fairly to gather information rather than leading with assumptions. And indeed, the gathering turned out to be perfectly pleasant. At the meeting the students created an open and welcoming space, and the faculty member took time to talk about their classes and their students' projects and the kind of support they were hoping we would offer. My students asked fair and challenging questions, the answers to which set some of my students at ease, whereas others remained concerned. Despite the friendly nature of the meeting, what we had hoped would be a dialogue really turned into simply a presentation. The expression of curiosity was mostly unidirectional; my students asked information-gathering questions but were not asked much about their own work and ideas in return. This alone was telling to them. We ended the meeting with a plan to reflect together as a staff and then to follow up with the faculty soon after.

In our next meeting we reflected on the conversation. Students' personal positions with respect to social entrepreneurship itself still varied—the faculty's presentation had complicated some of their views, though the majority were still critics, some fiercely so. Where there was a good deal of consensus, however, was in how the program should respond to the request—and future requests from any potential partner—for support. Central to their work, they agreed, was the need for radical dialogue in all their partnerships and workshops/sessions. If radical dialogue involves problem-posing questions, examining the sociopolitical contexts that create existing conditions, and exploring opportunities for students to have agency in resisting oppression (including dominant discourse practices), the students couldn't simply be passive or neutral stewards in teaching a standardized convention.

As such, we decided that rather than simply turning down the requests, we would renegotiate them. The first request had been for a workshop on women and speech, with the aim of encouraging women students to speak up more. We agreed the subject of women and speech was one that could fit into our mission of changing the world for the better but that the assumption that it was the fault of the women and their responsibility to speak up more was flawed. Instead, we agreed to lead a workshop about gender and communication more broadly, one that invited all students—of any gender identity—to think critically about their role in creating conditions supportive of many voices within a system that often suppresses the voices of women. With this new aim, the peer mentors were excited to facilitate, seeing this workshop as an opportunity to have a positive influence in a course that might not otherwise be reflecting in this way.

As to the second request, to receive professional training in pitch making and then copy those trainings for other students, we decided to decline. The trainings did not appear to support a reflective dialogue about pitch making itself. The peer mentors wanted to explore the ways standard pitch-making formulas implicitly privilege white male discourse patterns and the ways listener biases about the speaker's race, gender, age, ability, and so on impact the ways people respond positively or negatively to pitches. They wanted to explore the ways the fast-paced, performative nature of pitch making undermines the opportunity for genuine human connection and relationship building. The activities that had been proposed to us did not allow for this. We offered instead to meet individually with students who were working on their pitches, encouraging them to come to our center's drop-in hours. In those sessions, we could offer radical dialogues, not to unilaterally talk all students out of making pitches but to invite them into a critical reflection they might not be getting elsewhere and to open up opportunities to engage differently with the pitch-making process or even, if necessary, to abandon it.

In the end, we did go on to lead the workshop on gender and to work with a few students on their pitches, and those conversations were well received. To my knowledge, there has been no real fallout from the decision, either. Of importance, the process was highly energizing for the student staff and for me. At the end of that first staff meeting when the problem-posing question was raised, one student sat nodding her head and smiling and simply stated to her peers, "I am so proud of y'all." Indeed, the experience with the social entrepreneurship program has gone down in the program's history among the student staff as a defining moment in which they really came into being as radical mentors. For me, it was an awesome lesson in shared leadership. Trusting the students to share in the decision making had proven to be critical to the program's integrity.

Beyond simply being responsive to student concerns, however, shared leadership also involves proactive, anticipatory dialogue. To those ends, student staff can be invited into the process of helping set the agenda for their gatherings with the director, choosing topics of interest to them, and indeed sharing in facilitating. In my current program, for example, in past years students have each signed up for a date during the semester for which they will identify a topic of interest to them and facilitate a discussion for a brief part of our staff meetings. Depending on the number of students on staff in a given term, sometimes students work together to cofacilitate, and we have had more than one facilitation at each meeting. These facilitated moments have ranged from discussions prompted by a single question related to communication (e.g., Is it possible to communicate the story of a culture accurately to people outside that culture who have no context to understand it?); to reflections on the relevance or usefulness of various mentoring strategies (e.g., reviewing a handout on choreographer Liz Lerman's Critical Response Process for artistic works in progress and guiding a discussion about its usefulness to speaking mentoring); to activities inviting hands-on practice (e.g., facilitating the group in trying out speaking warm-up exercises used in improv comedy). More recently, students have collaborated to colead hour-long workshops for the rest of the staff. Critical to these moments is that the students have chosen topics and questions that have emerged organically from their own work and interests and that they have prepared a facilitation that invites a critical dialogue with their peers and their director, who can always weigh in and bring further expertise to bear such that the conversation remains focused in a critical direction. In a conservative model, the director always sets the agenda and facilitates. In a liberal model, there is no agenda—the director stays quiet and discussion is a free-for-all in absence of critical guidance that could otherwise lead in the direction of problem-posing and radical agency. In a radical model, the director and students cocreate the agenda, and the director guides and intervenes when necessary according to their critical knowledge.

Beyond staff meetings, students can participate in shared program leadership by communicating in a range of other forums. In my program, in addition to the meetings I attend, I have paid the students to hold regular staff meetings *without* me. Several students are the designated facilitators, and they use the meetings as they see fit—to discuss their mentoring experiences with one another, to discuss challenges and concerns about the program, and to collaborate on program projects. This space, just like the peer-with-peer writing or speaking sessions, allows for a kind of conversation unencumbered by the dynamics of a professor-student or director-mentor relationship. The facilitators then selectively update me with information and questions the staff thinks I should know about. Other opportunities for creating dialogue between the staff and the director might include staff surveys, individual conferences between the director and peer mentors, session-reflection reports, communication notebooks, wikis, and social gatherings. Of importance, if the director is not learning from and responsive to the staff's ideas in tangible, observable ways, the staff will quickly see they are not true collaborators in the work of the program and their commitment will wane.

When they are committed, in contrast, they can be supported in imagining and implementing new activities on behalf of the program that strengthens its collective work. In Catherine Savini's writing center at Westfield State University, for example, students in the tutor-education course are invited to create social justice projects, which they are then supported in developing and sustaining in future semesters through the writing center. Such recent projects included creating support systems for LGBTQ students and designing a visual display about different pronouns for the writing center; researching racial migroaggressions on campus and creating a visual display in the writing center and an interactive online resource to raise awareness; and creating materials to educate visitors to the writing center about language use that can help destigmatize mental illness and express support. In my own center this year, students proposed and facilitated discussion groups for students to reflect on their experiences with communication and conflict on campus; others have proposed and launched a workshop series for masculine-identified students to deconstruct internalized gender dominance; and yet others are working to develop a discussion series for women of color about having a voice at the college.

While these kinds of projects may be embraced at some institutions, they would likely be controversial and downright unimaginable at others. Indeed, despite the progressive leanings of my current institution and the often (though not always) supportive environment for such initiatives on campus, our institutions do not exist in a vacuum untouched by the outside world. Indeed, in the wake of inaccurate and reckless media reporting about my campus's student-initiated dialogues about the US flag, my own institution this year came under assault by a nationwide mob of bigots who swarmed the campus by the hundreds in caravans of trucks with Confederate flags, bombarded us with vile hate mail and phone calls by the thousands, terrorized students by shouting racial slurs and calling for their imprisonment, and made terrifying death threats. Even the (forty-fifth) president of the United States joined in the mob by tweeting a threat to revoke the citizenship of anyone who burns the flag. I raise this point to emphasize that there are no completely safe spaces to engage in radical work. The pushback we experience may come from different places and take different forms, but it will always be actively working against us—such is the motivation for radical praxis. We all must negotiate risks and rewards and make decisions that protect our safety while searching for opportunities to resist. A radical philosophy compels us to share leadership with students in analyzing the sociopolitical moment and devising opportunities for intervention.

To share leadership with the staff is not to pretend the director does not have more structural power in the program (as they surely do). To ignore or try to downplay the director's power is a liberal strategy that undermines the ability of students to articulate the specificities of their experiences within the power dynamics of the program and that misses important opportunities for the director to make use of their platform and resources. Rather, shared leadership requires that the director exercise their power in ways that create platforms for students' voices, that demonstrate listening to students, that direct resources to them, and that reveal their value in action. Doing so might mean, for example, when resources are tight, prioritizing morale-building and community-strengthening interests over staff size increases, material production, or services offered; doing so suggests people matter more than objects or efficiencies.

This kind of shared leadership will undoubtedly be threatening at institutions that operate with conservative bureaucracies, in which competition and isolation among faculty and departments or programs breeds suspicion and fear of one another. I once led a program in which the start of each semester was marked with a formal brunch for the student staff during which we discussed the goals and activities of the upcoming semester and students shared inspirational words about their experiences with the program. The students relished these brunches, as they were a key opportunity for relationship building, emotional connection, confidence building, and community support. One student, for example, practically hyperventilated in excitement at her first such gathering as she clutched her staff handbook and told me how eager she was to start her work. Other professional staff who were invited to join us commented that the spirit of community and depth of vision for their work expressed by the students at these gatherings were "breathtaking." Indeed, after one such gathering, a student staff member sought me out to tell me she had learned from watching my leadership style about the type of leader she wanted to be and the type of workplace she wanted to help create in her career after graduation. This demonstrable valuing of students, of saying they were worth the cost of a meal and the extravagance of cloth napkins and flowers in vases (which, at that institution, we had the privilege of affording), was a threat to other administrators who hadn't yet found the courage to put people first. As it was, I was scolded by my superiors for "treating the students too well." Faculty, after all, didn't get a brunch. A radical reading would lead us to see, however, that the flaw was in the system—an institution that did not treat its community as well as it might—rather than in my own use of resources to create a caring environment for my students. Rather than trying to take the brunch (or some other humanizing forum) away from students, a radical critic would ask why faculty couldn't get a brunch too.

Certainly, many programs struggle without a budget or with very limited resources or the restrictions of institutional policies, so sharing this example is not to suggest that in order to run a radical writing center one must regularly host brunches. Of course not! Rather, the radical project compels us to ask, when we are struggling to make difficult decisions about how to make the best use of our resources, why the choice between people and products is able to masquerade as a choice to begin with. When love is the motivating value, the sustenance of life—not the proliferation of profit-driven services—always takes precedence.

In my current program, for example, which has a much smaller budget, I have prioritized people over service transactions in different ways. In a recent semester, for example, due to a significant amount of internal turmoil across campus (and, I suspect, the stress of the presidential election), my student staff members were emotionally exhausted. With little patience for each other's imperfections, a number of interpersonal conflicts developed that took a toll on the morale of the whole staff. A more conservative approach might have been to tell the students to leave the drama at home, be "professional" at work, and move forward with business as usual. Instead, I prioritized their mental health and the needs of the staff community, cutting back on the activities we had planned for the semester and turning our attention inward on healing and group resilience. We had hard conversations about the power dynamics across students on staff, about the mistakes people had made in trying to make things better, and about the responsibilities and opportunities for different people to engage (or disengage) in different ways. It was difficult work. But through it the staff slowly began to redevelop trust, and most important, by attending to their humanity in the context of critical and immediately practical questions about communication and justice within the group, they were able to deepen their understanding of the work they sought to do with the larger campus community. If I had failed to center the students and instead asked them to continue to host their workshops, run their meetings, and recruit more visitors to the center, I may very well have lost a number of staff members, and those who stayed would have lost a significant opportunity to approach their work with a greater understanding of the relationship between radical theory and practice.

Finally, as programs that study the relationships between language and politics, we can be critical and purposeful about the ways we use everyday language to describe and therefore create or limit the conditions for shared leadership. What happens when students are invited to say they work *with* the writing or speaking center, for example, rather than *for* it? What would happen if the *it* with which we work became *us*? What would happen if we were conscious of the dehumanizing effects of capitalism and did away with the language of *work* altogether?

"You Move Me"

Demaris and Landsman (2016a) propose that in a culture of radical engagement, people strengthen bonds, cultivate collective resonance, and build trust and reciprocity. How might these activities be fostered in a writing center?

Trust and Reciprocity with Colleagues

Directors can seek out opportunities to forge relationships with students, staff, faculty, and administrators that resist the competitive dynamics our institutional systems might otherwise pressure us to assume. Research has consistently shown, for example, that compared to men, women receive considerably less mentorship in their careers, which has a negative impact on their ability to take on important projects, assume leadership positions, and receive promotions. When examined in a critical context, however, we can see the ways our broader gendered systems influence this phenomenon regarding mentoring. In particular, because of the striking lack of leadership positions available to women in numerous fields, the competition among women for the few token spots is often significant. Women hesitate to mentor other women for fear that doing so may jeopardize their own careers. If another woman is getting ahead, the assumption goes, their own opportunities are threatened.

On the other hand, when women do recognize their success is all bound up with each other's and do make the choice to mentor other women, different consequences emerge. Due to sexist assumptions, women who spend a good deal of time together in the workplace can be written off as gossiping, presumably about gendered issues like shopping or romantic relationships, or they are viewed suspiciously as conniving or scheming. Certainly, women can express their agency by thumbing their noses at these assumptions and supporting other women. But people with greater structural power, in this case men, can also mentor women and can use their influence to improve hiring practices so there is not simply a single token position for which women must compete, to advocate for greater resources and opportunities for women, and to change workplace climates that breed prejudice and hostility.

What can writing center directors do to strengthen bonds and reciprocity on campus? Perhaps we can more intentionally reach across disciplinary boundaries and mentor other faculty or staff who are in need of greater support, not simply in their writing but in navigating their relationships and campus communications. In what ways can we be champions of or advocates for others who have less support, less institutional power, less cultural capital than we do? Perhaps we might make the decision that the writing center will stand with those on campus demanding positive changes by adding our center's name to petitions, by showing up at critical meetings or events, by sharing resources, and by reaching out to various folks and asking how we can support them. What if we personally are in dire need of this support? How can writing centers support other writing centers? Recent online petitions that have gathered hundreds of signatures in protest of schools threatening to shut down their writing centers is one hopeful example. Perhaps the field might think about how our professional organizations can more proactively communicate with institutions where directors are vulnerable or grow the budding professional mentoring resources piloted in recent years. How can we reach across disciplinary lines to find this support? How can we give to others what we aren't getting ourselves?

Collective Resonance in Campus Partnerships

Many writing centers describe themselves as "interdisciplinary," referring to their openness to working with students on projects in a variety of disciplines and on topics across the curriculum. Given the climates of many campuses, however, many directors would never dream of purposefully sharing writing center leadership itself across the disciplines. Focusing on others' general ignorance of writing center theory and pedagogy, we frequently insist, it would be foolish and reckless to share power across departments and programs who misunderstand what we do and who might impose their own agendas! Rather than handing over our power to those we don't trust (a liberal assumption), how might we instead search for opportunities of shared agency in resisting the territorial structuring of the institution itself? How might we learn across disciplines? How might we trust what our fellow teachers tell us about their experiences? How might we build a culture of radical engagement, share leadership, and decentralize agency with them?

Cultures of radical engagement build resonance through storytelling, so our centers have the potential to facilitate this relationship building. How might we create more spaces for stories? One possibility is to host community conversations. Those might be in the form of a writing center advisory committee comprised of invited instructors and students from a range of departments, a day of open dialogue hosted by the center, a visit by the director to a departmental faculty meeting, or a small-group gathering with faculty who have expressed interest or even complaints. The idea would be to gather a group of people assumed to be outside the writing center discipline with those from inside it (which we know to be a false binary) in order to find resonance. People might be asked to share their stories about challenges with writing (or reading or speaking or listening or teaching or anything else), as well as their experience of support (who helped them through the challenge?) and the values that emerged (what principles were learned or affirmed through the experience?). The role of the listeners is to offer resonance. When Demaris and Landsman (2016a, 2016b) facilitate these kinds of storytelling gatherings, they often invite someone experienced in the process to tell a story (modeling vulnerability) to the entire group and then guide the group in sharing moments of resonance from the story with the storyteller. Then, participants break into small groups of five to seven people and take turns telling their own stories and resonating. A seemingly simple process, the results can be deeply profound.

Rather than thinking of these gatherings as problem-solving or strategizing meetings (e.g., "Let us convince you to send your students to the writing center!" or "Teach us about writing in the physics department so we can better serve your students!"), these gatherings can be culture-building moments in which we come together as human beings, resonate our points of empathy, make connections, identify our shared supports (from individuals to campus resources), collaborate on sharing a vision of outcomes, name shared values, and create next steps together. With that radical foundation, we can be better positioned to share leadership in creating a vision and practices for our institutional work together.

Students Trusting Students

Beyond the trust and shared leadership between a director and their colleagues or student staff, here I explore opportunities for building trust among student peers. To do so, I explore the ways radical praxis—critical reflection and action intended to name and resist systems of oppression—can be operationalized. Interestingly, the word *praxis* is everywhere in the field when it comes to directors and tutors reflecting on their scholarship and tutoring practices—we even have a journal named for it—but the idea is not consistently evoked as an integral component of tutoring and writing pedagogy itself. In other words, while scholars and tutors recognize the value of reflecting on their own practice, tutors are not always prepared to offer this opportunity to the students with whom they work. Students are not always asked to discuss the social and political implications of participating in certain types of classroom work, accepting certain kinds of lessons by teachers, conforming to the requirements of certain paper assignments, and making certain choices in their writing. Rather, in liberal writing centers, tutors are generally taught to assume the infallibility of the paper assignment (or to withhold their political critiques as a matter of etiquette) and to help writers—even if they acknowledge that the assignment is perhaps challenging or undesirable—to perform most effectively in the way the professor wants. Tutors are not always supported in helping students interrogate the underlying assumptions and cultural values of the assignments they bring to the center and imagine ways they can act with agency to reconfigure their writing choices to better reflect their values, to use their writing as a tool of resistance, to negotiate with the professor, to explore alternatives to the assignments, or to participate in a liberatory process in other forums. Radical praxis, ultimately, is not always imagined as a possibility for students in the writing center.

While the needs and ideas of the student are certainly often centered in the dominant paradigm, the student's agency with respect to oppressive systems is not. Instead, the agency of the professor and the institution remain central. Dominant liberal practices result in an ambivalence towards students as agents of change more so than we might desire in theory. Rather than trusting student agency and seeing students as collaborators in a liberatory process, tutors are often left to take on an almost missionary approach in order to forge the struggle (of liberation or assimilation) for students, as a gift. This may sound counterintuitive given the way writing center tutors characterize their work—not wanting to impose their ideas on students; nevertheless, the work done for the students happens not at the level of the "superficial" content of individual writing assignments but at the level of determining on the students' behalf the educational values and imperatives the students should adopt.

In other words, while students may be trusted to create their own thesis in response to a novel by Toni Morrison, to choose their own list of authoritative scholars to cite in support of that thesis, and to pick whichever vocabulary words they prefer in constructing their standardized English sentences, students are not always trusted to decide whether they even want to create a thesis itself (if their views cannot be expressed with integrity through that convention), whether they even want to cite scholars explicitly (to reinforce a particular Western culture of individualism and capitalism that imposes an understanding of intellectual property counter to that of the student), or whether they even want to write in standardized English (if another language variety would best convey their ideas). Even more, students are not always trusted to determine whether they want to write the assignment at all—whether there are ideas and values implicit in the assignment the student would rather not perpetuate. Students are not always trusted to question the teacher, to imagine alternatives, or to propose new projects of their own design. Students are not always trusted to determine what is in their own best interests—for a particular assignment or their educational strategies at large. Rather, tutors—as stewards of the writing center and of the institution under the dominant paradigm—implicitly often make this decision for them. This lack of trust is evidenced perhaps most obviously in the way many writing center tutors are given a hierarchy of concerns they are expected to address (HOCs versus LOCs), regardless of the concerns the writer brings to the table; in centers where students submit their papers to be read and reviewed in advance by a tutor, prior to any conversation; or in centers where tutors have resigned themselves to advocating for standardized English usage, believing it is ultimately in students' best interests. Radical writing center praxis requires that we abandon the assumptions that lead us to believe the decision about students' language use or anything else is ours to make.

One such assumption, as is critiqued in earlier chapters, is that tutoring practice can be reduced to a simple binary of directive (assumed to be bad) and nondirective (assumed to be good). Indeed, the field's subscription to this false binary serves to perpetuate conservative and liberal methodologies and inhibit any possibility of radical praxis. To be sure, what the field describes as *directive tutoring* is indicative of all the shortcomings of conservative education. Talked about synonymously with "banking" education, this methodology positions the tutor as an authoritarian who imposes the agenda and the ideas on the student. This tutor-centered, text-centered methodology, the field assumes, separates students from their own decision making. The tutor isn't listening. The student isn't really learning. The liberal alternative to this, the field celebrates uncritically, is *nondirective tutoring*. Here, the student is centered, the student determines the direction of the session, and the student makes all the decisions. Necessarily, the tutor is meant to be as hands off, removed, and neutral as possible. Grimm and others have critiqued the failings of this liberal approach, which, in the absence of any substantive participation by the tutor, can become a directionless, anything-goes conversation in which little critical work or learning actually takes place, serving to perpetuate a system that in many cases privileges white middle-class students.

> If, on the other hand, writing centers were focused on challenging systems of privilege, then we would acknowledge that the bigger the gap between the real background and the imagined background of a particular student, the more "work" a *tutor* needs to do to understand the perspective the student brings to the writing task and the more work a tutor needs to do in order to clearly articulate the usually tacit values, beliefs, assumptions, methods, genres, and citation practices of the task at hand. (2011, 85)

Whereas scholars such as Steven J. Corbett (2013) have argued for flexibility along a continuum of directive and nondirective tutoring styles, radical writing center praxis requires us to do away with the binary altogether, putting to rest once and for all the language of *directive* and *nondirective*. In its place, we need a new paradigm from which to develop radical methodologies. Such a paradigm might draw on the language of *collaboration, interdependence, negotiation, engagement, dialogue*, and other such terms that communicate shared leadership, decentralized agency, and deep relationship.

Radical education theory already offers possibilities for alternative models. Critical pedagogy is one of them. Critical pedagogy, working from a radical politics, supports teaching and tutoring methods in which educators work with students to develop a critical awareness that oppression is not natural, that oppressive systems can be changed, and that students themselves can be change agents. In the context of a writing center session, tutors work from a critical-pedagogy framework by asking problem-posing questions to denaturalize students' assumptions about writing or their assignments (e.g., But *why* is your teacher requiring that you write in standardized English? Why are we told that standardized English is superior or necessary? Whose agenda is served when we believe this? What is lost when you conform to this standard?). Tutors explore with students ways the ideas they have assumed to be absolute are indeed vulnerable (e.g., sharing examples of writers who use language other than standardized English in "formal" writing, introducing them to code meshing, sharing histories of language systems and the evolution of various Englishes, making connections between language standardization and systems of racism or sexism, and so on.). Finally, tutors support students in identifying opportunities for exercising their agency in the face of what they are examining. In the context of critical consciousness, tutors trust the students to exercise their agency how they see fit—be it an informed decision to perform the standard after weighing the stakes carefully; an informed decision to explore opportunities for code meshing or in some other way rewrite the assignment on their own terms (or even refuse to do it); or an informed decision to resist the system beyond the assignment itself, such as embarking on independent research on language prejudice, writing an op-ed piece for the student newspaper, organizing a campus dialogue, or some other action.

In such a process the tutor is neither the driver nor a passive passenger in the process but an engaged collaborator asking purposeful problem-posing questions, providing critical information the student might not have access to, participating actively in dialogue and reflection, sharing a range of ideas and feedback, listening for resonance, and listening to learn. Notably, this radical process requires that tutors come to understand the role of *questioning* differently than what is advocated through nondirective methodologies.

The centrality of the *question* in writing center pedagogy has radical potential but falls short when it is interpreted through a nondirective, liberal lens. We see this liberal interpretation in Leigh Ryan and Lisa Zimmerelli's advice that tutors use "guiding questions" to help students "recognize their difficulties and come up with their own solutions" (2015, 1); in Jeff Brooks's privileging of "leading" questions (1991, 4); in Nick Carbone's suggestion that tutors "ask questions . . . the way an interested friend will ask questions" (quoted in Gillespie and Lerner 2008, 37); and in the pervasive resolution of the "open" question in writing center lore as the ultimate catalyst for conversation. The list goes on. It's not that these kinds of questions can never be helpful in tutorials. Indeed, Isabelle Thompson and Jo Mackiewicz (2014) have shown in their research that tutors frequently use these kinds of questions—most notably questions that establish common ground and that lead to or provide scaffolds for students in brainstorm and revising—in ways that serve specific and useful functions. The problem comes when tutors use questions in order to avoid the liberal writing center taboo of imposing ideas on students but do not have a sophisticated understanding about how questions can function pedagogically. Often times, as numerous scholars have noted (Kiedaisch and Dinitz 1993; Reigstad 1981), the resulting conversation does not result in an improved analysis. When tutors ask questions absent a purposeful radical framework, the resulting conversation has little hope for a robust critical consciousness—or radical praxis—to develop. Tutors and students might report that their sessions are satisfying, but are they bringing us closer to justice and peace?

In contrast, a radical framework would center problem-posing questions, the sort of doubt-stimulating questions Freire describes, in order to challenge assumptions that may be leading students to accept (often covert) injustices in their assignments and their own ideas as somehow natural or neutral. It would center questions that seek to increase the tutor's understanding of the student's experiences, beliefs, assumptions, and values so as to better support a critical examination of the assignment and the ideas. It would center questions that elicit the student's reasoning, intentions, and goals so the mentor can be engaged in the student's process of development, avoiding appropriation of the student's ideas and texts but also providing a foundation from which the tutor can negotiate and advocate for possibilities. Understanding the student's values and intentions can also be instructive when a tutor is deciding whether or not to make the difficult (but sometimes necessary) decision to disengage and not support a project or process the tutor understands to be violent or oppressive. These kinds of questions support tutors in being able to trust *themselves.*

Finally, a resonant relationship between the tutor and student in a session could be informed by Demaris and Landsman's (2016a, 2016b) storytelling process itself. What would happen if sessions included solicitation of students' stories—stories of challenge (e.g., ideological conflict between the assignment and their voice), support (e.g., places and communities where their voices have been valued), and values (e.g., virtues they hold dear in response)? Tutors could listen for moments of resonance to strengthen bonds with the student and then use those values as a starting point to engage in a radical dialogue.

"You Change Me"

Demaris and Landsman (2016a) propose that in a culture of radical engagement, people build bridges and ensure full inclusion, representation, and accessibility across diversity. How might these activities be fostered in a writing center?

Radical Listening and Change

The previous section explored the ways tutors can radically trust students to make their own critically conscious decisions and to engage in the kind of dialogue that supports such consciousness-raising. Important to a radical process, however, is that students are not the only ones changed by the process. Instead, tutors can see their goal—indeed their fundamental purpose—as to be changed by the student during the same process. Tutors are familiar with the idea of being changed by liberal tutoring—learning more about different subjects, different points of view, and different strategies for writing that in turn strengthen their own writing processes. Radical change, however, goes a step further. When tutors listen radically, they emerge from sessions as different people, with their understanding of the world fundamentally altered and their commitments reoriented towards greater ethical alignment. They emerge with greater resonance across difference, more critically aware of the interconnectness of systems (both of life and of injustice), and more courageous in exercising their own agency in order to bring greater peace and justice and love into the world.

Accordingly, radical tutors do not paternalistically seek to empower students by sharing what the tutors believe to be their ethically superior reading of the world. Tutors are not bearers of truth, no matter how enlightened they (or we) think they are. Their own ethics must be critically, relationally engaged. They must be committed to seeing where their own values, assumptions, and practices are in contradiction and open to new action in response.

Radical Representation

Radical praxis is not exclusionary. Cultures of radical engagement seek opportunities to expand representation. In writing centers, we can explore ways representation must be expanded and, as radical listeners and partners, be changed through that expansion. Who is represented in the readings assigned in our tutor-education offerings? Who authored the tutoring guides, the writing center articles, the essays on education theories we use to introduce students to the field? Who is represented in the library of resources our centers offer to students? Who authored the writing guides, the chapbooks, the handouts we hold up as authoritative tools for writing processes? What experiences, views, languages, and possibilities are represented as central, given such authorship? What links appear on our center's Facebook pages, implicitly communicating a message about a dominant identity, a dominant story? Part of this revision process means questioning the centrality of the scholars we have for so long taken for granted and looking a little more carefully into the expanding archives of writing center collections to find voices and views that disrupt the dominant paradigm. Much of this work is already there, simply waiting (demanding) to be heard. We may also need to cross disciplinary boundaries (and here our resonance across our institutions will prove particularly useful) to gather stories that haven't yet been told in our field.

Beyond the texts, who comprises our staff? In what ways do the demographics of our tutors serve to reinforce the dominance of a particular kind of voice and view? It is not merely enough to seek to mirror the demographics of our campus, being satisfied, for example, that 5 percent of the staff are students of color if the broader college population is roughly the same. In most instances, it is a gross injustice that a predominantly white college population is so racially exclusive to begin with, so why would we try to replicate that? In what ways might we go beyond token representation to create a truly heterogeneous ecosystem in our centers? How might the writing center be changed when there is greater heterogeneity of identities, views, experiences, and positionings within power structures working together?

Radical Accessibility

Whereas liberalism seeks opportunities to accommodate difference within a normative space or practice, radicalism seeks to fundamentally alter the spaces and practices themselves such that access is universal across differences. Accordingly, radical writing centers ask, Who has access to our space and who doesn't? How is the physical location inaccessible? (e.g., Are there stairs leading up to the door? Is it in a basement with no elevator?) How is the space configuration a barrier? (e.g., Are there partitions set closely together such that a wheelchair might not pass? Are the chairs so small a fat-bodied person cannot sit comfortably within its arms? Are there restrooms and water nearby?) How is the quality of the space a barrier? (e.g., Are there flickering fluorescent lighting that might trigger seizures or migraines? Is there no escape from the distracting sound of chatter in the open-floor concept? Does the lack of ventilation make the smells from a new carpet or the perfume of a visitor potent for someone with allergies?) How is the process of accessing the space a barrier? (e.g., Are students required to register through an online schedule system with their legal names, leaving some trans students in the painful position of having to out themselves in order to access a tutorial? Do tutors with mental illnesses have a clear means of communicating and being supported if they need to cancel their shift at the last minute without being penalized?) How do resources present barriers to learning? (e.g., Is there room for students who learn spatially to spread their papers out across the floor? Are there markers, and scissors, and Post-its, and clay, and transcription machines, and headphones available?) What kinds of health-restricting protocols and rules limit engagement? (e.g., Do you prohibit eating in the space? Do you make rules that tutors can't step out in the middle of a session?) What kinds of cultural norms are perpetuated that make the center less safe for some students? (e.g., Do you have stated expectations about sexual harassment? Have tutors discussed plans for how to intervene in overt and covert instances of racial discrimination? Are there processes and protocols in place for filing a grievance? Do you have a history of being responsive in turn?)

As we explore these questions and continue to change our work in order to expand our accessibility, we can turn again to the storytelling process of radical engagement. How might we create space for people to share their stories of inclusion and exclusion, their stories of accessibility and support? How might writing centers listen radically, resonate, and change with these stories?

Building Bridges beyond the Center
When we remember that radical writing center work exceeds space, exceeds all boundaries really, we can look for opportunities to build bridges in order to share resonance with others who desire greater ethical transformation as well. Within our institutions, we can initiate and nurture relationships with entities engaged in radical work. Of importance, we can go beyond the helpful but nevertheless myopic activities of diversity trainings and multicultural workshops to align with efforts to revolutionize our schools altogether. How might we partner with people advocating for deep structural changes, such as free tuition for Black students or Native students at predominantly white institutions as a step towards reparations for slavery, genocide, colonization, and disenfranchisement; or changing teaching loads and providing compensation to account for the de facto mentoring work faculty of color often provide to students of color in predominantly white institutions; or radically altering the curriculum such that every college course (not simply a single multicultural course requirement) is required to meet a certain standard of representation in materials and explicit sociopolitical engagement; or radically altering hiring practices such that competent teaching across differences is a condition of employment and promotion; and so on? Perhaps representatives from the writing center might join in such discussions, send representatives to serve on committees, add their names to petitions, or participate in campus discussions or demonstrations. How else might we build bridges?

Beyond our institutions, how might writing centers build bridges with people from broader social and political movements? What ethical causes are in need of critical support? The movement for Black lives, reproductive justice, civil rights and freedom from violence for trans people, environmental justice, immigration justice, and economic justice are but a few of the many contemporary causes calling for our attention at the time I am writing this text. We might explore opportunities and resources for our students to speak out as activists, writing letters, modeling productive civic discourse, traveling to marches or protests, or speaking with the media. The writing center at the University of Oklahoma, for example, recently hosted a workshop on effective public-advocacy writing, including letters to public officials, which was cosponsored by their Gender + Equality Center and the Women and Gender Studies Center for Social Justice. A group of students in my mentor education course last year proposed replacing a study group meeting with a trip to a local city council meeting where they spoke during the public commentary section to oppose a funding proposal that appeared to benefit the police department to the detriment of actual public safety. I attended and spoke at the meeting as well, in the hopes of inspiring courage and demonstrating public speech in action. Further, we might lend our resources to various movements, offering competitive compensation for community leaders to speak to our students, doing research into stories already available, and initiating dialogues to learn more about what is needed in such movements so we as individuals and our centers as collective support systems might participate meaningfully. My current program, for example, has for multiple semesters sponsored talks and workshops led by a representative from an indigenous and immigrant women's movement from East Harlem, New York, called Movement for Justice in El Barrio that has been mobilizing in powerful ways for tenant rights and other social justice issues of pressing importance to that community.

Writing the Body and the Earth

Explicit in Demaris and Landsman's (2016a) work is the necessity not only of nurturing deep relationships between and among people but in returning to an awareness of the profound and inextricable connectedness between our vitality and the ecosystem itself. Building bridges for collective resonance in writing centers, I argue, can mean a reorientation that encompasses the body holistically as part of the learning process, the writing process, the relationship-building process, the liberatory process. Through attention to the body, we necessarily bring our attention to the earth.

At the level of the individual, radical writing center praxis might involve opportunities to move away from our processes as purely rooted in the mind ("mind over matter") and instead devote attention to the self as a fully embodied being. How are we nourishing our bodies? Do writing center staff meetings consist of pizza, chips, cookies, and soda, or might we support ourselves with more healthful fruits and vegetables and other whole foods?

In what ways are we, or our student staff, or our student visitors carrying trauma and stress in our bodies? What would happen if mentoring sessions began with deep breathing or stretching exercises, if staff meetings began with guided mindfulness meditation, or if the writing center provided workshops that taught strategies for holding and touching the body in ways that settle a triggered nervous system? Are our bodies getting enough rest? What if the writing center shut down operations for an hour every afternoon and turned into a nap space for students? How might we nurture an environment in which students feel safe to hold hands and to hug?

In what ways are our sessions and gatherings rooted in static positioning, restricting blood flow, stiffening muscles, deteriorating our cardiovascular systems? What if the writing center were to offer walking sessions around campus in which the tutor and student stroll or wheel across the green as they talk rather than remain confined to the indoor space of the center (or even down building hallways in city campuses)? What if the director offered such an alternative to office hours? What if sessions involved more regular kinesthetic learning, exploring opportunities for purposeful movement, rather than privileging conversation as the dominant learning style? What if staff meetings involved movement games, included warm-ups and backrub trains, or dance? Beth Godbee, Moira Ozias, and Jasmine Kar King's "Body + Power + Justice: Movement-Based Workshops for Critical Education" (2015), for example, offers a creative and compelling analysis of their attempts to approach racial justice work as a purposefully embodied practice.

In addition to caring for our bodies, radical writing center praxis compels us to build bridges with the ecosystem itself. Recently, for example, I hosted a beginning-of-the-year retreat for my student staff. Together we drove to a local park where we spent the day in various forms of activities and conversations, moving about and connecting with the environment in a range of ways. In the morning, we sat in small groups on blankets in the grass, still damp with the morning dew, telling stories about the experiences that led us to our work in the speaking program. We paused and laughed together as several students were chased away from their spot by a gaggle of assertive geese. Later we dispersed among the trees in new groups to tell new stories, sitting on benches and leaning against trunks with a vast canopy of leaves providing patches of shade from above.

Later we made our way to a long wooden picnic table in a different area of the park, our feet pressing upon the ground of dirt and stone softened with a blanket of dried red pine needles that had fallen many months earlier. Together we talked, and laughed, and sat in quiet contemplation as we shared a lunch, the bubbles of a nearby river at our backs, the wind in the trees above providing a backdrop of ambient sound.

After lunch we walked together around the large curve of the pond, crossing the wooden bridge and observing the rushing of the water over a small fall at its edge, and then made our way up a hill to a lovely wooden pavilion perched at the edge of a small cliff overlooking an expansive field at the heart of the park. There we sat in a circle, closed our eyes, and conjured up visions of our center, of our community, of our world in the years to come.

Later, we dispersed, some of us on our own, some in pairs, others in groups, to explore the park and simply spend time together—no prompts, no agendas, other than simply to be. As the day drew to a close, we gathered at the river. Taking off our shoes, rolling pants up to our knees, and helping one another down the steep slope to the river's edge, we entered the river itself. Some stayed close to the shore while others ventured further out, using a scattering of large stones as a makeshift path. Others stepped deep into the water, letting their toes sink into the soft cold wet mud of the river's bed. Together, we searched for stones to bring home with us to the speaking center as a reminder of the day but also as gifts for the community not there with us, a symbol of our deep interconnectedness.

When understanding our work with writing centers as indivisible from systems of oppression, our ethical engagement requires us to work not simply for justice and peace for humans but also for the right to livable lives for all beings on the planet, and indeed for the life of the planet itself. As Demaris and Landsman remind us, the survival of our very ecosystem is dependent upon this story of connection. The systems destroying our relationships are the same systems destroying the planet by exploiting our natural resources, polluting the environment, and perpetuating a myth that human beings can conquer the environment without consequence. In what ways might our writing centers instead advocate for the earth, for life? How do we collectively tell this story?

CONCLUSION

Through the frame of cultures of radical engagement, radical writing center praxis compels us to ask whose stories of writing (and speaking and listening and learning and life) are circulated as normal and how we might complicate and expand those stories in order to create greater resonance across differences and transform ourselves and the world in the process. Those of us who love writing centers fiercely, as I do, may be tempted to keep these stories to ourselves, to hunker down and protect this beautiful and special thing we are creating, not to be touched by the scary unknown world beyond. Demaris and Landsman (2016a) call this "hoarding resonance," a tempting yet destructive decision that ultimately separates us from our world, its vitality, and our potential for radical transformation. The radical work I am calling on the field to do, then, requires courage because ultimately we must relinquish control over the outcomes by trusting the inherent ethical value of the process.

As I think about what draws me to writing center work, and what drives me to imagine and create this work through a radical framework, it is this strong desire to connect, to feel and express and receive empathy, to participate in a world constituted by love. Butler (2004) reminds us that radicalism requires a comfort in unknowingness, a willingness to engage in a process the outcomes of which no one can surely know in advance. We might not know what the world will look like, but in many ways, that ending is not the point. Radical writing center praxis is not a utopian future but an immediate, love-inspired, reflective action we commit to again and again and again. Martin Luther King Jr.'s words "the arc of the moral universe is long, but it bends towards justice" are often quoted. Despite King's radical politics, this quote is decidedly liberal in its assumption of a natural order to the universe. Recently, when the Massachusetts House of Representatives was debating a bill to affirm civil rights in public accommodations to transgender people, Representative Byron Rushing added this important radical addendum to the quote about bending that moral arc: It only bends "because courageous people grab it and bend it down" (*Boston Globe*, June 1, 2016). May we all continue to have such courage.

NOTE

1.   Readers interested in learning more might read Fairfield 2018, Ganz 2011, and Wheeler 2011 or visit the *Healing Justice* podcast (March 20, 2018; March 22, 2018; June 19, 2018) for interviews with Mark Fairfield, Lucien Demaris, and Cedar Landsman.

REFERENCES

Adichie, Chimamanda Ngozi. 2013. "We Should All Be Feminists." YouTube video, 1:31. Posted by *TEDx*, April 12. https://www.youtube.com/watch?v=hg3umXU_qWc.

American Psychological Association. 2016. "Abuse of Women with Disabilities." http://www.apa.org/topics/violence/women-disabilities.aspx.

Alexander, Michelle. 2012. *The New Jim Crow: Mass Incarceration in the Age of Colorblindness*. New York: New Press.

Amnesty International. 2007. *Maze of Injustice: The Failure to Protect Indigenous Women from Sexual Violence in the USA*. https://www.amnestyusa.org/pdfs/mazeofinjustice.pdf.

Amurao, Carla. 2016. "Fact Sheet: How Bad is the School-to-Prison Pipeline?" *Beat the Streets, Inc.* July 15. https://www.beatthestreetsca.org/single-post/2016/07/15/Fact-Sheet-How-Bad-Is-the-SchooltoPrison-Pipeline.

Anderson, Benedict. 1991. *Imagined Communities: Reflections on the Origins and Spread of Nationalism*. London: Verso.

"Audio of Fanny Lou Hamer's Testimony." 2010. YouTube video, 8:12. Posted by Pamela Cook, June 10. https://www.youtube.com/watch?v=ML3WaEsCB98.

Babcock, Rebecca Day. 2015. "Disabilities in the Writing Center." *Praxis: A Writing Center Journal* 13 (1): 39–50.

Bakhtin, M. M. 1981. *The Dialogic Imagination: Four Essays by M. M. Bakhtin*. Edited by Michael Holquist. Translated by Caryl Emerson and Michael Holquist. Austin: University of Texas Press.

Barron, Nancy, and Nancy Grimm. 2002. "Addressing Racial Diversity in a Writing Center: Stories and Lessons from Two Beginners." *Writing Center Journal* 22 (2): 55–83.

Bawarshi, Anis, and Stephanie Pelkowski. 1999. "Postcolonialism and the Idea of a Writing Center." *Writing Center Journal* 19 (2): 41–58.

Benjamin, Medea. 2016. "President Obama Can Help Save Saudi Youth Facing Beheading." *CODEPINK*. http://www.codepink.org/president_obama_can_help_save_saudi_youth_facing_beheading.

Berenholz, Maya. 2016. *They Didn't Know We Were Seeds: Growing Heart-Centered Movements from the Ground Up*. Senior thesis, Hampshire College.

"Bernie Sanders Rally—Black Lives Matter Interruption." 2015. YouTube video, 4:21. Posted by Soaring Moments, August 8. https://www.youtube.com/watch?v=BWOuCfdJYMM.

Berrey, Ellen. 2015. "Diversity Is for White People: A Big Lie behind a Well-Intentioned Word." *Salon*. http://www.salon.com/2015/10/26/diversity_is_for_white_people_the_big_lie_behind_a_well_intended_word.

Bizzell, Patricia. 1988. "Arguing about Literacy." In *Academic Discourse*, 238–55. Pittsburgh, PA: University of Pittsburgh Press.

Bizzell, Patricia. 1990. "Beyond Anti-foundationalism to Rhetorical Authority: Problems Defining 'Cultural Literacy.'" In *Academic Discourse*, 256–76. Pittsburgh, PA: University of Pittsburgh Press.

Bizzell, Patricia. 1992. *Academic Discourse and Critical Consciousness*. Pittsburgh Series in Composition, Literacy, and Culture. Pittsburgh, PA: University of Pittsburgh Press.

"Black Lives Matter Protesters at Netroots Nation Town Hall Meeting." YouTube video, 20:50. Posted by James Roguski, July 18. https://www.youtube.com/watch?v=tMg2oT5Fgdo.

Blau, Susan, and John Hall. 2002. "Guilt-Free Tutoring: Rethinking How We Tutor Non-Native-English-Speaking Students." *Writing Center Journal* 23 (1): 23–44.

DOI: 10.7330/9781607328445.c006

Bonilla-Silva, Eduardo. 2014. *Racism without Racists: Color-Blind Racism and the Persistence of Racial Inequality in America.* 4th ed. Lanham, MD: Rowman & Littlefield.

Boquet, Elizabeth. 1999. "'Our Little Secret': A History of Writing Centers, Pre- to Post-Open Admissions." *College Composition and Communication* 50 (3): 463–82.

Boquet, Elizabeth. 2014. "It's All Coming Together, Right Before My Eyes: On Poetry, Peace and Creative Placemaking in Writing Centers." *Writing Center Journal* 34 (2): 17–31.

Bray, Mark. 2017. *Antifa: The Anti-Fascist Handbook.* Brooklyn, NY: Melville House.

Brooks, Jeff. 1991. "Minimalist Tutoring: Making the Student Do All the Work." *Writing Lab Newsletter* 15 (6): 1–4.

brown, adrienne marie. 2017. *Emergent Strategy: Shaping Change, Changing Worlds.* Chico, CA: AK Press.

Bruffee, Kenneth. 1984. "Collaborative Learning and the 'Conversation of Mankind.'" *College English* 46 (7): 635–52.

Butler, Judith. 2004. *Undoing Gender.* New York: Routledge.

Cain, Susan. 2012. *Quiet: The Power of Introverts in a World That Can't Stop Talking.* New York: Broadway Books.

Canagarajah, Suresh. 2013. *Literacy as Translingual Practice: Between Communities and Classrooms.* New York: Routledge.

Carino, Peter. 1996. "Open Admissions and the Construction of Writing Center History: A Tale of Three Models." *Writing Center Journal* 17 (1): 30–48.

Carter, Shannon. 2009. "The Writing Center Paradox: Talk about Legitimacy and the Problem of Institutional Change." *College Composition and Communication* 61 (1): 133–152.

Center for Disease Control. 2015. "Fact Sheet: National Violent Death Reporting System." http://www.cdc.gov/violenceprevention/pdf/nvdrs_factsheet-a.pdf.

Center for Reproductive Rights. 2016a. "Romani Women Subject to Forced Sterilization in Slovakia." http://www.reproductiverights.org/press-room/romani-women-subject -to-forced-sterilization-in-slovakia.

Center for Reproductive Rights. 2016b. "Forced Sterilization in Chile." http://www.repro ductiverights.org/feature/forced-sterilization-in-chile.

Clark, Irene L., and Dave Healy. 1996. "Are Writing Centers Ethical?" *WPA: Writing Program Administration* 20 (1/2): 32–48.

Coates, Ta-Nehisi. 2015. *Between the World and Me.* New York: Spiegel and Grau.

Cogie, Jane. 2001. "Peer Tutoring: Keeping the Contradiction Productive." In *The Politics of Writing Centers,* edited by Jane Nelson and Kathy Evertz, 37–49. Portsmouth, NH: Boynton Cook/Heinemann.

Condon, Frankie. 2007. "Beyond the Known: Writing Centers and the Work of Anti-Racism." *Writing Center Journal* 27 (2): 19–38.

Corbett, Steven J. 2013. "Negotiating Pedagogical Authority: The Rhetoric of Writing Center Tutoring Styles and Methods." *Rhetoric Review* 32 (1): 81–98.

Costa, Antonio Maria. 2009. "Global Report on Trafficking in Persons: Executive Summary." *United Nations Office on Drugs and Crime.* http://www.unodc.org/documents/human -trafficking/Executive_summary_english.pdf.

Crenshaw, Kimberlé. 1991. "Mapping the Margins: Intersectionality, Identity Politics, and Violence against Women of Color." *Stanford Law Review* 43 (6): 1241–99.

Crowley, Sharon, and Debra Hawhee. 2004. *Ancient Rhetorics for Contemporary Students.* 3rd ed. New York: Pearson Longman.

Crowley, Sharon, and Debra Hawhee. 2004. *Ancient Rhetorics for Contemporary Students.* 3rd ed. New York: Pearson Longman.

Demaris, Lucien, and Cedar Landsman. 2016a. "The Culture of Radical Engagement Residency." Hampshire College. February 21–26.

Demaris, Lucien, and Cedar Landsman. 2016b. "Transformative Change Making and Relational Leadership Training." Hampshire College. November 11.

Denny, Harry. 2005. "Queering the Writing Center." *Writing Center Journal* 25 (2): 39–62.

Denny, Harry. 2010. *Facing the Center: Toward an Identity Politics of One-to-One Mentoring.* Logan: Utah State University Press.

Diab, Rasha. 2008. "Rhetorics of Peace and Manifestations of a Peaceable Pedagogy in the Writing Center." Plenary speech at the *International Writing Centers Association* and the *National Conference on Peer Tutoring in Writing*, Las Vegas, NV, November 1.

DiNuzzo, Brian. 2014. "On Tutoring a Visually Impaired Student." *Dangling Modifier* 22 (1). http://sites.psu.edu/thedanglingmodifier/?page_id=2258.

DiPardo, Anne. 1992. "'Whispers of Coming and Going': Lessons from Fannie." *Writing Center Journal* 12 (2): 125–44.

Durling, Megan, Mika Kie Wiessbuch, and Judith Frank. 2009. "Where Do We Stand? Responding to Ideological Conflict and Ethical Dilemmas in the Writing Center." Workshop facilitated at the *National Conference on Peer Tutoring in Writing*, South Hadley, MA, November 7.

Eagly, Alice, and Linda Carli. 2007. *Through the Labyrinth: The Truth about How Women Become Leaders.* Cambridge, MA: Harvard Business School Press.

"Editor of Gay-Themed Magazine Hacked to Death." 2016. LGBTQ Nation. http://www.lgbtqnation.com/2016/04/editor-of-gay-themed-magazine-hacked-to-death/.

Elbow, Peter. 2002. "Vernacular Englishes in the Writing Classroom? Probing the Culture of Literacy." In *Alt Dis: Alternative Discourses and the Academy*, edited by Patricia Bizzell, Chris Schroeder, and Helen Fox, 126–138. Portsmouth, NH: Boynton/Cook Heinemann.

"11 Facts about Global Poverty." 2016. https://www.dosomething.org/us/facts/11-facts-about-global-poverty.

Erard, Michael. 2006. "Writing Centers in Professional Contexts." International Writing Centers Association. http://writingcenters.org/writing-centers-in-professional-contexts-by-michael-erard/.

"Factory Farming and the Environment." 2016. Farm Sanctuary. http://www.farmsanctuary.org/learn/factory-farming/factory-farming-and-the-environment/.

Fairfield, Mark. 2018. "The Ground for Inclusion: Diversity and Interdependence." *Gestalt Journal of Australia and New Zealand* 14 (2): 19–44.

Fallon, Brian. 2011. "Why My Best Teachers are Peer Tutors." Keynote address at the *National Conference on Peer Tutoring in Writing*, Miami, FL, November 5.

"Fanny Lou Hamer's Powerful Testimony." 2014. YouTube video, 3:40. Posted by American Experience PBS, June 23. https://www.youtube.com/watch?v=07PwNVCZCcY.

Frazer, Timothy C. 2006. "An Introduction to Midwest English." In *American Voices: How Dialects Differ from Coast to Coast*, edited by Walt Wolfram and Ben Ward, 101–5. Walden: Blackwell.

Freire, Ana Maria Araújo, and Donaldo Macedo, eds. 1998. Introduction to *The Paulo Freire Reader.* New York: Continuum.

Freire, Paulo. 1996. *Letters to Cristina: Reflections on My Life and Work.* Translated by Donaldo Macedo. New York: Routledge.

Freire, Paulo. 1998. *Pedagogy of Freedom: Ethics, Democracy, and Civic Courage.* Lanham, MD: Rowman & Littlefield.

Freire, Paulo. 2003. *Pedagogy of the Oppressed.* Translated by Myra Bergman Ramos. 30th anniversary ed. New York: Continuum.

Freire, Paulo, and Donaldo Macedo. 1987. *Literacy: Reading the Word and the World.* South Hadley, MA: Bergin and Garvey.

Ganz, Marshall. 2011. "Public Narrative, Collective Action, and Power." In *Accountability through Public Opinion: From Inertia to Public Action*, edited by Sina Odugbemi and Taeku Lee, 273–89. Washington, DC: The World Bank.

Gardner, Tyler. 2016. "Through the Ears of Another: Talking Privilege with a Deaf Writer." *Dangling Modifier* 23 (1). https://sites.psu.edu/thedanglingmodifier/?p=3501.

Garza, Alicia. 2014. "A Herstory of the #BlackLivesMatter Movement." *The Feminist Wire.* http://www.thefeministwire.com/2014/10/blacklivesmatter-2/.

Gates, Henry Louis Jr. 2014. "Did Lincoln Really Free the Slaves?" *The Root.* http://www.theroot.com/articles/history/2014/01/did_lincoln_really_free_the_slaves.1.html.

Geller, Anne Ellen. 2009. "The Difficulty of Believing in Writing Across the Curriculum." *Journal of the Assembly of Expanded Perspectives on Learning* 15 (Winter): 27–36.

Geller, Anne Ellen, Frankie Condon, and Meg Carroll. 2011. "Bold: The Everyday Writing Center and the Production of New Knowledge in Antiracist Theory and Practice." In *Writing Centers and the New Racism: A Call for Sustainable Dialogue and Change,* edited by Laura Greenfield and Karen Rowan, 101–23. Logan: Utah State University Press.

Geller, Anne Ellen, Michele Eodice, Frankie Condon, Meg Carroll, and Elizabeth H. Boquet. 2007. *The Everyday Writing Center: A Community of Practice.* Logan: Utah State University Press.

Gillespie, Paula, and Neal Lerner. 2008. *The Longman Guide to Peer Tutoring.* 2nd ed. New York: Pearson Education.

Gilyard, Keith. 1991. *Voices of the Self: A Study of Language Competence.* Detroit, MI: Wayne State University Press.

Gilyard, Keith. 1996. *Let's Flip the Script: An African American Discourse on Language, Literature, and Learning.* Detroit, MI: Wayne State University Press.

Giridharadas, Anand. 2014. *The True American: Murder and Mercy in Texas.* New York: Norton.

Giroux, Henry. 1997. *Pedagogy and the Politics of Hope: Theory, Culture, and Schooling: A Critical Reader.* Boulder, CO: Westview.

Giroux, Henry. 1988. *Teachers as Intellectuals: Toward a Critical Pedagogy of Learning.* Granby, MA: Bergin & Garvey.

Giroux, Henry. 2001. *Theory and Resistance in Education: Towards a Pedagogy for the Opposition.* Westport, CT: Bergin & Garvey.

Godbee, Beth. 2005. "A (Re)cognition of Peerness as Friendship." *Writing Lab Newsletter* 29 (6): 13–15.

Godbee, Beth, and Moira Ozias. 2011. "Organizing for Antiracism in Writing Centers: Principles for Enacting Social Change." In *Writing Centers and the New Racism: A Call for Sustainable Dialogue and Change,* edited by Laura Greenfield and Karen Rowan, 150–74. Logan: Utah State University Press.

Godbee, Beth, Moira Ozias, and Jasmine Kar King. 2015. "Body + Power + Justice: Movement-Based Workshops for Critical Education." *Writing Center Journal* 34 (2): 61–112.

Gore, Jennifer M. 1993. *The Struggle for Pedagogies: Critical and Feminist Discourses as Regimes of Truth.* New York: Routledge.

Graham, David A. 2015. "Violence Has Forced 60 Million People From Their Homes." *Atlantic,* June 17. http://www.theatlantic.com/international/archive/2015/06/refugees-global-peace-index/396122/.

Green, Neisha-Anne S. 2016. "The Re-Education of Neisha-Anne S. Green: A Close Look at the Damaging Effects of a 'Standard Approach,' the Benefits of Code-Meshing, and the Role Allies Play in This Work." *Praxis: A Writing Center Journal* 14 (1): 77–87. http://www.praxisuwc.com/green-141.

Greenfield, Laura. 2011. "The 'Standard English' Fairy Tale: A Rhetorical Analysis of Racist Pedagogies and Commonplace Assumptions about Language Diversity." In *Writing Centers and the New Racism: A Call for Sustainable Dialogue and Change,* edited by Laura Greenfield and Karen Rowan, 33–60. Logan: Utah State University Press.

Greenfield, Laura, and Karen Rowan. 2011a. "Beyond the 'Week Twelve Approach': Toward a Critical Pedagogy for Antiracist Tutor Education." In *Writing Centers and the New Racism: A Call for Sustainable Dialogue and Change,* edited by Laura Greenfield and Karen Rowan, 124–49. Logan: Utah State University Press.

Greenfield, Laura, and Karen Rowan, eds. 2011b. *Writing Centers and the New Racism: A Call for Sustainable Dialogue and Change.* Logan: Utah State University Press.

Grimm, Nancy Maloney. 1999. *Good Intentions: Writing Center Work for Postmodern Times.* Portsmouth, NH: Heinemann.

Grimm, Nancy M. 2011. "Retheorizing Writing Center Work to Transform a System of Advantage Based on Race." In *Writing Centers and the New Racism: A Call for Sustainable Dialogue and Change,* edited by Laura Greenfield and Karen Rowan, 75–100. Logan: Utah State University Press.

"Gun Violence by the Numbers." 2014. Everytown for Gun Safety. https://everytownresearch.org/gun-violence-by-the-numbers/.

Grutsch McKinney, Jackie. 2013. *Peripheral Visions for Writing Centers.* Logan: Utah State University Press.

Halperin, David M. 1995. *Saint Foucault: Towards a Gay Hagiography.* New York: Oxford University Press.

Harris, Muriel. 1988. "SLATE (Support for the Learning and Teaching of English) Statement: The Concept of a Writing Center." International Writing Centers Association. http://writingcenters.org/writing-center-concept-by-muriel-harris/.

Harris, Muriel. 1995. "Talking in the Middle: Why Writers Need Writing Tutors." *College English* 57 (January): 27–42.

Hewett, Angela, and Robert McRuer. 2001. "Composing Student Activists: Relocating Student Writing." In *Public Works: Student Writing as Public Text,* edited by Emily J. Isaacs and Phoebe Jackson, 97–108. Portsmouth, NH: Boynton/Cook.

hooks, bell. 2003. *Teaching Community: A Pedagogy of Hope.* New York: Routledge.

Horner, Bruce, and John Trimbur. 2002. "English Only and U.S. College Composition." *College Composition and Communication* 53 (4): 594–630.

James, Marlon. 2016. "Are You Racist? No Isn't A Good Enough Answer." YouTube video, 2:15. Posted by the *Guardian,* January 13. https://www.youtube.com/watch?v=jm5DWa2bpbs.

Johnson, Michelle T. 2011. "Racial Literacy in the Writing Center." In *Writing Centers and the New Racism: A Call for Sustainable Dialogue and Change,* edited by Laura Greenfield and Karen Rowan, 211–27. Logan: Utah State University Press.

Jordan, June. 1997. "Nobody Mean More to Me than You and the Future Life of Willie Jordan." In *Living Languages: Contexts for Reading and Writing,* edited by Nancy Buffington, Marvin Diogenes, and Clyde Moneyhun, 194–209. Upper Saddle River, NJ: Prentiss Hall.

Kail, Harvey. 2003. "Separation, Initiation and Return: Tutor Training Manuals and Writing Center Lore." In *The Center will Hold: Critical Perspectives on Writing Center Scholarship,* edited by Michael A Pemberton and Joyce Kinkead, 74–95. Logan: Utah State University Press.

Kail, Harvey. 2009. "Innovation, Repetition, Tradition: Where We Are Now." Keynote address at the *Northeast Writing Centers Association conference,* Hartford, CT, April 4.

Kiedaisch, Jean, and Sue Dinitz. 1993. "Look Back and Say 'So What': The Limitations of the Generalist Tutor." *Writing Center Journal* 14 (1): 63–74.

Kiedaisch, Jean, and Sue Dinitz. 2007. "Changing Notions of Difference in the Writing Center: Possibilities of Universal Design." *Writing Center Journal* 27 (2): 39–59.

Lakoff, George. 2002. *Moral Politics: How Liberals and Conservatives Think.* 2nd ed. Chicago, IL: University of Chicago Press.

Lape, Noreen. 2008. "Training Tutors in Emotional Intelligence: Toward a Pedagogy of Empathy." *Writing Lab Newsletter* 33 (2): 1–6.

Lazere, Donald. 1992. "Teaching the Political Conflicts: A Rhetorical Schema." *College Composition and Communication* 43 (2): 194–213.

Lazare, Sarah. 2015. "Body Count Report Reveals at Least 1.3 Million Lives Lost to US-Led War on Terror." *Common Dreams.* http://www.commondreams.org/news/2015/03/26/body-count-report-reveals-least-13-million-lives-lost-us-led-war-terror.

Le Guin, Ursula K. 1986. "Bryn Mawr Commencement Address." Serendip Studio. https://serendip.brynmawr.edu/sci_cult/leguin/.

Lerner, Neal. 2009. *The Idea of a Writing Laboratory.* Carbondale: Southern Illinois University Press.

"List of Ongoing Conflicts." 2016. Wars in the World. https://www.warsintheworld.com/?page=static1258254223.

Lu, Min-Zhan. 2004. "An Essay on the Work of Composition: Composing English against the Order of Fast Capitalism." *College Composition and Communication* 56 (1): 16–50.

MacAskill, Andrew. 2013. "India's Poorest Women Coerced into Sterilization." *Bloomberg.* http://www.bloomberg.com/news/articles/2013-06-11/india-s-poorest-women-coerced-into-sterilization.

Macedo, Donaldo. 1994. *Literacies of Power: What Americans Are Not Allowed to Know.* Boulder, CO: Westview.

Macedo, Donaldo, and Lilia I. Bartolomé. 2001. *Dancing with Bigotry: Beyond the Politics of Tolerance.* New York: Palgrave.

"Malachi Larrabee-Garza on Purity Politics in Activism." 2016. YouTube video, 1:48. Posted by *Yerba Buena Center for the Arts.* https://www.youtube.com/watch?v=p2TG9Qn44VM.

"Malalai Joya: The Woman Who Will Not Be Silenced." 2009. Independent. http://www.independent.co.uk/news/world/malalai-joya-the-woman-who-will-not-be-silenced-1763127.html.

McDonald, James C. 2005. "Dealing with Diversity: A Review Essay of Recent Tutoring-Training Books." *Writing Center Journal* 25 (2): 63–72.

McKenzie, Mia. 2014. "Why I'm Not Really Here for Emma Watson's Feminism Speech at the UN." *BGD.* http://www.blackgirldangerous.org/2014/09/im-really-emma-watsons-feminism-speech-u-n/.

McKinnon, Catherine. 2010. *Women's Leadership and Social Justice.* President's inauguration panel discussion, Mount Holyoke College, South Hadley, MA.

McLaren, Peter, and Ramin Farahmandpur. 2005. *Teaching against Global Capitalism and the New Imperialism: A Critical Pedagogy.* Lanham, MD: Rowman & Littlefield.

Meerloo, Joost. 1956. *Rape of the Mind: The Psychology of Thought Control, Menticide, and Brainwashing.* Cleveland, OH: World.

Messner, Michael. 2000. "White Guy Habitus in the Classroom: Challenging the Reproduction of Privilege." *Men and Masculinities* 2 (4): 457–69.

Moore, Clare. 2016. "Coming Out in the Writing Center." *Dangling Modifier* 23 (1). https://sites.psu.edu/thedanglingmodifier/?p=3484.

NAACP. 2016. "Criminal Justice Fact Sheet." http://www.naacp.org/pages/criminal-justice-fact-sheet.

National Sexual Violence Resource Center. 2015. "Statistics about Sexual Violence." http://www.nsvrc.org/sites/default/files/publications_nsvrc_factsheet_media-packet_statistics-about-sexual-violence_0.pdf.

Nhat Hanh, Thich. 1987. *Being Peace.* Berkeley, CA: Parallax.

Neale, Jonathan. 2015. "Why Radical Academics Often Find it Hard to Write, and What to Do about It." Anne Bonny Pirate (formerly *WordPress: Sexism Class Violence*). https://sexismclassviolence.wordpress.com/2015/04/29/why-radical-academics-often-find-it-hard-to-write-and-what-to-do-about-it/.

Nelson, Cary, and Stephen Watt. 1999. *Academic Keywords: A Devil's Dictionary for Higher Education.* New York: Routledge.

Nelson, Jane, and Kathy Evertz, eds. 2001. *The Politics of Writing Centers.* Crosscurrents. Portsmouth, NH: Heinemann.

North, Stephen. 1984. "The Idea of a Writing Center." *College English* 46 (5): 433–46.

North, Stephen. 1994. "Revisiting the Idea of a Writing Center." *Writing Center Journal* 15 (1): 7–19.

Odom, Mary Lou. 2016. "Local Work: Identity and the Writing Center Director." *WLN: A Journal of Writing Center Scholarship* 41(1–2): 25–28. https://wlnjournal.org/archives/v41/41.1–2.pdf.

Olson, Bobbi. 2013. "Rethinking Our Work with Multilingual Writers: The Ethics and Responsibility of Language Teaching in the Writing Center." *Praxis: A Writing Center Journal* 10 (2): 66–71.

"185 School Shootings in America Since 2013." 2016. Everytown for Gun Safety https://everytownresearch.org/school-shootings/.

"Our Mission." Relational Uprising. http://relationaluprising.org/mission/.

Perry, Andre. 2016. "Black and Brown Boys Don't Need to Learn Grit; They Need Schools to Stop Being Racist." *The Root*. http://www.theroot.com/articles/culture/2016/05/black_and_brown_boys_don_t_need_to_learn_grit_they_need_schools_to_stop/.

Peskin, Joy. 2017. "Why the Milo Yiannopoulos Book Deal Tarnishes the Publishing Industry." *Publishers Weekly*. https://www.publishersweekly.com/pw/by-topic/columns-and-blogs/soapbox/article/72695-why-the-milo-yiannopoulos-book-deal-tarnishes-the-publishing-industry.html.

Powell, Kevin. 2016. "Will Racism Ever End, Will I Ever Stop Being a Nigger?" *Utne Reader*. http://www.utne.com/community/kevin-powell-will-racism-ever-end-zl0z16szsau.aspx.

Prendergast, Catherine. 2003. *Literacy and Racial Justice: The Politics of Learning after* Brown v. Board of Education. Carbondale: Southern Illinois University Press.

RAINN: Rape, Abuse, and Incest National Network. 2009. "Victims of Sexual Violence: Statistics." https://rainn.org/get-information/statistics/sexual-assault-victims.

Reigstad, Tom. 1981. "The Writing Conference: An Ethnographic Model for Discovering Patterns of Teacher-Student Interaction." *Writing Center Journal* 2 (1): 9–20.

Rickford, John Russell, and Russell John Rickford. 2000. *Spoken Soul: The Story of Black English*. New York: John Wiley & Sons.

Rousculp, Tiffany. 2014. *Rhetoric of Respect: Recognizing Change at a Community Writing Center*. Urbana, IL: NCTE.

Ryan, Leigh, and Lisa Zimmerelli. 2010. *The Bedford Guide for Writing Tutors*. 5th ed. Boston, MA: Bedford/St. Martin's.

Ryan, Leigh, and Lisa Zimmerelli. 2015. *The Bedford Guide for Writing Tutors*. 6th ed. Boston, MA: Bedford/St. Martin's.

Saifi, Sophia, and Greg Botelho. 2014. "In Pakistan School Attack, Terrorists Kill 145, Mostly Children." *CNN*. http://www.cnn.com/2014/12/16/world/asia/pakistan-peshawar-school-attack/.

Schendel, Ellen, and William J. Macauley Jr. 2012. *Building Writing Center Assessments that Matter*. Logan: Utah State University Press.

Schroeder, Christopher, Helen Fox, and Patricia Bizzell, eds. 2002. *Alt Dis: Alternative Discourses and the Academy*. Portsmouth, NH: Heinemann.

Severino, Carol. 2005. "Crossing Cultures with International ESL Writers: The Tutor as Contact Zone Contact Person." In *A Tutor's Guide: Helping Writers One to One*, 2nd ed., edited by Ben Rafoth, 41–53. Portsmouth, NH: Boynton/Cook.

Shafer, Gregory. 2001. "Standard English and the Migrant Community." *English Journal* 90 (4): 37–43.

Shamoon, Linda K., and Deborah H. Burns. 1995. "A Critique of Pure Tutoring." *Writing Center Journal* 15 (2): 134–51.

Shelley, Lynn. 2014. "'You Can't Get Anywhere without Relationships': Marginality and Mattering in the Writing Center." *Writing Lab Newsletter* 39 (3–4): 1–5. https://wlnjournal.org/archives/v39/39.3–4.pdf.

Shor, Ira, and Paulo Freire. 1987. *A Pedagogy for Liberation: Dialogues on Transforming Education*. South Hadley, MA: Bergin & Garvey.

Simpson, Jeanne. 1985. "What Lies Ahead for Writing Centers." International Writing Centers Association. Last updated 2006. http://writingcenters.org/what-lies-ahead-for-writing-centers-position-statement-on-professional-concerns-by-jeanne-h-simpson/.

Sloan, Jay. 2003. "Centering Difference: Student Agency and the Limits of 'Comfortable' Collaboration." *Dialogue: A Journal for Writing Specialists* 8 (2): 63–74.

Sloan, Jay. 2004. "Collaborating in the Contact Zone: A Writing Center Struggles with Multiculturalism." *Praxis: A Writing Center Journal* 1 (2): 8–10.

Sloan, Jay, and Andrew Rihn. 2013. "'Rainbows in the Past Were Gay': LGBTQIA in the WC." *Praxis: A Writing Center Journal* 10 (2): 81–93.

Smith, Eric Steven. 2012. "Making Room for Fat Studies in Writing Center Theory and Practice." *Praxis: A Writing Center Journal* 10 (1): 17–23. http://www.praxisuwc.com/smith-101.

Smitherman, Geneva. 2001. *Talkin that Talk: Language, Culture, and Education in African America.* Illustrated ed. London: Routledge.

Southern Poverty Law Center. 2016. "Active Hate Groups 2016." https://www.splcenter.org/fighting-hate/intelligence-report/2017/active-hate-groups-2016.

"Students' Right to Their Own Language." 1974. Special issue, *College Composition and Communication* 25 (Fall): 1–32.

Terry, Don. 2015. "In the Crosshairs." *Southern Poverty Law Center.* https://medium.com/hate watch-blog/in-the-crosshairs-3700fbf2203d#.ptyn61kct.

Thompson, Isabelle. 2009. "Scaffolding in the Writing Center: A Microanalysis of an Experienced Tutor's Verbal and Nonverbal Tutoring Strategies." *Written Communication* 9 (4): 417–53.

Thompson, Isabelle, and Joe Mackiewicz. 2014. "Questioning in Writing Center Conferences." *Writing Center Journal* 23 (2): 37–70.

Tinson, Christopher M., and Javiera Benavente. 2017. "Towards a Democratic Speech Environment." *Diversity and Democracy* 20 (2/3). Association of American Colleges and Universities. https://www.aacu.org/diversitydemocracy/2017/spring-summer/tinson.

Trimbur, John. 1987. "Peer Tutoring: A Contradiction in Terms?" *Writing Center Journal* 7 (2): 21–28.

Trimbur, John. 2000. "Multiliteracies, Social Futures, and Writing Centers." *Writing Center Journal* 20 (2): 29–32.

Turse, Nick. 2013. "Rape Was Rampant During the Vietnam War. Why Doesn't U.S. History Remember This?" *Mother Jones*, March 19. http://www.motherjones.com/politics/2013/03/rape-wartime-vietnam.

Unicef. 1996. "Sexual Violence as a Weapon of War." *The State of the World's Children.* http://www.unicef.org/sowc96pk/sexviol.htm.

Unicef. 2015. "Statistics and Monitoring." https://www.unicef.org/search/search.php?q=Statistics+and+Monitoring.

United States Census Bureau. 2015. "Income and Poverty in the United States: 2014." https://www.census.gov/library/publications/2015/demo/p60-252.html.

Villanueva, Victor. 2006. "Blind: Talking about the New Racism." *Writing Center Journal* 26 (1): 3–19.

Wahlstrom, Helena. 2013. "Imposter in the Writing Center—Trials of a Non-Native Tutor." *Writing Lab Newsletter* 38 (3–4). https://wlnjournal.org/archives/v38/38.3–4.pdf.

Wang, Qian. 2017. "Will You Trust Me?" *WLN: A Journal of Writing Center Scholarship* 41 (9–10): 26–29. https://wlnjournal.org/archives/v41/41.9–10.pdf.

Weber, Jessica L. 2016. "Workplace Writing Centers." International Writing Centers Association. http://www.writingcenters.org/wp-content/uploads/2017/01/IWCA_Work place_Writing_Center_Resource_2016.pdf.

Wells, Ida B. 1909. "Lynching Our National Crime." *BlackPast.org.* http://www.blackpast.org/1909-ida-b-wells-awful-slaughter.

Wescott, Lucy. 2015. "Eight Suspects in Malala Yousafzai Assassination Attempt Acquitted." *Newsweek*, June 5. http://www.newsweek.com/eight-suspects-malala-yousafzai-assassina tion-attempt-acquitted-339857.

Wheeler, Gordon. 2011. "Who Are We? Narrative, Evolution, and Development: Our Stories and Ourselves." In *Relational Child, Relational Brain: Development and Therapy in Childhood and Adolescence*, edited by Robert G. Lee and Neil Harris. Santa Cruz, CA: Gestalt Press.

White, Hayden. 1982. "The Politics of Historical Interpretation: Discipline and De-Sublimation." *Critical Inquiry* 9 (1): 113–37.

"Who We Are." The Relational Center. http://www.relationalcenter.org.

Williams, Jesse. 2016. "BET Awards Acceptance Speech: Jesse Williams Spits Knowledge like a Seasoned MC." BET. http://www.bet.com/video/betawards/2016/acceptance -speeches/jesse-williams-receives-humanitarian-award.html.

Wolfe, Lauren. 2016. "Syria Has a Massive Rape Crisis." *Atlantic*, April 3. http://www .theatlantic.com/international/archive/2013/04/syria-has-a-massive-rape-crisis/274 583/.

World Health Organization. 2016a. "Violence against Women." http://www.who.int/media centre/factsheets/fs239/en/.

World Health Organization. 2016b. "Female Genital Mutilation." http://www.who.int /mediacentre/factsheets/fs241/en/.

Yamamoto, Traise. 1999. *Masking Selves, Making Subjects: Japanese American Women, Identity, and the Body*. Berkeley: University of California Press.

Young, Vershawn Ashanti. 2011. "Should Writers Use They Own English?" In *Writing Centers and the New Racism: A Call for Sustainable Dialogue and Change*, edited by Laura Greenfield and Karen Rowan, 61–72. Logan: Utah State University Press.

Young, Vershawn Ashanti, Rusty Barrett, Y'Shanda Young-Rivera, and Kim Brian Lovejoy. 2013. *Other People's English: Code-Meshing, Code-Switching, and African American Literacy*. New York: Columbia University Teachers College Press.

ABOUT THE AUTHOR

DR. LAURA GREENFIELD is the founding director of the Transformative Speaking Program at Hampshire College, where she serves as a faculty associate of communication and education in the School of Critical Social Inquiry. Her research and teaching interests include the intersections of language, power, and education, with a particular focus on race and gender. Her book *Writing Centers and the New Racism: A Call for Sustainable Dialogue and Change* (USUP 2011) with Dr. Karen Rowan was the winner of the International Writing Centers Association Outstanding Book Award in 2012. Dr. Greenfield is the founder and former executive director of the education-based nonprofit Women's Voices Worldwide, Inc., and before that she served as the associate director of the Weissman Center for Leadership and the Liberal Arts at Mount Holyoke College, where she brought its Speaking, Arguing, and Writing Program into international prominence. In 2018 she was honored with the Ron Maxwell Leadership Award by the National Conference on Peer Tutoring in Writing.

INDEX